Major Sanderson's War

Fig. 1: Map 1. Overview map of the second Civil War

MAJOR SANDERSON'S WAR:

DIARY OF A PARLIAMENTARY CAVALRY OFFICER IN THE ENGLISH CIVIL WAR

by

P.R. Hill and J.M. Watkinson

First published 2008

Spellmount Publishers
The History Press Ltd.
The Mill, Brimscombe Port
Stroud, Gloucestershire, GL5 2QG
www.thehistorypress.co.uk

Spellmount Publishers are an imprint of The History Press Ltd.

British Library Cataloguing in Publication Data.
A catalogue record for this book is available from the British Library.

ISBN 978 1 86227 468 6

Typesetting and origination by The History Press Ltd.
Printed in Great Britain

Contents

PART I

CHAPTER ONE

INTRODUCTION

In 1919 the manuscript diary of a parliamentary officer, written on an interleaved copy of William Lilly's *Merlini Anglici Ephemeris 1648*, was exhibited by Mrs Wynne-Jones at the January meeting of the Society of Antiquaries of Newcastle upon Tyne. A transcript was produced the following month, and published in the Society's *Proceedings* in 1921.[1] The diary starts on 11th January and finishes on 30th December. Reference to other accounts of events mentioned show that the year covered is indeed 1648, the period of the Second Civil War.

Nowhere is the name of the diary's author given but, from the nine references to Hedleyhope, the editor of *PSAN* was able to deduce that he was one of the Sandersons of that place, an estate some eight miles west of Durham City bought by the Sandersons in or before 1623 (map 1 (*1*) and *plate 2*). The identification is backed by other sources which describe the movements of Major John Sanderson in 1648 and confirm details given in the diary. His Will (Appendix 4) places him firmly in the Hedleyhope family.

Much has been written on the better-known campaigns of the English Civil War. Many commanders have left both contemporary and later letters and accounts but fewer of the junior officers have done so. Diaries written by participants in the Civil War in the true sense of a more or less daily account, are very rare. Memoirs are more common, but were usually written after the passage of some years, and tended to concentrate on what hindsight saw as important.

In many ways the most significant account is this diary for 1648 of Major John Sanderson, who was an officer in Colonel Robert Lilburne's regiment of horse, originally part of the Northern Association of the parliamentary army. Of major importance is the sheer number of entries, all made within a few days at most of the events recorded, and the way in which they can be collated with other accounts to give a narrative thread. It is at times concerned with well-known events, but is also a remarkably detailed record of the endless day-to-day minutiae of patrol and skirmish. There is no other published source which allows the day-by-day reconstruction of a year in the Civil War.

Of other accounts which have been published, Captain Hodgson's *Memoir* is not a diary and only occasionally mentions dates. It was probably not written until the 1660s,[2] although the details may have been taken from a contemporary diary. He is telling a story, and concentrates very much on Happenings rather than the mundane everyday events. Atkyns *Vindication* is a document full of points of interest, but was written 25 years after he had served in the army. Gwyn is somewhat similar but is even less reliable as he wrote when advanced in years, some 35 years after the Civil War.[3]

Prince Rupert's Journal[4] is a simple record of where the prince went with very little detail given. For example, "23. Sunday, the Battle of Edgehill. The armyes all night in the feild" does not add anything to the history of the campaign. Its value, not inconsiderable in itself, lies largely in the detail of distances marched by an army.

The closest parallel to Sanderson's Diary is that of Captain Birch, a parliamentary infantry officer. This is a genuine diary, which runs from 16th May 1648 to March 1650; it thus covers a longer period but there are only 83 entries in nearly two years, whereas Sanderson has 270 for the one year. He is generally more descriptive than Sanderson, chiefly on the subject of the weather and quarters, and his records of pay are especially useful, as will be seen. It is possible to plot Birch's progress almost as closely as Sanderson's, although he spent days and even weeks together in the same quarters and there is nowhere near the same sense of movement and activity.

John Sanderson's Diary

Major Sanderson did not write his Diary as a history of the campaign in Northumberland and elsewhere. It seems to have been written more as an *aide-memoire*, very terse notes of where he went to and, sometimes, what he was doing (*plate 1*). It usually relates where he and his troop were quartered, it occasionally explains the reason for the journeys and, very rarely, tells us what other forces were doing. Sanderson concentrates on where he and his men were going; he has little interest in the activities of others. As Oxberry has commented "We could wish . . . that he had been endowed with just a touch of . . . a Boswell or a Pepys."[5]

And yet, the very brevity of the entries, usually written within a day or two at most of the actual events, gives an immediacy and accuracy which would be missing if they were written at leisure much later, reviewing events in the light of history. Frustrating though it is, "today I did this" is in many ways of greater value than "this day ten years ago I did this because . . ." A history would be unlikely to relate what he paid for a yard of hay on 7th March, or that on 15th May "every Soldyer a bottle [a bundle of hay] under him."

His Diary is not the only information on the Civil War which John Sanderson has left us. Two manuscript letters survive in the Baynes correspondence in the British Library, and his *Relation* of the battle of Preston was printed in 1648, the only known copy now in the library of Worcester College Oxford. Two letters of his from 1648 have already been published. All these contribute to the picture of the parliamentary major and his view of the war presented in this book, and are reproduced in Appendix 4. Some of the actions in which Major

Sanderson was involved are reviewed in detail for the light they shed on the activities of the parliamentary army.

The Diary provides an unrivalled framework for a view of the Second Civil War but, just as it sheds occasional light on known events, so other sources are needed to explore its full potential. Chapter 5 uses the Diary in conjunction with all available sources to give a rounded view of the Civil War in the north in 1648.

This is a book written for the general reader, and can be read without recourse to the notes, which are largely devoted to the sources of information and quoted material.

The weather

The summer of 1648 was said to have been the worst in living memory with frequent rain, cold, storms, and bitter winds.[6] In March there was a storm at Sherburn in Elmet with hailstones the size of walnuts and nutmegs, which broke windows, and killed ducks and geese.[7] From mid-June to mid-July Capt. Birch complains of "extreame foul weather . . . in extreamity of wet and foul weather . . . Such a wet time this time of the yeare hath not been seen in the memory of man . . . extremely wet as it was."[8] In July Lambert wrote of "miserable marches", "illness of weather", and "bad weather."[9] In early August there was an "extraordinary storm, wind at North-East, with abundance of rain."[10] In his description of the battle of Preston, Burnet describes "the Rains which fell continually; for all the while there were such deluges of Rains not only over England, but over all Europe, that every Brook was a River."

The weather was so bad that Parliament took notice of it: owing to "abundance of Rain and such unseasonable Weather, the like whereof hath scarce been known at this season of the year" the Lords and Commons "set apart a Day for Solemn Humiliation".[11]

In the Isle of Wight "from Mayday to 15th September, we had scarce three dry days together. . . . When a dry day came they would reap [wheat] and carry it into the barns although they mowed it wet. . . . I told [the king] that in this 40 years I never knew the like before. . . .The rivers . . . have overflown . . . the rich vales stand knee deep with water . . ."[12]

There will not have been continuous heavy rain or no campaigning at all would have been possible, and the weather was certainly good enough for haymaking, as Sanderson was able, on 15th May, to obtain 100 country cart loads of hay. Rather, the records sound very like the weather experienced in 2007 as this text was being prepared, when violent storms, which caused serious flooding in June and July with up to two months' rain falling in 24 hours, could ceased abruptly and give way rapidly to sunshine and scattered white clouds. Likewise, the retreat of the Scots from Preston to Wigan took place in very heavy rain and yet that night there was a full moon (see chapter 5, August). Unlike almost all other contemporary writers Sanderson mentions the weather only once, when rain caused a change of quarters on 20th June.

The calendar

In the middle of the seventeenth century the Julian calendar, in which the year began on 25th March, was still in use in England but the modern Gregorian style was also being used. Dates given in direct quotations are in their original style, which could be either, and sometimes both are used in the same document. Where there is room for doubt the old style is as quoted with the addition of the modern year in brackets: thus 1st January 1647[8]. A calendar for the Julian year 1648 is given in Appendix 1.

The maps

The sketch maps show most of the places listed in the 'To' column of the Transcript (Appendix 3), together with a few other towns as a guide to location. The general location of some small places for which there was no space on the maps is given in the Notes column of the Transcript, except where the distance from the previous place is only a few miles. No attempt has been made to differentiate the size of towns.

On small scale maps it is impossible to show but a small indication of where roads may have been in the mid-seventeenth century, and some of those shown may not have existed then. A few modern road numbers are shown, although the routes are not necessarily those followed in Sanderson's day. Some relevant rivers are also shown.

For readers who wish to follow Sanderson's travels closely, the relevant map number is given in the Notes column of the Transcript. Where the place is not named on the map, the reference is in brackets.

People

In Appendix 7 are notes on all those mentioned in the Diary and the *Relation at Large* about whom it is been possible to discover information. For reasons of space most of these biographical notes have been condensed to a few essential details and in general do not go beyond 1648. Information has been taken from Furgol, GEC, Hedley, NCH, Newman, *ODNB*, Paul, and Welford 1905, and other specialised sources given in the Bibliography.

A few people are discussed only in the text, and appear in the index. Troopers and servants are not listed individually but a few, about whom some information has been found, appear at the end of the alphabetical listing under *Soldiers and Servants*.

Officers of Lilburne's are not included as they are briefly discussed in the notes on that regiment, chapter 3. The one exception is Major Cholmley, whose identity is the subject of discussion in Appendix 7a.

Acknowledgments

It proved possible to trace the current owners of the Diary and through their great kindness, and that of a member of their family, the original was made available to the writers for study. The owners prefer to remain anonymous. Sincere thanks are extended to Dr C.D. Watkinson for assistance in locating the Diary and with the pedigree of the Sanderson family. Mr & Mrs D.H. Flintham gave advice on, and much help with, equipment for photography of both the Diary and the illustrations in this book, and Mrs Flintham kindly commented on the text. The writers are grateful to the Provost and Fellows of Worcester College Oxford for permission to reproduce the text of Sanderson's *Relation at Large*, and to the Librarian Dr Parker for her assistance. Mr Peter Young, Archivist, York Minster Library kindly made available for study the Record of Council of the Northern Parliamentary Army (Order Book). Sanderson's letter and Will, from *Skirmish in Northumberland*, and two sheets of the Quartermasters' Map are reproduced by permission of Durham University Library which also provided the photographs of the map. The text of the two letters of Sanderson's from Add. Mss 21,417 are reproduced by permission of the British Library. The Argass family gave ready access to Cartington Castle. Mrs McCreath gave essential guidance to the ford over the Tweed at Twizel. Mr N.M. Croll kindly advised on the use of planetary symbols for days of the week and on some of the obscure place names.

Material was consulted also in the National Library of Scotland, Edinburgh Public Library, and Newcastle Literary and Philosophical Society, and thanks are accorded to the staff in these institutions. Particular thanks are due to the Special Collections staff in the libraries of Durham, Edinburgh, and St Andrews Universities.

CHAPTER TWO

THE SANDERSON FAMILY

There were at the time several Sanderson families in the Northeast of England, seemingly not directly connected. This particular family came originally from Newcastle, where Thomas Sanderson, a leading hostman (an agent who arranged the shipping of coal from the Tyne), was Sheriff in 1506 and John Sanderson Mayor in 1537. They were related to the Brighams, Chaytors, Lewens and Mitfords, all eminent in Newcastle civic and commercial life. As the century progressed power became concentrated in the hands of families such as the Andersons, Brandlings, Claverings, Jenisons, Liddells, and Selbys, who were involved in the coal mining industry on the south bank of the Tyne. Although the son of a merchant, Henry Sanderson, Major John's grandfather, became a customs official for Queen Elizabeth and had some success in hunting down priests and recusants in the area.[1] He was also leader of the Non Grand Lessees, the group of Newcastle freemen who were excluded from local government in the town by the faction which owned the Grand Lease of the coal mines under the Bishop of Durham's manor at Gateshead and Whickham.[2]

In December 1603 Henry and his son Samuel were rewarded for their service to the Crown by being appointed Constables of Brancepeth Castle and Keepers of the Forest for life under James I, and granted an annuity of £200 the following month[3], although a letter written by Henry to Lord Burghley in September 1597 suggests that he was already living there, as guardian of the recusants lodged in the Castle.[4] His coat of arms (paly of six argent and azure, a bend sable) was augmented by a sword proper, hilted and pommeled or on the bend, granted to him as Constable. A similar coat was used by the Sanderson family of Eggleston, Co. Durham, who were not entitled to it, and no immediate connection between the two families has yet been traced.[5]

Samuel married Barbara, daughter of Thomas Liddell of Ravensworth and half-sister of Sir Thomas, 1st baronet, in December 1610, and went on to have a large family of sons and daughters (Family Tree, 2). It was through this marriage that the Sandersons of Hedleyhope rejoined the mercantile and land-owning elite of Newcastle.[6]

No birth or baptismal date is known for John Sanderson, but it is most likely that he was the second son. The Visitation of 1615 records an

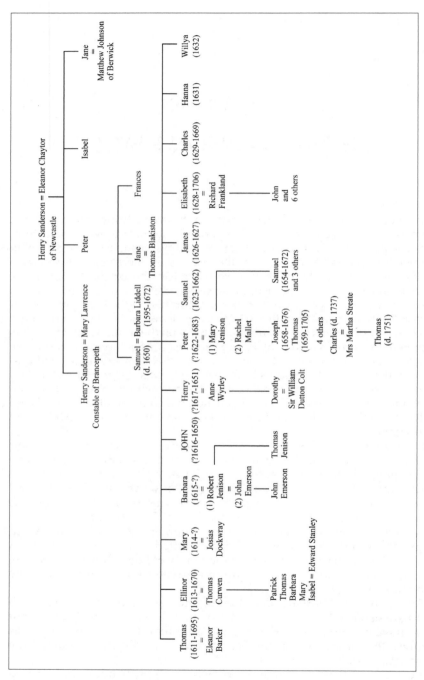

Fig. 2: Family Tree of the Sandersons of Hedleyhope

only son Thomas aged four who was 54 in 1666.[7] Surtees includes this information in his pedigree but lists another son, Samuel, baptised on 3rd November 1611,[8] and other writers have copied him.[9] However the Brancepeth Parish Register clearly shows that Thomas was baptised on that date, with no mention of a son Samuel.[10] The first daughter, Ellinor [sic], was baptised on 25th February 1612[3], and a second on 14th June 1614, having been born on 31st May. Surtees names this latter Margaret, and postulates another daughter Mary, birth date unknown. But as one of "Margaret's" sponsors is given as John Sanderson of London who, in his will dated 30th June 1624, proved 3rd March 1627, bequeathed £100 to his goddaughter Mary on her reaching 18,[11] it is suggested that these are one and the same, the name Mary being misread on some occasion as Marg. On 10th May 1615 a third daughter, Barbara, was baptised. The next child of Samuel and Barbara Sanderson listed in the Brancepeth register is Samuel, baptised on 29th June 1623.

A son Henry was apprenticed to a Newcastle boothman on 11th November 1633[12], and another, Peter, to John Blakiston of Newcastle on 1st March 1639[13]. Since no-one could be bound apprentice under the age of 16,[14] (and Samuel is described on the memorial in the chancel of Lanchester Church as fifth son of Samuel and Barbara[15]) 1617 and 1622 are the probable years of birth of these two, but as in the case of John, neither birth nor baptismal records have been found for them. It may be that the three were baptised at Lanchester, but the parish register for 1603-1653 is missing. One other son and another daughter are listed in the Brancepeth register: James was baptised 18th April 1626 and died the following January; Elsabeth [sic] was baptised 20th January 1627[8]. The baptisms of three further children are recorded in the register of St Nicholas Church, Newcastle: Charles on 26th March 1629; Hanna on 25th May 1631; and Willya [sic] on 3rd July 1632, one of whose godparents was John Sanderson. This helps to confirm John's birth in 1616 as it is unlikely that he would have been a godparent before the age of 16.

Thomas inherited £50 from his grandfather, Thomas Liddell, and he and Ellinor are the only two from their generation to be mentioned in their great-aunt's will, dated 10th August 1619[16] (Jane, widow of Matthew Johnson of Berwick, was Constable Henry's sister). John Sanderson of London (see above) left his godson, John, the rent of some land in Ireland and £100 on his coming of age. If, as has been accepted in Foster, Hunter, and the Hodgson Pedigrees, Thomas was the eldest son, and John the second, he must have been born in 1616, with Henry as the third one year later. Henry and Samuel are further discussed below, *Army careers of John Sanderson's brothers*.

The family illustrates some of the difficulties experienced in the early Stuart era, with divided loyalties during the Civil War. Constable Henry was short of money and borrowed from Nicholas Salter, an acquaintance of his "cosen" John in London.[17] Mary had not received all of her legacy, and two bonds owed by Constable Henry's son to Robert Jenison were still unpaid when Samuel's wife Barbara made her will in March 1672.[18] In June 1620 Henry petitioned for arrears of fees of £170 15s 10d.[19] By

1623 some at least of the family were living at Hedleyhope.[20] Complaints were lodged against Henry,[21] but in 1635 he stated that he had served as Constable of Brancepeth for 40 years, and claimed money owing to him for repairs to the Castle. John's Will (Appendix 4) shows that he had lent his father £170, although he did secure a 99 year lease of part of Hedleyhope in return. There is no record of Constable Henry's death. The suggestion that he was tried and executed for neglect of his duties is improbable;[22] it is more likely that he was buried at Lanchester in the period for which there are now no registers.

John's father Samuel and brother Thomas were admitted to Sidney Sussex College Cambridge in 1603 and 1628 respectively. There is no evidence that any of Samuel's other sons attended university, but their bequests and inventories suggest that John and Charles were well educated, and their mother Barbara left books worth 40 shillings including her Bible which she "dayly read on".

Samuel and his sons Thomas, Henry and Samuel took the Protestation (the declaration to "maintain and defend ... the true, reformed, Protestant religion" which was to be taken by all males aged 18 or over) at Lanchester on 20th February 1641[2], while John took it three or four days later at Ryton in the company of Toby Dudley father of Sanderson's "dear friend" Jane Norton whose husband supported the royalist cause.[23]

Three of John's sisters married clergymen. Mary's husband was Josias Dockwray, son of Robert Dockwray, headmaster of Giggleswick School. Josias, having been ejected in 1662, conformed and was curate of Lanchester from 1663 until he succeeded his brother Thomas as Vicar of Newburn, Northumberland, in 1668. He was buried there in July 1683.[24] Mary survived him but they had no children.

Barbara was married twice: she was the third wife of the Puritan Dr Robert Jenison (1583-1652), Vicar of Newcastle from 1645 until his death, and her second husband was John Emerson, Sheriff of Newcastle 1639-40 and Mayor 1660-61. Of her two sons, one from each marriage, Thomas Jenison, Sheriff of Newcastle 1661-2 and Mayor 1674-5, married Emerson's daughter, Alice, by his first wife, and they were grandparents of Elizabeth Newton mentioned in the codicil to the will of Barbara's nephew Thomas.[25]

Elizabeth, the youngest surviving sister, married the nonconformist Richard Frankland (1630-1698), who had been a pupil at Giggleswick. He preached at Lanchester and elsewhere in the northeast before being ordained in 1653 by presbyters in Durham, but having refused to conform he was ejected in 1662 and went on to open a dissenting academy at Rathmell near Giggleswick. His first pupil was George, youngest son of Sir Thomas Liddell, Bart, of Ravensworth Castle, great nephew of Elizabeth's mother, and Elizabeth's nephew Charles, Peter's son, is said to have attended the academy.[26] The Franklands had four daughters and three sons, only one of whom, John, is mentioned in his grandmother's will.[27] Elizabeth died in 1706.

The eldest Sanderson sister, Ellinor (or Helena), married Thomas Curwen (1590-1653) of Sella Park in 1639[40]. He represented Cumberland on several Committees: for Assessment 23rd June 1647; for Assessment for Ireland 16th February 1647[8]; and for Settling the Militia in the Northern Counties 23rd May 1648.[28] They had ten children, of whom four died young, and five are mentioned in Barbara Sanderson's will, Patrick, Thomas, Barbara, Mary, and Isabel. Thomas (1646-1683[4]) was apprenticed to his uncle, Peter Sanderson in 1661 and became a merchant in Newcastle. Isabel (1641-1693) married, probably in 1665, Edward Stanley of Dalegarth, Cumberland, who, as High Sheriff of that county, proclaimed William III as king in 1688.[29]

While his younger brothers, John, Henry and Samuel, were in the army during the Civil War, Thomas Sanderson seems to have remained at Hedleyhope, dealing with family matters and serving on local committees. He was appointed, with his father and others, to represent the Bishopric of Durham on the Northern Association Committee set up by ordinance of 20th June 1645,[30] and Sir Arthur Hesilrige, in a letter to the Speaker of the House of Commons dated 18th May 1648, requested that Thomas be "added to the committee for sequestrations" together with five other "gentlemen of good quality".[31] Twelve years later Thomas was appointed to the Committee for Settling Militia in Co. Durham while his brother Peter represented Newcastle.[32] In November 1653, acting as guardian of the infant Thomas Howard, he put in a claim for Tursdale manor in Co. Durham,[33] and a year later petitioned for a reduction in rent on Winlaton Colliery which had been sequestered for the delinquency of his mother's sister Jane Liddell,[34] wife of Sir John Mennes, commander of Charles I's navy and, after the Restoration, a colleague of Pepys on the Navy Board.

Thomas is said to have rebuilt Hedleyhope Hall in 1646,[35] presumably the modest house with two hearths recorded in the Hearth Tax assessment records of 1666.[36] On 10th February 1656[7] he married Eleanor, daughter of Francis Barker of Topcliffe Manor in Yorkshire, and died without issue in April 1695, having outlived all his brothers.

Although granted a militia commission as Captain of foot in 1659,[37] Peter Sanderson, like his eldest brother, seems to have played a civilian role in the Civil War, not in Durham but in Newcastle, where in 1665 he owned a house with 11 hearths in Pink Tower Ward, at the end of the Tyne bridge.[38] He was admitted Freeman of the town at the beginning of March 1649, some ten years after being apprenticed to the regicide John Blakiston, and remained a merchant there until his death in January 1682[3], taking on many apprentices himself, some of whom appear to have caused him trouble. He was fined £100 in August 1658 'for certifying the court at Hamburg improperly on behalf of his apprentice, John Shadforth, who was refused his freedom'. In October 1651 he was appointed Sheriff in Newcastle, served as an alderman 1652-55, and was appointed to committees for Assessment and for Settling Militia in July 1659, and in January and March 1660. [39] Although he inherited part of the Somborne estate from John, £50 from his mother, and £10 from Charles, and held money for his sister Mary, unlike his brothers he is not a witness to, or executor of, any of the known family wills. But a copy of John's will now in Durham

University Library,[40] written before the original was sent for proving at Canterbury, appears to have been made for Peter.

He married, as his first wife, in May 1649, Mary, daughter of Dr Robert Jenison (whom his sister Barbara later married) and they had four children only one of whom, Samuel, survived infancy. After her death in January 1656[7], he married a widow, Rachel Mallet, in September of that year. Four of their sons, Joseph, Thomas, Charles and Henry, are mentioned in their grandmother's will, and Thomas appears to have lived at Hedleyhope.[41]

Charles, of the Inner and Middle Temple, became one of the leading London attorneys and a noted pupil-master in the first quarter of the 18th century, acting as legal agent for his friends and relatives among the north eastern coal owners.[42]

On his death in 1737, his only son Thomas, of Lincoln's Inn Fields, London, admitted to the Middle Temple in 1714, inherited the Hedleyhope estate which he still owned in 1745. He died childless in 1751, seemingly the last male descendant of this branch of the family. The farmer Henry Sanderson, "formerly of Hedleyhope", mentioned in a copyhold document dated 8th November 1835 (Durham County Archives D/X614/33) will have been a member of one of the later families of that name in the area.

Little is known of John's youngest brother Charles, apart from his will in Durham University Library, in which he left 'that Tenement called Dicken house' at Hedleyhope[43] (possibly the house with nine hearths in the 1666 Hearth Tax Assessment[44]) to his mother. Together with Henry and Samuel, he was named as an executor in John's will, and was present, with Samuel, when the will was proved at Durham on 19 November 1650. Henry was absent as he was serving in the parliamentary army in Linlithgow.[45]

Army careers of John Sanderson's brothers

The family was not untypical of the officers of the parliamentary army, and in accordance with Cromwell's stated preferences and background. "It had been well that men of honour and birth had entered into these employments, but why do they not appear? . . . But seeing that it was necessary the work must go on, better plain men than none . . ." [46] Hence "I had rather have a plain russet-coated captain . . . than that which you call a gentlemen and is nothing else".[47]

Two brothers are mentioned in the *Diary* by name: Peter and Samuel. Henry is not named in the Diary, but some examination of his career is relevant in order to separate references which could be either to him or to John. He may have been in the army by the middle of 1642, if he can be identified with Lieutenant Henry Saderson [*sic*] in the troop of Captain Francis Dowett.[48]

The first reasonably certain reference is found in August 1646, when it was ordered that "Colonel Henry Sanderson do forthwith march to London, with his Regiment of Reformadoes . . . for further service or disbanding . . ."[49] This reference allows identification with another, one year earlier, approving payment for " . . . reduced officers who marched . . . under the command of Lieutenant-Colonel Sanderson . . . for the relief of Taunton."[50] An even earlier reference, November 1644, to Lieutenant-Colonel Sanderson is presumably to the same man. The rank indicates that it was a foot regiment.

As shown above, he was probably born in 1617, and thus achieved his rank by the age of about 27. There are numerous other references to him in the Journals of the Lords and the Commons claiming his arrears of pay as late as March 1650, both as Sanderson and Saunderson (sometimes in the same document[51]) but always referring to his regiment of reformadoes. Another Colonel Sanderson appears in the same Journals, but he is clearly a colonel of horse and not the same person.[52]

In May 1647 the Committee at Derby House, which was considering the disbanding of the army, discharged Colonel Lilburne and Major Sanderson from further attendance.[53] Robert Lilburne was at that time commanding a regiment of foot, and "Major Sanderson" may be Henry, but the identification is by no means certain.

There is a possible reference to Henry on 10th September 1648 when "Lieut. Gen. Cromwell having received intelligence of a party of Monroes horse that were designed for Berwick, commanded out Major Sanderson a Gentleman of known integrity with a party of horse . . ."[54] On 18th it was reported that Cromwell "sent the Bishoprick horse commanded by Major Sanderson . . . to dissipate the English enemy about Barwick."[55] At first sight these reports might refer to John Sanderson, but the Diary shows that from 1st to 13th September he was marching from Ecclesfield to Durham. Henry Sanderson is the most likely candidate.

On 29th August 1650 "Col Hy Sanderson" received a commission as major in Sir Arthur Hesilrige's newly raised militia regiment of horse; three days earlier he, with the rank of major and with Captains Hutton and Shepherdson, had received 14 days pay for his "new raised" troop. [56] He was made governor of Linlithgow in September of that year,[57] but died there in February 1651 and for reasons which are not clear was buried at Newcastle.[58] He may have been killed in an attack in January,[59] but there is no record of the circumstances of his death.

The identification of Colonel Henry Sanderson with John Sanderson's brother was first made by Surtees, and accepted as such by Sharp. Sanderson's will left Leicester Castle to his brother Henry, and it does appear to have come into the possession of Colonel Sanderson.[60]

Henry's younger brother Peter is mentioned in John's Diary as drawing certificates and debentures on 4th February. As he was not in the army during the Civil War he was helping in a civilian capacity.

On 16th April Sanderson writes "my brother sent Robert Bell to me with an order from generall Lambert". It is not known which brother this was. The introduction to the original publication of the Diary says that Henry is mentioned in it, but his name does not appear; this reference could be to Henry but no confirmation has been found. Samuel is the more likely brother as he is known to have acted for Sanderson.

Samuel is mentioned by name only once, when sent to pay quarters on 29th February. It is not clear from this entry whether Samuel was acting in a civilian capacity on behalf of his brother or was part of the military, but there are some clues. It will be convenient to start with the most certain references and work backwards.

In January 1652 Cornet Baynes wrote: "I bought it [a debenture] of Sam. Ellis; it was his brother Joseph Ellis's of Major Smithson's troop in Collo. Lilburne's regiment, and was in Major Sanderson's hands, and now in his brother's Lieu[t] Sanderson's;"[61]

A little earlier there is a record naming Samuel Sanderson with, *inter alia*, four officers of Lilburne's (George Smithson, Thomas Lilburne, William Bradford and Francis Wilkinson) making a contract in June 1651 to buy the Manor of Holm Cultram (Holme Cultram, Abbeytown, Cumberland NY177508). A record of an obstruction to the sale dated April 1652 names Lt Sanderson and Col. Lilburne's regiment.[62]

In May 1651 Colonel Lilburne, referring to recruits, wrote " . . .(if Corn[t] Sanderson come from London) desire that he only may have the conduct of them."[63] This again confirms that Samuel was in Lilburne's regiment.

A month earlier Colonel Lilburne asked that Captain Adam Baynes "confer with Capt. Peavarell and Cornt Sanderson."[64] In 1659 Parliament passed a revised list of officers for Colonel Lilburne's regiment, which included Captain Peverell.[65]

A letter from a Captain Lister to Captain Adam Baynes on 9th March 1650[51] " . . . beg your trouble in speaking to Cornett Sanderson about it [a debenture]",[66] probably refers to Samuel's activity as attorney for the purchase of land on behalf of Lilburne's and Fenwick's.[67]

The record of the Council of Officers meeting at Pontefract on 12th December 1648 included among those present Cornet Saunderson.[68]

It is clear that in January 1652 John's brother Samuel was a lieutenant in Lilburne's, promoted from cornet at some time after May 1651, which rank he probably achieved during 1648. As he was sent on military business by John, it is probable that he was in his troop. Sanderson mentions his cornet seven times (19, 21 March, 3, 13 April, 14, 17 May, 9 Aug) but only by rank and, even though the Diary tends to be impersonal, the cornet was probably not then Samuel. Presumably he was serving in some lower rank, either trooper or, conceivably, quartermaster, and was perhaps transferred to another troop on promotion. One might expect that even the taciturn Sanderson would have mentioned that his brother was promoted to cornet under him.

There is no record of when Samuel joined the army; he does not appear in any records after 1652 and presumably returned to civilian life. He died in 1662.

In his account of the battle of Preston (Appendix 4), Sanderson records that "both my Brothers and all my Officers are well, in health, and unhurt." He asks for a copy of the letter to be given to Henry, who was thus clearly not in the battle. As discussed above neither Thomas nor Peter was in the army, and the likely candidates are Samuel and Charles. No record has been found bearing on the life of Charles, but by default it seems that he was in the army during the second Civil War.

At some date unknown John Sanderson himself joined the parliamentary army. If he were born in 1616 he would have been aged 26 at the start of the Civil War in 1642, and 32 in the Diary year of 1648.

CHAPTER THREE

Background to the Diary

The Civil War background

The first Civil War was effectively over by the middle of 1646 (Harlech held out until March 1647) and the king, having surrendered to the Scots, was handed over by them to English custody in January 1647. Over the next year the various parliamentary interests argued among themselves and with the army, whose own factions were in dissent and mutinous. The king was negotiating with Parliament while at the same time gaining the support of the Scots for his restoration by force. "The king raised a Parliament he could not rule, and the Parliament raised an army it cannot rule, and the army has raised Agitators they cannot rule, and the Agitators are setting up the people whom they will be unable to rule. Things are in great confusion."[1]

In this extremely unsatisfactory state of affairs the governor of Pembroke Castle declared for the king on 23rd March 1648, followed by uprisings in the king's favour in several parts of the country including north Wales, Kent, Essex, Leicestershire and Northamptonshire. The towns of Berwick and Carlisle were seized by royalists on 28th and 29th April respectively. Castles and strong points in many parts of the country were held by royalists, and on 8th July a Scottish army under the Duke of Hamilton invaded through Carlisle in support of the king. Major-General Lambert defended Stainmore against their attempts to cross the Pennines by that route, and then marched to Knaresborough to join Cromwell who had brought troops up from the siege of Pembroke. The army crossed the Pennines through Skipton to Clitheroe. Hamilton's army was defeated at the battle of Preston, and in September Cromwell took an army into Scotland. Lambert's and Lilburne's regiments returned from Scotland in November to join Cromwell at the siege of Pontefract castle, which did not fall until March 1649.

In December 1648 the army sent a Remonstrance to Parliament against treating with the king, and the forces at Pontefract sent a letter in support of this. The king was tried and executed in January 1649.

In 1650 Cromwell invaded Scotland in a pre-emptive strike. Lilburne's was one of the regiments involved but, as will be seen, Major Sanderson remained in England for a time.

After Cromwell's death in 1658 Major-General Lambert attempted to maintain the power of the army against parliament, and General Monck brought his army down from Scotland to restore order, a move which led to the restoration of the monarchy.

The Parliamentary Army

At the start of the Civil War the parliamentary army was commanded by the earl of Essex. Other armies grew up, supported by Associations of counties, particularly the Western, Eastern, and Northern. The Northern Association, to which Lilburne's belonged, was set up in 1645[2] and originally commanded by Ferdinando, Lord Fairfax, then by Major-General Poyntz, and from July 1647 by Major-General Lambert, who is mentioned in the *Diary* four times by name and 13 times by his rank. All the armies consisted not only of formal regiments of horse and foot, but also independent troops and companies.

The fortunes of both sides fluctuated, and in an attempt to find a decisive solution a new parliamentary army was formed out of parts of the Association forces. This New Model Army was established in February 1645, and was to consist of 11 (later 12) cavalry regiments 600 strong, divided into six troops, 12 regiments of foot, each of 1,200 men divided into ten companies, with one regiment of dragoons 1,000 strong.[3] It was commanded by Sir Thomas Fairfax (ennobled on the death of his father in March 1648) with Cromwell, mentioned seven times in the *Diary*, as Lieutenant-General in command of the horse. Cromwell's appointment was not made until the eve of the battle of Naseby, June 1645, and then by the Commons alone.[4] The army was reorganised in 1647[5] and again in 1648 when on 9th February the Commons voted that "the Horse shall be divided into Fourteen regiments; and every Troop consist of Eighty."[6] Ten days later the Lords voted for the pay of the existing army from 3rd November 1647 to 21st February 1648; very usefully they give a precise list of rates for every rank, with numbers, summarised overleaf.[7]

A cavalry regiment of the New Model was commanded by a colonel, with a major below him, both ranking as field officers. The six troops were severally commanded by these two officers and four captains. Each troop had as junior officers a lieutenant, a cornet, and a quartermaster. The colonel's troop was in practice commanded by his lieutenant with the title of captain-lieutenant, who ranked as a captain for some purposes, and was so referred to. The major was still technically known as Serjeant Major, but in practice was normally referred to as Major.

Lieutenants and captains had one third of their pay withheld to a later date, more senior ranks had half withheld, and even troopers were paid one quarter short. Pay in the New Model was reasonably regular from its founding in 1645 until the middle of 1647, and most of the arrears about which the army complained were from pre-Model or from the Association armies. New Model foot were paid more regularly than the better-paid horse; in the period referred to the foot received around three quarters of their pay, the horse just under 60%.[8]

Pay scales at the beginning of 1648

Rank	Pay per day	
	s	d
Colonel	12	0
As captain	10	0
Allowance for 4 horses at 2s each	8	0
Major	5	8
As captain	10	0
Allowance for 3 horses at 2s each	6	0
Captain	10	0
Allowance for 3 horses at 2s each	6	0
Lieutenant, 1 per troop	5	4
Allowance for 2 horses at 2s each	4	0
Cornet, 1 per troop	4	8
Allowance for 2 horses at 2s each	4	0
Quartermaster, 1 per troop	4	0
Allowance for 2 horses at 2s each	4	0
Corporals, 3 per troop, each	2	6
Trumpeters, 2 per troop (3 in colonel's troop), each	2	6
Farrier, 1 per troop	2	
Saddler, 1 per troop	2	
Troopers, 600 in 6 troops, each	2	

All ranks above trooper were usually referred to as officers, i.e. office holders, although there was the distinction between those holding a commission from the Parliament (quartermaster and above) and those appointed by the colonel. The given strength of a regiment excludes the 43 office holders and 24 officers. Also with each regiment were a Preacher, a Surgeon with two mates, and a Provost Marshal with two men.

Firth implies that the reduction from 100 to 80 troopers was the peacetime establishment with the war footing remaining as 100 men to a troop.[9]

Regiments and loose troops in the Association armies were either disbanded or added to the New Model until by 1649 it was the single army of the country. Among the forces from the Northern Association brought in to the New Model after July 1647 were the cavalry regiments of Lambert and Lilburne and the loose troops of Major Sanderson, Captain Lilburne, Captain Wilkinson, and Major Cholmley. Their complete absorption will have taken some time, and was still in progress during the early period of the Diary: "the Reducement of the Soldiery goes on very well, and the Model will quickly be finished."[10] This is further discussed below, *Lilburne's regiment.*

Although the House of Lords Journal gives the nominal establishment of the new regiments, it is difficult to find confirmation of actual troop numbers. A list from October 1647 gives the strength for quartering purposes of the army of the Northern Association. For the only regiment which gives numbers of troops (Copley's) it is an average of 80 men per troop.[11] The list names Major Sanderson's and Capt. Lilburne's troops but does not give numbers. At the same date, the troops of Major Cholmley and Captain Bayer averaged 85 men each.[12]

Early in 1648 Parliament decreed that the Northern Forces were to conform to the New Model; on 27th January Lambert informed the Council of War of the Northern Army "of the Parliament's resolutions of new modelling the army and reducing to a lesser number."[13] Among the reductions were "40 troopers a piece (or the worst) out of Major Sanderson and Captaine Lilburnes troops."[14]

This not only gave an interesting degree of latitude, but as Sanderson discharged 30 men and soon afterwards mustered 77, his strength must have been 107 troopers. Major Cholmley's troop was to lose the excess over 60 men "which will be "44. and 30 Foot"[15] showing that at this point he seems to have had a mixed command. In July 1648 Major Cholmley is said to have had 80 men in his troop,[16] so he must have been recruiting following his reductions in February. The fact that the reductions were dealt with by named troops confirms that these were loose troops and not part of a regiment.

On 2nd March 1648 Sanderson received pay for 80 soldiers. On 13th he mustered 77 men with 20 men still to join him, perhaps to put it on a war footing. When Cromwell went into Scotland in July 1650, Lilburne's had a strength of 603 "so that the troops were at their war strength of 100 apiece."[17] On 20th May 1651 Major Goodrick was paid £91.10.0 "for each souldr and non-commission officer in Major Genrall Lambert's Regimt of Horse att 3s p man," which works out at 610 men.[18]

On 16th June of the same year there were 586 non-commissioned officers and men in Lilburne's, and 628 in Lambert's, and on 24th June Lilburne's had 599 men.[19] Allowing for the 43 non-commissioned officers in a regiment, these regimental figures give between 92 and 95 men in a troop: the establishment had clearly reverted to a nominal troop strength of 100.

A letter from Lambert concerning the disbanding of regiments in early 1649 shows that the number of troops had also become variable: "viz. 3 regiments of horse, consisting of 22 troops . . ."[20]

There is a lesson here in the diary of Captain Birch, who twice gives not only the amount of pay but details how much to the numbers in each rank.[21] He receives 7s 6d a day for himself, although it appears he should have been paid 8s 0d a day. All other pay rates are as laid down for the New Model, although Birch was in the Lancashire Militia regiment of Colonel Asheton, but instead of three corporals he has four and 135 soldiers rather than 100. In the absence of a Birch it is easy to make false assumptions about ranks and unit strength.

Sanderson uses the term "squadron" four times in the Diary, but not in the usual modern sense of two or more troops under one command. Twice he refers to "my owne squadron", 20th January and 8th December, in reference to quarters and means a part of his troop. On 3rd April he refers to "my squadron . . . coronets Squadron . . . Leeuetents squadron" and is clearly talking about subdivisions of the troop under each of the three fighting commissioned officers. Monck also refers to the three sub-divisions of a troop of horse.[22]

When on the march it was normal for soldiers to be billeted on house-holds by the system known as "free quarter." This does not mean that soldiers were billeted at the householders' charge. Instead, the host might be paid, or more likely given a ticket to be redeemed at a later date, according to rates laid down by Parliament.[23] Punishment for breaking the rules could be severe: "no Officer or Soldier (upon Pain of Death) shall do the Contrary hereof ."[24] Despite these restrictions the system caused much hardship and was very unpopular.

Parliament's troops seem in general to have been rather better than the royalists when it came to discipline in the matter of quarters and paying for them. On the few occasions Sanderson mentions paying for quarters he seems to have been as prompt as funds would allow. On 26th February he paid his men and they paid for their quarters two days later. On 29th February he paid for quarters for 19th and 20th. The longest interval occurred when on 10th March he paid Bamburgh ward for 4th-18th February. Oddly enough, after his payment to Mr Swinoe of Chatton on 14th April, he makes no more reference to paying for quarters: perhaps the money had run out.

Lambert was so concerned about the effects of quartering that he put out an Order running to 15 sections and including revised rates for quartering – or, more accurately, rates to be paid by householders to avoid having soldiers quartered on them.[25]

Much has been written on the arms and armour of the Civil War period,[26] and it is unnecessary to go deeply into the topic here. In brief, during the second Civil War the cavalry were armed with swords and pistols, although a few may still have carried carbines.[27]

Their defensive armour consisted of relatively small but thick iron plates to protect front and back, known as back-and-breast, and an iron helmet, or pot, with three vertical bars to protect the face from a slashing blow.

Some may have worn a thick buff leather jacket, which could turn a sword, instead of, or even as well as, the back-and-breast, and leather boots would have helped to protect the leg from sword cuts.

Lilburne's regiment[28]

Robert Lilburne was a member of the well-known County Durham family; the Leveller Lt.-Col John Lilburne was his elder brother and Lt.-Col Henry Lilburne his younger.[29] His war service began in 1642 in the army of Essex, as a cornet in Lord Brooke's troop under the command of the General of horse, William, Earl of Berford.[30]

In 1643 he was lieutenant in Richard Crosse's troop in the same army. From June 1644 to June 1645 he commanded a regiment of harquebusiers (cavalry) raised in Durham, the following year he became colonel of a regiment of foot in the New Model, and in August 1647 was appointed governor of Newcastle upon Tyne.

He was replaced as both colonel of foot and as governor by Sir Arthur Hesilrige at the close of 1647,[31] after which he was appointed to the cavalry regiment which he had previously commanded from 1644 to 1645.[32] It was to this regiment that Sanderson (with Captain Lilburne, Captain Wilkinson, and Major Cholmley) was transferred in March 1648.

There is some difficulty in reconciling the number and ranks of officers in Lilburne's with the normal establishment of six troops. Apart from Major Sanderson's own troop, Col. Lilburne's troop is mentioned twice, Major Smithson's five times, Captain Bradford's ten, Captain Thomas Lilburne's five,[33] and Major Cholmley's[34] and Captain Wilkinson's once each, a total of seven troops.

As already noted, the regiment was in process of being absorbed into the New Model and regiments of the Northern Association had a different structure. For example, in October 1647 Col. Copley's regiment had eight troops with an average of 80 men in each.[35] It is thus theoretically possible that Lilburne's had seven troops, but Sanderson twice gives the number as six.[36]

Sanderson mentions Captain Wilkinson's troop only once, when 20 of the latter's men were to be transferred to his own troop, and never in connection with operations. It may be that Wilkinson was Col. Lilburne's Captain-Lieutenant.

Captain Wilkinson's troop is mentioned in operational terms in 1647: "Captain Wilkinson's and Captain Bradford's troops, and Sir Robert Collingwood's Regiment, are to march out of that County [Northumberland] into the county of York."[37] Firth says that Lilburne's was kept up to strength by the incorporation of other northern regiments, and in 1647 Wilkinson probably commanded an independent troop. In March 1648 "Capt. Wilkinsons, and some others yesterday desired the Commander in chief that they might have his consent to be reduced . . . which was assented to."[38]

It was probably at this point that Captain Wilkinson was brought into Lilburne's, and some of his men were transferred to Sanderson. On 13th March, presumably referring to these 20 men, the Diary gives the number at muster "besides ye Leeuetents men who are not com'd yet," perhaps an indication that they came from the now Captain-Lieutenant Wilkinson.

This still leaves three majors instead of one, and two captains in place of four. In March 1648 a list of officers to be continued in the North of England was published.[39] The officers in Lilburne's are given as: Col Lilburne, Major Smithson, Capt. Sanderson, Capt. Lilburne, Capt Cholmley, Capt. [blank]. The list for Lambert's includes Capt Bradford. These lists raise at least two questions.

First, it appears that Sanderson and Cholmley were substantive captains in Lilburne's, probably carrying over a previous rank which did not strictly still apply. For example, Colonel Henry Sanderson was referred to by his superior rank when appointed to be major in Hesilrige's regiment, (chapter 2, see note 56).

This would certainly solve the excess number of majors, although apart from this reference their given rank of major is reasonably consistent. In the records of the Northern army Sanderson is mentioned four times: three as Major and once as Captain.[40] Cholmley appears once, as Major.[41]

Secondly, Bradford appears in a muster of Lilburne's in 1645,[42] is mentioned several times as working with Sanderson in 1648, and was with the regiment in 1651 when "11th January To Capt. Bradford for the sicke souldrs of Col. Lilburnes Regimt extraordinary 60.00.00."[43] It is perhaps possible that Bradford was temporarily attached to Lambert's in March 1648, but the evidence available suggests that his listing with Lambert's is a clerical error.

There is ample scope for further investigation, but this is not the place to go any more deeply into the history of the officers of Lilburne's and Lambert's. Firth's plaint that "the history of the northern forces is obscure and chaotic" finds a ready echo.

Lilburne's regiment took part in the battle of Preston, and the advance into Scotland in autumn 1648, and was then part of the force besieging Pontefract. That castle surrendered in March 1649, and by July 1649 the regiment was at Northallerton, where Cornet Baynes took the muster.[44]

In July 1650 it was part of the army with which Cromwell invaded Scotland, and on July 31st was engaged in fighting at Musselburgh. The regiment was in reserve at the battle of Dunbar and not directly involved. It took part in the pursuit of the royalist forces but remained in Lancashire while the rest of the army marched south to the battle of Worcester, 3rd September 1650. Lilburne, with a mixed force including his own "wearied and somewhat shattered regiment, through our tedious march from Scotland",[45] defeated the Earl of Derby and the Lancashire royalists. The regiment had returned to Scotland by November, and remained there until October 1653, after which it was stationed in the north of England. When Lilburne supported Lambert against Parliament in 1659-60, Major Smithson took four of the six troops over to support Fairfax.

PART II

CHAPTER FOUR

HIS EARLY CAREER

In 1643 a Captain John Sanderson was appointed Commander of Holy Island, with leave to recruit 300 soldiers from London and surrounding counties.[1] This may or may not be the diarist: the location is appropriate, although the recruiting area is strange unless he were serving in the south when appointed. In November 1644 a royalist attempt to raise the siege of Helmsley was foiled in part by a Major Sanderson, commanding "240 of the Lord Fairfax his horse."[2] Again the identification is uncertain, but the reference cannot be to Henry, whose regiment of reformadoes remained in service until at least 1646.[3]

In August 1647, when Major General Lambert took over command of the Northern Forces, he met some of his officers at Sherburn [in Elmet] and ordered his regiments to rendezvous on Peckfield Moor, some 4 miles to the west (SE435315). Present at the rendezvous were six regiments of horse and foot "and the Two Troops commanded by Major Sanderson."[4] The sense is of two independent troops, command of which would attract the rank of major. The second troop was probably commanded by Captain Lilburne with whom he was consistently operating later in the year.

On 29th and 30th September 1647 Sanderson attended meetings of the Council of War at Ripon, as did Captain Lilburne on 29th.[5] Rushworth quotes from a letter from Ripon that "Major Sanderson's and Colonel [*recte* Captain] Lilburne's troops are appointed to march into Northumberland . . . to suppress the Moss-Troopers"[6] At the same time "Major Cholmley's and Captain Bayer's horse . . . are appointed to quarter in [Cumberland] . . .for their [moss troopers] suppression." A letter from York, 30th October 1647 reported that Sanderson sent 40 men to Bewcastle to apprehend moss troopers, and that he and Captain Lilburne "preserve the countrey" and had taken Thirlwall Castle when "the old thieves fled by night, and quit it."[7] (*plates 3, 4*) The area of these events is shown on map 2 (3).

Both Rushworth and Thomason report that on "the last of September" Sanderson was in action,[8] but this date calls for some explanation. Rushworth and Thomason are using the same source, "By letters from the North, dated Novemb. the 8th," that is apparently some five weeks after the event. Throughout the Thomason collection letters almost invariably refer to very recent news, rarely more than a week old. Rushworth reports that on 1st October a petition had been received complaining of the activities of the moss troopers, and it was on this date that the troops of Sanderson, Lilburne, Cholmley, and Bayers were "appointed to march" to deal with the problem.[9] He is clear that on 8th October Major Cholmley and Captain Lilburne marched through Ripon on their way to Cumberland and Northumberland respectively,[10] difficult to believe if they had already been active there at the end of September when in any case they had both been at meetings of the army council.[11] It is most unlikely that the records of the Northern Army meetings are incorrect, and the probable explanation is that the correspondent from the North wrote September when he meant October. The date of the following action is taken to be 31st October.

Sanderson's and Captain Lilburne's troops raided Liddesdale,[12] following an attack by Major Cholmley the night before. They met up at daybreak at "Newcastle" (Newcastleton, on the Liddel), after Sanderson had marched over Was-moors (probably West Moors, but unlocated), presumably overnight. They marched seven miles to Liddelside, but Lilburne's horses were tired, having been caught up in "foul mosses"[13] and Sanderson made the raid with his own troop alone, divided for the attack into three columns. The thieves were chased over the Scottish border leaving behind saddles, boots, swords, and pistols, as well as 60 stolen sheep. Sanderson did not pursue them across the border "lest exceptions be taken from thence", an indication that he was not simply a thrusting cavalryman but one who was aware of political implications of his actions. Instead, he "marched east-northerly, &c. seven miles up along the border of Scotland" (Rushworth) or "marched to Esk-Netherby, &c seven miles" (Thomason). He would have quartered at Lanton but decided against it owing to it being "inconvenient and unsafe; and therefore marched eight miles more into the country, within four miles of Carlisle." (Rushworth)

No direction is given for the first seven miles to Liddelside, the location of which is unknown,[14] but the later reference to "east-northerly" and "up the border" suggest that the whole march was to the north east. However, if he marched up the dale a total of 14 miles from Newcastleton he would have been about 30 miles from Carlisle, and another eight miles into the country cannot have brought him within four miles of that place.

If, on the other hand, the whole march was down the dale "up to" (i.e. as far as) the border the picture is much clearer. Seven miles down the Liddel would bring them to the area near Cauldside, and seven miles from there is close to Netherby, which is on the Esk. "East-northerly" and "Esk-Netherby" could be two interpretations of a handwritten despatch. The distance from Newcastleton to Netherby is actually about 13 miles, which is near enough to fit the account. Lanton could be Longtown, eight miles from Carlisle.

On 6th November Sanderson was again reported as "active against the Mosse Troopers."[15] Early in 1648 he had further success against them, recovering stolen cattle. The report is dated 13th January, two days after the start of the Diary and presumably referring to an event just before then.[16]

The Diary begins on 11th January.

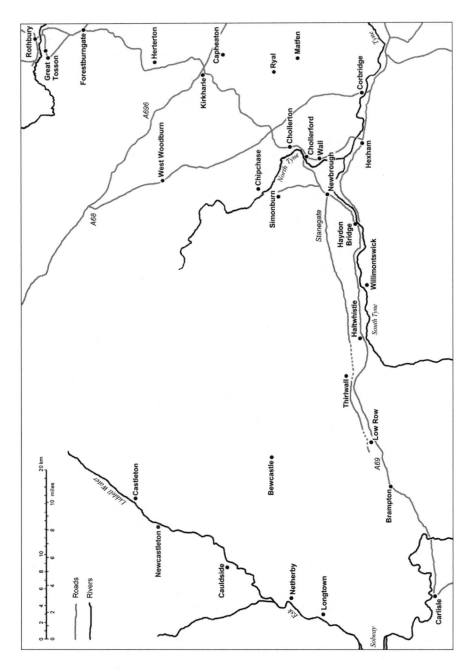

Fig. 3: Map 2. Rothbury and Corbridge to Carlisle

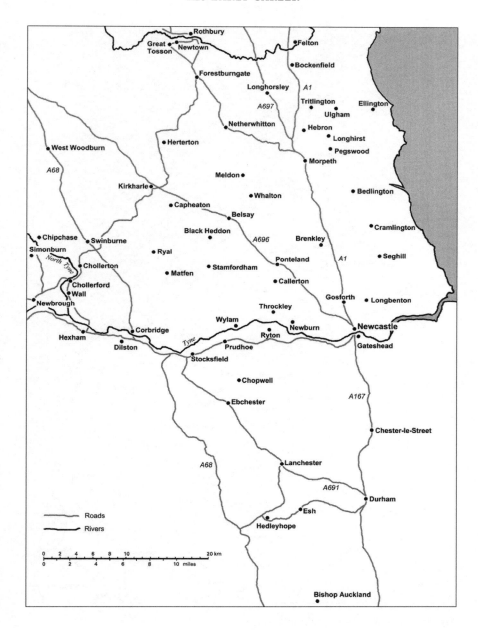

Fig. 4: Map 3. Rothbury to Bishop Auckland

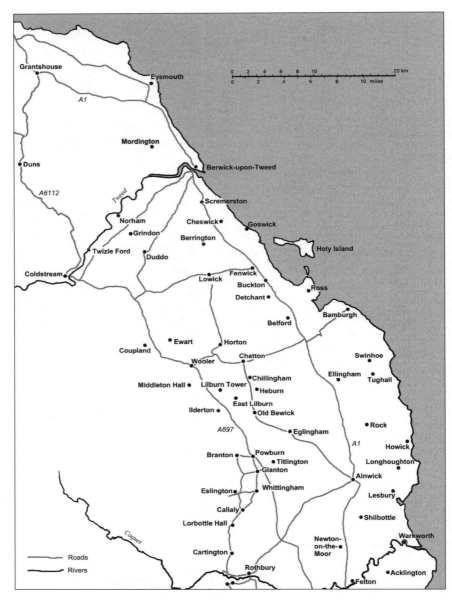

Fig. 5: Map 4. Rothbury to Grantshouse

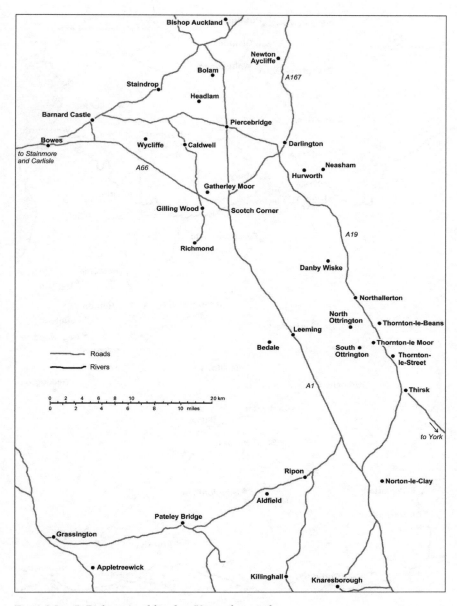

Fig 6: Map 5. Bishop Auckland to Knaresborough

Fig. 7: Map 6. Hexham to Branton, 1st July 1648

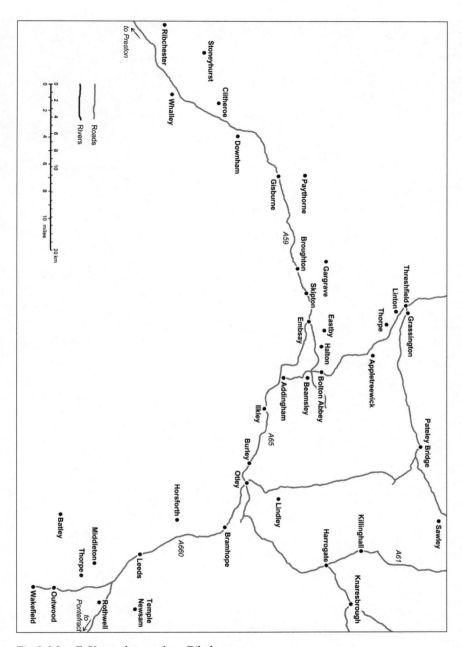

Fig 8: Map 7. Knaresborough to Ribchester

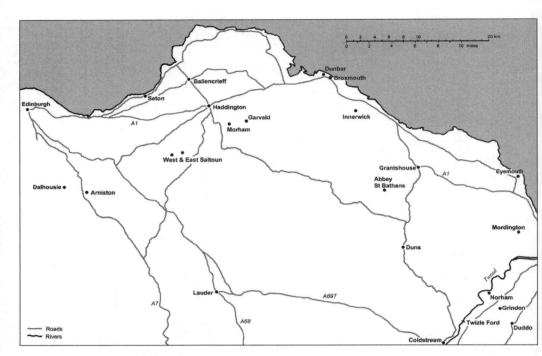

Fig. 9: Map 8. Berwick-upon-Tweed to Edinburgh

CHAPTER FIVE

CAPHEATON TO APPLETREEWICK: THE DIARY YEAR

January 1648

"I went to Capheaton."

The opening entry on 11th January is as enigmatic as any in the Diary. If the early pages had been preserved (see *The Diary volume*, Appendix 2) we would know where he had come from, but he does not feel it necessary to record why he made the journey. It is, incidentally, one of six visits he made there during the year, presumably for a purpose so obvious to him that he had no need to enter an *aide memoire*.

At Morpeth (*plate 6*) the "sesses" he was trying to raise were local taxes ("assessments") for the support of his troop. When he dispersed his troop from Simonburn to new quarters they may have gone as far afield as Haltwhistle and Woodburne, 25 miles apart, where he later paid for quarters, but he was more likely to be paying for previous quarters at one or both of these places. His comment "reseruing standerton p'ish" may show where his own squadron was quartered.

Following the entry for 25th, he seems to have recalled what he did on 21st and 24th and added them afterwards. The entry for 21[*sic*] should come before the entry for 21st, and on that day he went from Matfen to Haltwhistle, and from there to new quarters at Cheeseburne. This should be borne in mind when looking at the From and To entries in the transcript.

The payment to his squadron (for "squadron" see *Parliamentary Army* in chapter 3) on 27th is presumably something on account to help them in paying for their quarters, although the sense is not entirely clear. His visit to Newcastle on 31st will have been be in relation to the reduction in the size of the army.

February

On 2nd February 1647[8] there was a report from Durham about "Major Sanderson and Captaine Lilburnes troops, who are ordered to march thither to have their accompts ordered accordingly."[1] Lilburne may have gone with him on 3rd and 5th-8th, but he makes no mention of this or of troops accompanying them. The report to Parliament may refer to actions already undertaken before the start of the diary or, more likely, his " papers referd to Mr. Gilpin and Mr. Marchall" on 5th were his accounts.

When his troop was ordered north to Alnwick (*plate 5*) and Wooler they first came to a rendezvous, which does indeed suggest that they were widely scattered in their quarters. He sent them off while he was busy at Hedleyhope and Durham, where his brother Peter, a civilian, helped him to draw up debentures, a method of paying troops by promissory note.

When Sanderson's troop moved north without him it will have been under the command of his lieutenant. Sanderson rejoined his men on 12th February, and over the next three days disbanded his supernumerary soldiers. On 9th February Parliament had voted on the size of the army[2], but it is clear that a general reduction was already taking place. Rushworth quotes a letter from York: "We are proceeding here to the work of disbanding as fast as we can . . . which will both prevent Discontent, and take away the worst Members."[3] A Proclamation by Lambert recommended for disbanding (among others) "Those who are of debayst or dishonest conversation and demeanour, as in Drinking, Swearing, abusing their Quarters or Country, or other demeanours contrary to the Lawes and Ordinances of Warre."[4] As recorded in his Order Book, Lambert announced reductions at his Council of War on 27th January.

On 8th February Sanderson had been given £175 for two months pay for a corporal and 30 men. This is a useful confirmation of rates of pay given by the Lords on 19th February[5] as it amounts to 56 days' pay for one corporal at 2s 6d a day and 30 troopers at 2s 0d a day. Equally, the sum of £5 12s paid to each man (see entry for 15th) is 56 days' pay for one trooper. Pay was clearly given in lunar rather than calendar months. The figures show that Sanderson's men were on New Model rates rather than a different Northern Association scale. The fact that Corporal Racket received debentures as well as cash indicates that his pay was more than two months in arrears, a not uncommon situation; the entry for 7th shows that the troopers also received debentures.

No sooner had Sanderson discharged the men than he was ordered south again, to Barnard Castle (*plate 7*). He marched with his troop to Hilton, and left them for two days (see entry for 29th) while he went to Hedleyhope. Hilton is not identified; it could mean Hylton Castle, near Sunderland but that is eight miles from Chester-le-Street where he later paid for quarters. Hilton near Staindrop is only nine miles from Barnard Castle and is unlikely. It is not clear whether his lieutenant took them on to Barnard Castle or whether Sanderson rejoined them, but the fact that they stayed there for two days suggests they waited until he returned.

On 22nd February he left for York, arriving on 23rd, where the "ye generall *poferd* mee my troope, and gaue me 14 days pay for them . . ." The initial 'p' of 'poferd' is not drawn as any other such letter in the Diary and it is almost certainly meant for a 'p' with a bar across the tail to indicate 'pr' giving the reading 'proffered,' indicating that he was offered the command of a troop.[6]

The most likely meaning is that it was at this point that, his independent command of two troops having been abolished under the New Modelling of the army, he was brought into Lilburne's. The general was Major-General Lambert who commanded in the north, and it is noteworthy that it was to the general and not to his colonel that Sanderson reports on 18th April and 16th June. He received orders directly from the general as early as 15th February, and again on 16th April.

A report on 28th February refers to "The disbanding of Major Sandersons Troop of Horse, and Captain Lilburnes Troop of Horse."[7] This clearly refers to their disbandment as two independent troops even though they were immediately taken into Lilburne's.

The pay he received for his troop, £161.1s.2d is impossible to reconcile with the known pay rates and establishment. From the few figures Sanderson gives he should have had 82 troopers, but there is no indication of numbers of officers and office holders (see the reference to Captain Birch, *Parliamentary Army* in chapter 3,).

On 29th February he sent his brother Samuel off to pay for quarters "about Chester for $a & $u the 20 & 21 febr." He made an error here; those days were 19th and 20th (see Appendix 1).

March

Sanderson returned to York, arriving on 1st March and leaving on 3rd. The supplementary entry for 𝕸 [1st] shows that he travelled with his servant John Jackson. The order to pay off his surgeon, a post for which there was no establishment in a unit smaller than a regiment, will have been to do with the general reduction in numbers. It also reinforces the point that until this time Sanderson was not part of a regiment but commanding two independent troops for which a surgeon will have been useful.

The order to reduce his lieutenant in favour of a new man, Leven, raises the question of who held the post up to then. His accounts, (Appendix 3a), show payment to Lt. Shepperson "before he went", but he was also making payments to Lt. Strangeways. It is unlikely that Strangeways was reduced, as Captain (later Major) Strangways [sic] is recorded in the regiment from 1656-1660.[8] Strangeways is discussed further in chapter 7.

Incidentally, the amount shown as due per day, 9s 4d, is made up of 5s 4d a day for pay and 4s per day for the two horses allowed to a lieutenant, another useful confirmation of rates of pay actually in use. On 2nd Sanderson received pay for 80 soldiers, which tends to confirm the peacetime troop strength.

As he had been back in Barnard Castle for only two days there must have been some compelling reason for him to return to York so soon. During his visit, on 3rd March, 20 men of Captain Wilkinson's troop, then in York as shown by the entry for 6th, were ordered to join Sanderson's troop which would bring it up to wartime establishment. The royalist uprising did not begin until 23rd March, but Charles I had signed his Engagement with the Scots, by which they agreed to restore the king by military means if necessary, as early as 26th December 1647. There were already indications of coming trouble from north of the Border: "The Scots Soldiers are very chearful with Hopes of another Invasion and our English Ground adjacent to their Quarters, sends forth Echoes of their thundering Threats daily" There were also contra-indications: "Letters from Scotland, from a good hand, give us assurance That we need not fear a sudden Disturbance in England from thence".[9] Rumour and counter-rumour were no doubt a spur to a change of policy, and to have been behind his quick return to York and the increase in his troop strength. On his return to Barnard Castle, his lieutenant (probably Shepperson), his Chirurgion (surgeon), and another five troopers were paid off.

Sanderson went up to Bamburgh (*plate 8*) where he paid for quarters for mid-February, calling at Hedleyhope on the way back on 10th March. This was long ride of 58 miles.

When his troop was mustered on 13th, he had 77 troopers "besides ye Leeueten^ts men who are not com'd yet." These were presumably the men from Captain (-Lieutenant) Wilkinson's troop.

After another visit to Hedleyhope, he had orders on 23rd March to march to Belford and Wooler, only 17 miles from Berwick-upon-Tweed. This may be concerned with the general attitude of the Scots, as news of the royalist uprising, which began in the south, will not have reached the north for several days.

April

Leaving after an unexplained delay of four days he dispersed his troop to duties around his patrol area, including an inspection of the border when his cornet was sent to look at Berwick and he himself went to Grindonrigg.

At about this time there were further clear signs of trouble. A letter to William Clarke, Secretary to the Council of the Army, refers to the situation in Scotland, where "the moderate party are now the fewest, and that the generall resolution is to come into England."[11] Throughout April and May Sanderson was operating chiefly in the north of the county, often close to the border. Rushworth recorded in April that "The Cavaliers in Northumberland are a little curbed by Major Sanderson's Horse, quartered in that County, and do already fear they may be questioned again."[12] Referring to one or two troops detached from a regiment as "Major Sanderson's Horse" shows that the mind of the reporter was attuned to the Major's previous independent status and that the nature of his duties was little changed. The feelings of the local people must reflect the general fear throughout the country that troops of either army might descend on them at any time and take them in for questioning: "rounding up the usual suspects."

Sanderson then went to Hedleyhope, arriving there on 15th April, leaving his troop in the north. The only purpose seems to have been to go to the races at Gatherley although "I founde my gray nag lame". He entered his mare, which came second to Major Smithson. Captain Wilkinson provided the plate, as shown in Sanderson's accounts, but the meeting was probably a publicly organised rather than regimental event as Gatherley Moor was well known as a centre for horse racing.[13] It is clear that special, presumably light-weight, saddles, were used for racing, and the fact that Richard Robinson had a riding suit suggests that jockeys were already running in colours, although neither they nor the saddles had been paid for.

Horse racing was disapproved of by the Puritans, but there were certainly other races held. There was a meeting at Berwick in March under the guise of which an attempt was to be made on the town, and "At Chop Welledge on Wednesday next a great Horse race 14 Horses run, which hath not been usual of late times."[14] The location of Chop Welledge (Chopwell Edge?) is unknown. Cornet Baynes in a letter from York to Captain Adam Baynes, 24th March 1648, refers to a race meeting just held at Clifford.[15]

While at Hedleyhope "my brother sent Robert Bell to me with an order from generall Lambert to march with my troope into newcastle." The brother was presumably Samuel, who seems to have been in Lilburne's at this time. On the other hand, within a day or so he "lent my brother Sam[l] 4[li]. 00. 00". Samuel could already have been with him, which means that another brother (?Charles) brought the message, or the money could have been carried to Samuel by Robert Bell. The order must have been carried out in his absence as he did not rejoin his troop until eight days later, when together they moved from Newcastle to Rothbury and thence to Alnwick. The orders came from Lambert rather than from his colonel, showing that Sanderson was working to the general rather than his nominal commanding officer.

He does not explain why he went to York on 18th to see Lambert; it was a long ride but cannot have been important as he then sent a letter to the general who was elsewhere. When he stayed with William Lees on the way, as he had done before, he gives the location as Leeming Loning. This in not so much a place as an address: Inglis (Routes 8, 140) describes the Great North Road (A1) from Boroughbridge to Scotch Corner as Leeming Lane as late at 1911, and loaning is an old word for a lane. William Lees had a house on the side of the main road, probably in the vicinity of Leeming, but nothing more is known about him.

Berwick was seized by royalists under Sir Marmaduke Langdale and Sir Charles Lucas on 28th April, and Carlisle by Sir Thomas Glanton and Sir Philip Musgrave on 29th.[16] About this time, Langdale tried to bribe Capt. Batten, Governor of Holy Island.[17]

May

On 2nd May Sanderson garrisoned Warkworth Castle (*plate 9*) with 30 dragoons sent by Sir Arthur Hesilrige, Governor of Newcastle, as well as with the 18 troopers he left there. Hesilrige, in a letter to the Speaker of the House of Commons, William Lenthall dated 8th May, records that he sent men and ammunition to Warkworth as soon as he heard that Berwick had been taken.[18] Sanderson provisioned the castle for 14 days. It may have been about this time that his claim for expenses (Appendix 3b) records "Thos. Gooley, Mr. Ogle's man, for going into the enemy's quarters near Berwick presently after the taking of it, 5s."[19] Mr Ogle cannot be identified, unless he is the man Sanderson went to see on 31st March.

On 5th May he heard that Cartington (*plate 10*) was being garrisoned by royalists under Major Errington, and at once marched the 19 miles there from Morpeth with 120 horse. His own troop should have had about 90 men after leaving nine at Warkworth, and similarly Captain Lilburne's either 70 or 90 depending on its establishment; the balance of 40 or 60 men were presumably left in Morpeth as a garrison against any danger of marauding royalists capturing it.

Sanderson then "summoned" Cartington, a demand for immediate surrender as an alternative to wholesale slaughter. The term is best explained by extracts from two letters from Cromwell to the defenders of Farringdon in April 1645: "I summon you to deliver into my hands the House wherein you are . . .Which if you refuse to do, you are to expect the utmost extremity of war . . ." and later that day "I will not spare a man of you, if you put me to a storm."[20]

Errington refused, and 50 of Sanderson's troopers fought on foot for five hours, with only limited success. They then returned to Morpeth, presumably because he felt it was not safe to remain in the area. If it were an error not to take more men, Sanderson at least had the ability to recognise an impossibility and to reverse his decision. In fact it is not normally the job of cavalry to assault or to hold strong points and his next move clearly accepted this.

Two days later, Sunday 7th May, on hearing that Cartington had been abandoned the day before, he sent "post to the Governor of Newcastle for procuring dragoons to take Cartington".[21] The dragoons arrived in Morpeth on Monday 8th, and Cartington was occupied the same day. Sanderson "got horses in the Country for the foot." The sense is that the dragoons (mounted infantry) had marched on foot to Morpeth. It is not known at what time Sanderson's message reached Newcastle, but the men would have to be selected and make themselves ready before marching the 15 miles to Morpeth. It is possible that part of the distance was covered on 7th, but they did not reach Morpeth until 8th and then rode 19 miles on untrained horses to Cartington. It is not an extraordinary feat, but it does point up the organisation and discipline of the parliamentary forces. It also shows that, despite the problems the war must already have brought to the area, Sanderson was able to commandeer 40 horses in no more than 24 hours.

Rushworth makes no mention of the fighting, recording that Cartington was abandoned by the royalists on the approach of Major Sanderson's troop, and that "the Major hath got 40 Musketeers and put into it, who it's feared will not be able to hold it unless more be added.[22]" This forecast proved to be correct.

The garrison was strengthened on 12th May by the addition of one man from each squadron, that is, three men from each troop (see *Parliamentary Army* in chapter 3). On 11th May his troop and Captain Lilburne's had been joined by Major Smithson's and Colonel Lilburne's troops, under the command of Major Smithson, Col. Lilburne presumably being engaged elsewhere. This made 12 men, a useful addition under Major Smithson's corporal. Despite this, Cartington was abandoned by the parliamentary forces within a few days. "Newcastle May 18 . . . Cartington being not tenable, the men in it were called off, and the house dismantled . . . " [23] The castle was presumably not susceptible of quick demolition and was held briefly by the royalists on 1st July.

The situation in Northumberland was becoming dangerous for its inhabitants. "The high Sheriffe of Northumberland, and many Justices of Peace, are inforced to flie to Newcastle for the safety of their persons, leaving their houses and goods exposed to the danger of the enemy."[24] A few days later Sir Phillip Musgrave "hath marched [from Carlisle] as far as his own house, neer Kirby Stephen and to have forced Cholmley over Stainmore."[25] Cholmley was probably the Major Cholmley of Lilburne's, discussed in Appendix 7a.

It was when he came to quarter at Alnwick on 13th May that Sanderson wrote to Peter Denton of Lanchester[26] (Appendix 4). His plea that he had not had time to call at Lanchester when last at Hedleyhope (on 21st April) on his way to Durham does not ring true as the diversion would have added no more than four miles to a day on which he rode only 24 miles. The fact that he took three weeks to answer the letter, and then suggested that Denton come to Hedleyhope to see him, sounds as if he were in no hurry for the meeting.

There is a report dated from Newcastle on 11th May that Alnwick and Morpeth were taken by the royalists.[27] Sanderson does not mention it, and as he was quartered in Morpeth until 8th and in Alnwick from 13th it seems that there was no more than a very brief occupation of both places. It may have been because of this royalist raid that he was sent post to Newcastle on 15th, presumably on the order of Major Smithson. Whatever the reason, it must have been of some significance that he, the second most senior man present, was sent to report. It was on the same day that he had the satisfaction of recording that "every man a bottle under him." This was a bundle of straw or hay, used in this case for sleeping on, and suggests that they were not usually so fortunate. The fact that they were able to get 100 horse loads of hay from Chillingham shows that, although the summer was a bad one, the growing of some crops was still possible.

The rest of May was taken up with patrolling, occasionally taking prisoners. For most of this time he had Captain Bradford's troop with him instead of Captain Lilburne's. The entry for 16th shows that part of Lambert's regiment had also been operating in the area, as on this day Major Goodrick's troop marched away from Alnwick; and Goodrick is shown as a captain in Lambert's in March 1648.[28] This had presumably been a temporary strengthening of the garrison. The significance of the entries on 21st and 22nd about Col. Weldon's oats and rye is explained elsewhere: "our English Troopes at Anwick, have fetched in Colonel Weldons Wheat least the enemy at Barwick take it in; as they did him;"[29] A bowl or boll is an old measure equal (usually) to 2 bushels,[30] a bushel being equal to 2 gallons or 9 litres.

On 25th May he is known to have written to Hesilrige: "Sir Arthur Haslerige received a letter from major Sanderson at Alnwick, where he doth gallant service well approved on."[31]

If his claims for expenses (Appendix 3b) were listed in chronological order it will have been in the last part of May that he sent men to spy on the enemy at Twizle, Alnwick, Ford Castle, Tweedmouth, Norham, and Learmouth. Major Sanderson was clearly involved in the gathering of intelligence, but whether this was any more that the normal activity of the officer commanding a cavalry patrol is not clear.

The parliamentary forces certainly had to make themselves aware of what was happening as they were very thinly spread: "Wee have two Troopes of Horse, and two Companies of Foot lying at Alnwick Castle, and that is all we have in Northumberland."[32]

When, on 27th, his cornet and 30 horse took Mr Grey of Howick and Mr Reed of Titlington it is not clear whether they were found in the same place or in their houses. If the latter, it would have been a round trip of 44 miles.

June

At the beginning of June Sanderson and the foot at Alnwick got orders to hand over their provisions to Warkworth and march to Newcastle. This effectively abandoned Alnwick as a stronghold. There must have been some unexplained urgency, as they left Alnwick at 9 p.m., arriving at Felton, nine miles away, by 1.00 a.m. Progress was very slow, at just over two miles an hour, but the sun had set at 8.40 p.m, twilight was ended by 9.50, and the moon did not rise until a few minutes after 1 a.m.[33] If the night were overcast, darkness would have been complete by 10 p.m. At Felton he was told it was up to him whether or not he went to Newcastle (a very strange order), and his entries show that he did not go there. His claim for expenses records that "a man met us from Felton with a letter from the Governor of Newcastle which required us to stay." This contradicts the Diary. Why he had to send the messenger back riding post, at a cost of 5s 4d is not stated. The expenses also show that on 2nd June he sent a Mr Marshall's man from Morpeth "up to Ryall and Wall for intelligence upon the report of Langdale's coming thither." "Up to" sounds like a journey northward, but the only Ryall (Ryal) in the area is at NZ 015742, two miles north of Matfen, and Wall (NY917690) is two miles south of Chollerford. The probable meaning is "as far as." The two places are about eight miles apart and Langdale's suspected movements can be tied to events on 9th June. Who this Marshall was, and why his man was selected is not known.

There was a skirmish on 3rd June between Morpeth and Alnwick, during which Mr Baynes and Will Windsore were captured. In an exchange of prisoners, Windsore was released but Baynes was held until 14th. Although Sanderson does not say so, it seems likely that this was Commissary Baynes who mustered the troops at Alnwick on 1st June. He can safely be identified with Cornet John Baynes. Commissaries were responsible for musters, and Cornet Baynes also mustered the regiment in July 1649, at Northallerton.[34] Will Windsore is not so easily identified. Sir William Drummond of Hawthornden noted in his diary for 1657 that on 14 May: 'Mester Winsore, an English ferrier, cam and saw me in his jurney towards London'.[35] It is conceivable that he was Sanderson's farrier but this is very speculative.

It is worth noting that although the fighting between royalists and parliamentary forces could be bitter at times there are many instances of mannerly communication (see note 20, this chapter), and on 8th June Sanderson was able to send 12s to Baynes through his servant Thomas Atkinson.

Sanderson's expenses show that on 3rd he sent his quartermaster riding post to Newcastle. This does not appear in the Diary and the reason is unknown; it may have been to give news of the skirmish or of the taking of Cornet Baynes, or to report some new intelligence.

Sanderson has as usual left much unsaid here. A report in *The Moderate Intelligencer* says that, on hearing that Alnwick had been abandoned, royalists came down from Berwick to occupy it, and it was this news which caused Sanderson to march north from Morpeth with "three troops, one new raised." This last may possibly be Captain Ogle's troop, which was certainly with Sanderson about a week later, as will be seen.

The same report says that he had Captain Lilburne's troop with him, although Sanderson himself names Captain Bradford; perhaps the writer had been used to Lilburne being under Sanderson's command the previous year. It also mentions the two companies of foot left in garrison with Sanderson at Alnwick, given by him on 18th May as Major Legard's & Captain Challenor's.[36] The report goes on to say that Sanderson pursued the royalists almost to Berwick and went into quarters at Scremerston, although he himself says he quartered in Outchester, 12 miles to the south. A letter apparently written by someone under Sanderson's command also says that they "lay within four miles of Barwick"[37] (Scremerston is about three miles south of Berwick) which does suggest an error. On the other hand, the writer may have been in the other troop and Sanderson was concerned only with the whereabouts of his own men.

A letter gives the royalist numbers as 140 horse and 120 dragoons and the number of prisoners taken as 16 rather than the 3 of the Diary, and says that Sanderson met them on the march and forced them to fight.[38] The letter goes on to say that "the mist was so great wee could not see the enemies disorder nor retreat; we took four of them prisoners, kild two, and wounded about 12 or 14."

On 7th June Sanderson "put corne and fat beasts into holy Island," (*plate 11*) apparently provisions for six months,[39] and then moved south, first to

Chillingham and on the 8th to Cartington, which was no longer held (see above note 23). It may have been there that Mr Marshall's man brought intelligence of royalist troops around Chollerford, as there is no sense of urgency up to this point.

On 9th June he and his troop, presumably still in company with Captain Bradford's troop as they were again operating together six days later, set out for Chollerford. According to the letter referred to in note 37 he also had Captain Ogle and his troop, and the same letter says "Col George Fenwick being joined with Major Sanderson (the day before)". On 1st July, as will be seen, Fenwick appears to have had around 130 men with him, but how many he had at this point is a matter of speculation. The total force may have numbered around 400 men. After 19 miles they stopped to rest and feed and then covered the 12 miles to Chollerford and Simonburn where they encountered the enemy. The Diary is curt and matter-of-fact, but the letter adds the information that they rode as fast as they could, and that the force crossed the river North Tyne by fording ("wee ventured desperately to ride the water at Chollerford") (*plate 12*), but does not say why they did not use the fourteenth century bridge which survived until 1771. It may have been guarded by royalists, or may have been in an unrecorded state of disrepair.

When the enemy fled from Simonburn to Newbrough and split up, the parliamentary force divided, with Fenwick following one group the three miles to Haydon Bridge while Sanderson pursued others a further 20 miles to Haltwhistle. The Roman road known as the Stanegate (*plate 13*) passes through Newbrough and runs just over a mile north of Haltwhistle. The likelihood is that they were on the Stanegate all the way, and did not actually pass through the town. The letter says that they went beyond Haltwhistle "even within 14 miles of Carlisle." This would take them to the vicinity of Low Row, a hamlet half a mile south of the Stanegate, which would explain why the Diary says they "lay that night in the feild," and perhaps why Haltwhistle is named by Sanderson as being the only place of any size which they passed. The then population of Haltwhistle, which might have been expected to provided at least some quarter, is unknown as records were destroyed during the Civil War.[40] The Haydon Bridge group "took through the water", presumably the river South Tyne, and in the pursuit one of Captain Ogle's men was drowned (note 37).

In the day, assuming they did indeed pursue beyond Haltwhistle, Sanderson's men covered at least 58 miles which, considering they were skirmishing as well, was a significant ride. The following day, Saturday, they marched 15 miles to Hexham where, not surprisingly "wee stayed till munday".

This was no more than a minor skirmish, with the enemy retreating rather than stopping to fight, and with the only casualty lost in the river rather than by enemy action. But a body of around 400 horse descending on the royalists from over 30 miles away, and then chasing them for another 20, must have caused the enemy serious disquiet.

The difficulty in crossing the rivers is, on its own, surprising. The North Tyne at Chollerford is normally fairly placid in summer, and in places can be crossed on foot, but following heavy rain can become a raging torrent. It would seem that it was not unlike this on 9th June. The South Tyne at Haydon Bridge, where Capt. Ogle's trooper was drowned, is wider than the North Tyne at Chollerford and is also shallow in dry weather, but with pools of up to 5m deep. The level fluctuates rapidly with changes in rainfall, can rise by over a metre and is fast flowing when in spate.[41] The reason for the state of the rivers was the extremely wet weather, discussed in chapter 1.

After this raid Sanderson returned to patrolling in the neighbourhood of Warkworth, during which there occurred what seems to have been a half-hearted mutiny. The original transcript reads "memorandum that 13 my troope and Capt: Bradfords would needs go back and were like to mutinie". But there is a planetary sign before 13, and a better reading would be "memorandum that ♂ 13th my troope and Capt: Bradfords would needs go back and were like to mutinie." Thirteen unhappy men is one thing, but 200 disgruntled cavalrymen would have taken some facing down. However, there is no mention of any punishment, and it may have been no more than grumbling which went a little too far. He records this as occurring on Tuesday 13th, yet his entry for Wednesday 14th shows that it was only on the latter day that they went north of Morpeth to Acklington and so past Helm o' the Hill. The point is discussed below, *The writing of the Diary* in Appendix 2.

It was on 15th that he sent letters to the general, an indication that he was reporting directly to Lambert (who was in Penrith blocking Langdale[42]) rather than to Lilburne. The content is not disclosed, but may have contained intelligence which had a bearing on the events of the next few days.

On 19th they moved south towards Newcastle, for reasons which it is left to others to explain. "Upon Colonel *Tempests* coming into Northumberland, ours drew towards Newcastle"[43] because "Colonel Gregory [*sic*] Fenwick and Major Sanderson, who until now lay to strengthen Berwick, having notice that Langdale's horse intended to get between them and Newcastle, retreated . . ."[44]

They were in the Newcastle area when, on 20th June, "wee removed by reason of raine at night to Longbenton." This is his single, understated concession to what must have been atrocious weather for cavalry on patrol.

From 23rd to 30th June there was considerable activity covered by only brief entries. Again, it is only by reference to other sources, including a letter Sanderson wrote on 3rd July,[45] the letter from Hesilrige mentioned above (note 43), and two letters from 'gentlemen of quality',[46] that the full picture can be seen. The culmination was of such significance that the events are worth examining in some detail, both for their intrinsic interest and for the light they shed on the activities of the army of the period. To obviate a large number of notes, the letters are abbreviated in the text in parenthesis as Sanderson, Hesilrige, and G of Q. For convenience, the whole area of the action is shown on map 6 (7).

Late in June, Langdale sent Colonel Tempest from Carlisle with seven or eight hundred horse to join up with Colonel Grey coming down from

Berwick with more horse to make a total of around 1200 (Hesilrige). The "two commanders of quality" (note 46) give the royalist strength as 1000. This movement was clearly known to the parliamentary forces, and Hesilrige ordered Colonel Wren with 220 (Sanderson) of the Bishoprick horse to join Colonel Fenwick of the Northumberland horse. Wren came to Sanderson at Newburn on the evening of Sunday 25th (Diary). According to Sanderson (Diary and Sanderson), the royalist horse seem to have intended to rendezvous around Chollerton on the following day, but were prevented by the manoeuvring of the parliamentary horse which moved westward and quartered at Chipchase.

The royalists retreated, and made their rendezvous further north; Hesilrige says that this was about Alnwick, which had been abandoned by Parliament when Sanderson left there on 19th June. Sanderson and Wren moved eastwards again to Blackheddon on 27th and to Capheaton on 28th (Diary). There, Sanderson was joined by dragoons sent by Hesilrige; the latter says he sent 100, Sanderson's letter records receiving 50.

At Capheaton they were only 4 miles from the enemy, who would then be 24 miles from Alnwick. When the royalists closed to within a mile, the parliamentary troops pulled back towards Hexham both to meet additional reinforcements and to convince the enemy that they were retreating and posed no threat (Sanderson). Under 500 horsemen (including 50 dragoons) would certainly look very inferior to 1200 and the ploy appears to have worked, as the royalists marched north to meet up with 600 foot from Berwick and, as events showed, took no great precautions against attack.

The parliamentary horse reached Hexham on Thursday 29th: "viz. Col. Fenwick, and our two old troops" (Sanderson), that is to say his and probably Captain Lilburne's. Sanderson and Fenwick had been guarding Berwick (see note 45) which may mean that they were already together although Sanderson does not mention him earlier. It is more likely that there were acting in concert but did not actually meet up until they got to Hexham. There is no indication of Wren's location. At about the same time, Colonel Lilburne with three troops reached Haydon Bridge (Hesilrige, Sanderson). Lambert had sent Lilburne[47] as "the enemy there [Northumberland] increases much and summon in the country which come in freely." He also despatched ten troops with Colonel Harrison, who set out on 1st July.[48]

The parliamentary strength is worth analysing. Sanderson's letter gives some precise numbers. The whole of Lilburne's regiment appears to have been there, as Lambert says that he sent Lilburne "with the remainder of his regiment." (see previous note). Sanderson's, Captain Lilburne's, and Captain Bradford's troops all seem to have been operating in Northumberland in the weeks before, and Sanderson mentions Col. Lilburne having three troops with him. Sanderson certainly had about 100 in his troop, but one month later Cholmley had only 80. If all but Sanderson's troop had only 80 men the total comes to 500. Sanderson's figure of 50 dragoons and 220 for Wren's regiment brings the total to 770 men, leaving Fenwick's regiment with a strength of 130. Both Wren's and Fenwick's have remarkably low numbers, but as they were both newly-raised (Sanderson and Hesilrige respectively) they may not have been at full establishment, or perhaps only detachments were sent.

The Diary (29th June) then records that "I sent to Coll: Lilburne at Heydon bridge to meet us in the morning by nine at Chollerford". This sounds as though, however diplomatically his message was phrased, he is giving orders to his colonel. His letter merely says that "Friday, 30 Junii, according to agreement, we randevouzed". It may be that, owing to months of patrolling Northumberland, he knew more of what was happening than his superiors and was thus to some extent orchestrating, although not conducting, events. The various troops all rendezvoused at Chollerford to the number of 900 men (Hesilrige). The letter from Two Commanders of Quality (note 46) gives the parliamentary strength as 600. Rushworth, 1175, 4th July, gives the parliamentary strength as 600 and the royalists as 1000, corrected on 5th July to 900 and 1200.

Hesilrige gives the rendezvous as Chollerton but Sanderson is here accepted as correct when he gives Chollerford in both his letter and his Diary. With 900 cavalry, a meeting at Chollerford (*plate 12*) on the North Tyne makes more sense than Chollerton which has slightly less easy access to water.

Hesilrige says that "Col: *Lilburn* with three Troops of Horse, came to them to Chollerton, and that evening they marched towards the Enemy." The Diary is not entirely clear about the timing, but Sanderson's letter is a little better "we randevouzed, about eleven of the clocke, at Chollerford, three miles north of Hexam. We hasted away that night, and marched sixteen miles, from Hexam to Harterton; bated our horses two houres; then mounted again, and marched from thence." The Diary refers to meeting Colonel Lilburne at 9 o'clock and "marched to harterton. that night about eleaven a Clock we advanced . . ." It is not entirely clear whether they left Chollerford at 11 p.m, rather than earlier, but that seems to be the sense. Lambert in a letter says that Lilburne "drew near them [the enemy] in the night." (note 48).

It is not known why Col. Lilburne came to the rendezvous at 9.00 and yet the march did not begin for another 14 hours. It is possible that they may have been waiting for clear intelligence. Perhaps the most probable explanation is that they knew where the enemy was likely to be found and wanted to advance at night in the hope of surprising them.

As some aid to understanding the problems of a night march the route was followed (by car), on the equivalent day and at the same times, in 2006. Travel was in short stages, with long halts to allow, as it were, the column to catch up. Sunset and sunrise times were virtually identical to 1648 but the moon, which was full, rose earlier, at 9.45. The weather was dry, with light cloud cover.

July

On 30th June 1648 the sun set at about 8.30 p.m., and twilight ended about an hour later. The moon was about two thirds full, and rose just before

11.30, reaching a height of 10 degrees about half an hour after midnight. It would already have had an effect on the brightness of the night by 11.00, and it could be that a start was made at this time as it was known that the sky would be light enough to march.

The place of their halt, Harterton, appears on some maps as the house and park of Hartington Hall but is signposted Herterton House. The distance from Chollerford by road measured both from a large scale map and by odometer is 16 miles, which agrees precisely with the distance given by Sanderson's letter of 3rd July.

There he says "to Harterton; bated our horses two houres; then mounted again and marched from thence." The rate of march of cavalry at a mixed pace of trot and walk is 5 mph.[49] They were marching to attack the enemy, and there would have been good reason to make every effort to press on, but it would be unwise to proceed much faster than this at night, especially as the first half hour would have been in relative darkness. They had also to ensure that their horses were not exhausted when they met the enemy. When the moon was well up it may have been possible to put in short periods at the canter, and perhaps they could have reached Herterton in about two and a half hours although that may be a little too fast. This would bring the time to 1.30 a.m. or later on 1st July, by which time the moon was at an altitude of about 16 degrees.

A rest of two hours would no doubt have been welcome for both men and horses, but it unlikely that many of them had the full opportunity. Cavalry on the march in half-sections, that is two abreast, (likely as the roads would be narrow) take up a road space equal to 2 yards per horse.[50] Even with no allowance for pack animals, a column of 900 horse will have occupied at least 1800 yards (1650m), plus a little space between units to prevent minor checks being felt throughout the length of the column. The head of the column may have left Chollerford at 11.00 but, unless it was already formed up on the road, the last man will have left somewhat later, with a corresponding delay in reaching the halt. There, the horses will have been watered and fed, and ideally unsaddled and rubbed down: perhaps some of the men got a little sleep.

The two hour halt would take the time to 3.30 at the earliest. Sunrise at Herterton and Tosson that day was a few minutes before 4.00, and twilight began at about 2.45. The moon was at 27 degrees at 3.30 and even with cloud cover there will have been ample light for movement to begin. On the reconstructed journey in 2006, the sky was becoming light before 3.00, and by 3.45 had all the appearance of broad daylight even though the sun was not up (*plate 14*).

"[We] then mounted again and marched from thence. I commanded the forlorn hope." (Sanderson) "wee aduanced I had the forlorne hope" (Diary). There are two points to make here. A Forlorn Hope, incidentally, was an advance party of skirmishers, foot or horse, sent out in advance of the main body and usually referred to as "the forlorn."

First, Sanderson does not give the size of the forlorn hope. Captain Atkyns, in the royalist regiment of horse of Prince Maurice, twice gives numbers when he led a forlorn hope: respectively 2-300 and 160 men.[51] At

Preston (see below) the forlorn of horse was 200 on 17th and 72 on 19th. Although Lilburne's advance was intended as a deterrent rather than the start of a battle, the large numbers of prisoners and horses which the forlorn was able to capture suggests that Sanderson had a considerable number of men with him, perhaps up to 200. A forlorn hope was usually made up of officers and men selected for the purpose, rather than an existing formation. Sanderson explains this in his *Relation* (see below), and Captain Birch says in his entry for 26th June 1648: "sent out a party out of every company as forlorne."

Secondly, the records suggest that the enemy was not far way. In fact, this was far from the case, as their first objective was Great Tosson, 11 miles from Herterton by road.

As an aside, it must be asked why they went to the small tower at Tosson, where there could never have been a large garrison and from which an alert enemy could have got across the river to warn more important centres. Perhaps they took the shorter route on a minor road, described below, to avoid alerting or disturbing Rothbury, where the bridge may have been guarded, and received information on the way that Tosson was occupied.

Pushing the pace, but without exhausting the horses, Great Tosson (*plate 15*) could have been reached before 4.30 or 5.00. The garrison of 6 dragoons will have delayed them only for so long as it took them to get the men out of bed and, presumably, tied up and left under guard. Incidentally, the implication of the record is that not only was there no look-out but that the lieutenant in command had not taken the elementary precaution of bolting the door. Pressing on quickly (and by-passing Cartington), the forlorn might have reached Lorbottle by around 5.00 or 5.30, where they again found the enemy in their beds due to the fact of "the enemy having no Scouts out" (Hesilrige) This is not the same as "Our men . . .before break of day fell into their [the enemies] quarters" (G of Q), but to do that Great Tosson would have to have been reached well before 3.00, which would allow no more than one and a half hours to march to Herterton which is far too high a rate. Alternatively, they left Chollerford soon after 9 p.m. The "break of day" could be dramatic licence, and if the sky were heavily overcast it may have appeared not to be full daylight.

Sanderson's letter is more specific than the Diary about where he himself went. After Lorbottle (the hamlet not the Hall, which was not built until the eighteenth century) came Callaly and Whittingham and he then mentions actions at Eslington and Glanton, no more than three miles apart; it is unlikely that he was at both as they are at opposite corners of a square. One reading is that he went north from Callaly Castle to Eslington, while others went to Glanton. Callaly-Eslington-Branton is more or less a straight line.

Only "Cartington Castle . . . stood out two hours" (G of Q), but neither Sanderson nor Hesilrige mention Cartington (*plate 10*) which is nearly 3 miles north of Great Tosson and about 1¼ miles short of Lorbottle. The forlorn would not have had the numbers to invest a castle; it would have been the main body which dealt with it and therefore of no direct interest to Sanderson. Hesilrige's letter was written on 2nd July, probably before he was in possession of all the details. Cartington had been abandoned by the parliamentary forces early in June (see above, note 23).

Being "cloyed with prisoners and horse, and booty" they retired from Branton to Whittingham where Colonel Lilburne was rallying his troops in the face of royalist horse at Shawton (Sanderson). Shawdon Hill is 1½ mile NNE, Shawdon Hall 2 miles NNE, and Shawdonwood House about 2 miles N, of Whittingham. Lilburne would have been with the main body, advancing to Whittingham after leaving sufficient men to invest Cartington.

They then all pulled back to Newtown, where they halted for two hours. There are only two places with this name in the general area between Whittingham and Morpeth. Newton-on-the-Moor (NU173055) lies SE of Whittingham, but has no direct access from there owing to the steep slopes and broken ground near Eglingham and the route would not be an obvious one. The most likely is the hamlet of Newtown half a mile or so east of Great Tosson. This would carry the reasonable implication that the force retraced its steps to complete the mopping up of the enemy and to collect their prisoners. Although Sanderson says that he had prisoners with him at Branton, it is unlikely that he brought them all with their horses. More probably he brought the more important ones, leaving small detachments to contain the rest. From Newtown the whole force then marched south with their prisoners to Morpeth, almost 17 miles away.

It was a quite an achievement by the parliamentary forces, especially when numbers are taken into account. Small numbers can often move fast, but large bodies of men are invariably slower[52] and 900 is no small force. A night march of 16 miles, followed by a further advance of 23 miles involving at least six skirmishes, and a long march to Morpeth with prisoners, a total of 80 miles, and so many captured with so little loss, says much for the training of the army, the fitness of both men and horses, and the quality of their intelligence. It is not surprising that Col. Lilburne, in a letter to Hesilrige, asked him to acquaint Major-General Lambert of the event "because our horses are much wearied."[53]

None of the route was over very difficult countryside. From Chollerford to Herterton is rolling countryside (plates 16 and 17), much of it now agricultural land, rising gradually from about 175' (55m) to 620' (190m). From the distance given, they seem to have been marching by road, which gives a reasonably straight route and would have been much easier to follow at night. After crossing Herterton Park there are more signs of heath land with rocky outcrops, but the topography is still best described as rolling. The road at first heads north, but soon begins to describe a big curve to the east, avoiding valleys and boggy ground as well as aiming for the east side of Simonside Hill. The very minor road to Great Tosson which follows the foot of the north east slope of Simonside leaves the main road less than a mile north of Forestburn Gate at a height of 190m and rises by up to 20m in a climb of over a mile; this would have put pressure on the horses, which work better on short steep slopes than long, slow ones.[54] There then follows a series of undulations before dropping down a long slope to Great Tosson. The tower comes into view only about 400 yards before it is reached, which is perhaps one explanation for the garrison being surprised. There are, incidentally, unobstructed views between Tossons and Cartington (*plate 18*).

The tower stands some 70m above the river Coquet which runs about a kilometre away across a flat flood plain (*plate 19*). It is not a wide or deep river and should have been easy enough to cross by a ford which was still shown on early twentieth century maps. From there it will have been a long climb to Cartington, rising 100m in just under two miles, the last part particularly steep. Any alert defender will have had a very good view of the approaching column and this perhaps explains why the castle was able to hold out. They were not however sufficiently alert to pass the word on to Lorbottle and Callaly.

The road from Cartington to Whittingham skirts high ground with rocky outcrops, running along the southern lip of a valley with a few short, steep undulations. From Whittingham to Glanton the ground levels out, apart from the considerable hill of Glanton Pyke, and Branton lies in farmland which forms the flat bottom to a bowl of hills (*plate 20*).

The return from Newtown could, as suggested, have reversed the morning route past Simonside to Forestburn Gate (NZ065963), and then south east to Netherwitton (NZ101903), and from there to Morpeth. From Forestburn Gate there is a steep rise of some 70m over a mile, a long climb for tired horses. After a mile of flat heath land, the road drops down to Netherwhitton, after which the route is more or less level.

If they left Chollerford at 11 p.m. on 30th it is most unlikely that they reached Morpeth before 5 p.m on 1st, 18 hours of riding and skirmishing at the very least, with only two rest periods. The riders would probably have walked beside their horses at intervals, as was normal on the march, and with no adrenalin rush to spur them on it will have been a very weary column at the end of a very long night and day.

However, on the following day horses and men of Sanderson's troop, and perhaps others, were still in a condition to march the prisoners 15 miles to Newcastle. It must have been a slow march with 300 or so of the prisoners on foot as some of the soldiers were sufficiently active already to have begun taking the captured horses to Newcastle to be sold.

In these several actions the parliamentarians captured "three hundred private Soldiers, and between 5 and 600 Horses, and good store of Arms, without the loss of one man of either side." (Hesilrige). Sanderson says " 50 grand officers and 400 troopers" (Diary) and "we had 359 prisoners, besides many that escaped. We took about 600 horse, . . . We had but one horse shot dead, and one man shot through the thigh: and of the enemy there was five slaine, and Cap. Smith run through the body, and some others wounded." (Sanderson). It was a very light toll for the results achieved.[55]

Parliament was duly impressed. "Ordered, That a Letter of Thanks be written to Colonel Lilbourne, and Colonel Fenwicke, Major Sanderson, and Colonel Wrenn, for their good Services, in the great Victory obtained in the North."[56]. The news had travelled 300 miles to London in no more than four days. The mention of Major Sanderson in the same sentence as three colonels, including his own, gives him a status above his substantive rank, as though he still had an independent troop. Hesilrige's letter also mentions "Major Sandersons two Troops" as though they were an independent force. A letter from "one of our commanders" lists Sanderson's troops alongside the three regiments.[57]

Those sources which name Cartington say that it was held by Col. Sir Richard Tempest. Sanderson says that Sir Richard Tempest was taken at Eslington, along with Major Troulop [Trollop]. It seems either that Sir Richard Tempest got away from Cartington before the parliamentary forces arrived, or that by chance he was not there at the time. Both Sir Richard Tempest and Sir Francis Radcliffe are named elsewhere as commanding Cartington,[58] and they need not both been there at the same time.

There is another interesting point arising from the account. Both the Durham and Northumberland horse, under Colonels Wren and Fenwick respectively, were newly raised. Given that some of the troopers may already have had some experience, it is still remarkable that they managed such a ride and says much for their training and discipline. But as Hesilrige's letter says "Some of the foot Soldiers of this Garison, and some of our new raised Horse ran away to the Enemy, and we have taken divers of them". "Foot Soldiers " presumably refers to the 100 dragoons sent from Newcastle, which might explain why Sanderson received only 50 men. Hesilrige asks for directions as to their fate "if not, they will be suddenly knit up". By this expressive phrase he presumably means hanged, shot, or transported. Hesilrige was certainly keen on transporting recalcitrant royalist soldiers to "forraigne plantacions."[59] Desertion in the face of the enemy would presumably be more harshly treated, although Hodgson notes that in July 1648 deserters captured near Carlisle "were judged to be hanged; but mercy was used."[60]

It may be noted in passing that Colonel Lilburne was sent to Northumberland by Lambert with "instructions not to attempt anything upon the enemy, except God should put some clear opportunity into his hands by surprising, beating some quarters, or the like."[61] Lambert further explains that Lilburne "finding them in great security, and having either none or a very slight guard, fell into their quarters." This suggests that most of the royalists were as careless as the lieutenant in Tosson tower.

There is an error in the Diary for 4th July, when Sanderson says "marched my troope to duddo". Duddo is 57 miles from Newcastle, and his letter of 3rd says that "ten troopes of horse come to us this night, under Col. Harrison; they are to meet us at Meldon".[62] Duddo is presumably an error for Meldon which is about 6 miles west of Morpeth and about the same from Belsay where he quartered on 4th. The word is exceptionally clear in the Diary.

After two days in the Tyne valley with Captain Bradford and the dragoons, Sanderson moved back to Alnwick where some loot was obtained but on 13th he was ordered south by Colonel Lilburne to join the army. Although Sanderson does not discuss the reason, Lambert was collecting all his available forces to oppose the Scots army which had entered Carlisle on 8th July to the ringing of bells.[63] He had to guard against a possible advance over the Stainmore pass (*plate 21*) and to mask Pontefract which was still held by royalists, and could do little but delay the invaders.[64] On 4th July Lambert reckoned his army at around 2,600 horse and 2,200 foot,[65] against a Scots army which he estimated to be around 4,000 horse and 10,000 foot with more being raised, and gathered from Ireland. Lambert himself was fighting delaying actions around Penrith and Appleby. He was forced from the latter on Tuesday 18th, and retreated to Bowes and Barnard Castle on the same day.[66] Captain Birch and Captain Hodgson both cover these events, with much more detail given by the former.

It was not only the invading army he had to guard against. In order to forestall activity from Berwick, Northumberland could not be left without troops. A plaintive letter on 19th July from the governor of Holy Island, Captain Robert Batten, to Speaker Lenthall complains that he has "been in a besieged condition near these six weeks" and declared a lack of provisions.[67] The island was relieved in August by Major John Mayer who found there 200 sheep, a warren full of rabbits, and cobles bringing in a great store of fish, "besides that Major Sanderson not above two months before sent in provisions for at least six months." Later in the year Batten was accused of being ready to deliver up the island.[68]

By 18th July Sanderson was on duty at Bowes (*plate 22*) at the eastern end of the Stainmore Pass ("but this night at Bowes, we met with Major Sanderson, and Capt. Bradfords Troops, out of Northumberland,"[69]) guarding it against the invaders. There is no indication from the Diary that Sanderson was involved in any action during this period.

Some of his fellow officers were fighting, however. Major Cholmley and a party of horse garrisoned Rose Castle, 6 miles south of Carlisle,[70] from where "Major Cholmley, with 80 horse well armed" was forced to retreat to Appleby by the advance of the Sir Philip Musgrave.[71]

August

On 2nd August Sanderson, now presumably with the rest of Lilburne's, began the march south to meet up with Cromwell coming north. That night his quarters near Richmond were "at Mr Norton's" (Major Norton; this abbreviation for major is used elsewhere, e.g. 30th November), the father-in-law of his "dear friend Mrs. Jane Norton" (see chapter 7 and Appendix 7).

The amount he paid to his lieutenant and men on 2nd August can be only hypothetically related to pay scales. The lieutenant *may* have received 64 days' pay, including forage allowance for two horses, and 28 men *may* have received two days' pay. This sounds like very unfair discrimination in favour of the officer, but Gentles points out that distribution of pay was carried out very fairly. He found only one example, from 1649, of an officer withholding pay from his men, and quotes evidence that in times of shortage the officers often helped the men out from their own pockets.[72]

Indeed, the following day Sanderson paid 12s each to the corporals and men, but nothing to the officers. The fact that the corporals and troopers received the same amounts suggests that he was paying out on account whatever money was available.

On 9th, near Ripon "My great white gelding my Cornetts black horse & mich Dicksons meare stolne from oldfeild in the night." It says much for the spirit (or perhaps desperation) of the local people that they should steal horses from the army. On the other hand, it is not impossible that the horses may have been stolen by another unit in the army. Only five days later Cromwell was obliged to insist in writing that a Lieut. Swayne obey orders and restore two horses to a Captain Harrison, from whom he had taken them.[73] A major of horse received a forage allowance for three horses, so Sanderson presumably had at least two other horses available, while his Cornet had an allowance for two horses (see *Parliamentary Army* in chapter 3). Mich Dickson was probably a trooper.

The bulk of Lambert's army rendezvoused with Cromwell's in the Knaresborough-Wetherby area, but Lilburne's remained at Ripon for nine days, after which they "kept guard" at Sawley and Pately Bridge. On 13th they joined Cromwell near Otley and the combined army began the crossing of the Pennines, quartering around Skipton on 14th. That night part of Lilburne's, with Twistleton's, had the guard at Gargrave just over 4 miles to the west of Skipton but it is not clear from Hodgson's *Memoir* whether it was this night that Captain Henry Cromwell of Harrison's prevented Langdale taking the castle. Hodgson implies that it was on 16th that Colonel Richard Tempest and others were taken at Waddey. The place is sometimes modernised as Whalley, as given by Sanderson in his *Relation at Large* (see below), but Woolrych suggests that the place was Waddow Hall, just north of Clitheroe. It lies 7½ miles and Whalley 10½ miles from the overnight quarters at Gisburn, so either place is possible. Sanderson is clear that this event was on 15th, and it was the Earl of Cornewath and others who were taken on 16th.

The rendezvous on 15th was at Broughton where George Fell, tenant of Stephen Tempest, spent 8s on ale and bread and 10s on mutton for Cromwell's soldiers. Joseph Littlewood received 26s provisions for Capt. Peck and Capt. Cread when Cromwell reached Skipton, and 18s for provisions for "Lt General Croumwell" when "General Birch and his company lay at Carleton on their way from Otley to Stonyhurst".[74]

The night before the battle they "qrtered in the feilds about mr Sherburns great house." Sherburn was a noted royalist; the house is now Stoneyhurst College. Birch relates that the enemy had previously occupied quarters on the route and left them bare, although it is not clear whether he is referring to Stonyhurst itself. Sanderson makes no comment on matters of comfort.

The three days' marching, covering 19, 13, and 19 miles respectively, was no bad achievement for an army of around 10,000. Lilburne's seems to have been at the rear of the column for at least part of the way, as on the night of 15th Sanderson quartered some 5 miles to the east of Captain Birch, who lay at Downham near Clitheroe.

The Diary adds little of great moment to the published accounts about the battle of Preston, although his description "wee charged on to warrington brige" (from Winwick) gives a sense of the pace of the running battle not found elsewhere.

However, in his account Sanderson twice mentions his "Relation at large," a letter to his father, printed in 1648 but not published since then,[75] which has much more detail (see Appendix 4).

This letter, dated 20th August, has a postscript requesting that Hesilrige be shown it as "time will not let me write to you both" which may be an indication that it was Hesilrige who had it printed. Moreover, the fact that he seems to have been expected to write to Hesilrige carries the suggestion that he was reporting to him at intervals, and it may be that Sanderson's letter of 3rd July (note 45) was to Hesilrige. As a point of interest, the printed version of the *Relation* included, in brackets, what Sanderson for obvious reasons never mentions in the Diary, that his regiment was Lilburne's. It is most likely an interpolation by whoever had it printed for a wider readership.

Sanderson's reference to his "Relation at Large" is paralleled by Capt Birch who, in his description of the battle, also refers to a fuller description in the modern-sounding phrase "see the account on the file."

Bull and Seed have published a detailed and careful examination of the battle of Preston, but as the *Relation* is one of the very few contemporary accounts of the battle by one who fought in it, it is worth examining some aspects of the event. Unreferenced quotations in the following paragraphs are from the *Relation*, references to Cromwell are to his letter of 20th August,[76] and Hodgson is from Hodgson 1806. The principal places are shown on map 1.

In broad terms, Hamilton's army, given by some sources to have grown to some 20,000, was centred around Preston but spread out between Kirkby Lonsdale 37 miles to the north and Wigan 17 miles to the south, and protected on its left flank by English troops under Sir Marmaduke Langdale. The Scots infantry were to cross the Ribble at Preston where they could have combined with the main force of royalist cavalry who were foraging towards Wigan. When Langdale realised that a parliamentary force was approaching he drew up his troops to resist the advance.

The opening stages of the battle on Thursday 17th August are tersely described in the Diary, with Major Smithson having the 200 strong forlorn hope of cavalry and Major Pownall the 400 foot (Cromwell's figures). Hodgson was also in the forlorn of foot, and says that he shared the command with Pownall, a pardonable conceit as he was probably second-in-command. Cromwell says that the forlorn "marched within a mile, where the enemy was drawn up . . . and there, upon a Moor, about half a mile distant from the enemy's army, met with their scouts and outguard." The *Relation*, the Diary, and Hodgson all agree that the enemy was first encountered at Longridge Chapel (now Longridge), about six miles north east of Preston, and in sufficient numbers for Hodgson to say that "our horse gleaned up considerable parcel of the enemy." The *Relation* agrees that Smithson "took divers prisoners." The outposts were driven in, with

Hodgson and the *Relation* describing fighting and taking prisoners all the way to where Langdale's main body stood. There were clearly large numbers of skirmishers well in advance of that, if there were fighting all the way from Longridge.

Hodgson relates that he and the forlorn of foot caught up with the forlorn of horse near a little ditch within a mile of Preston. The *Relation* says that Smithson was held up at a bridge within a mile of Preston. There is no watercourse of any size in the area, but even a small stream with a bridge over it would make a fixed line for the royalists to hold. The stream was probably the one identified by Holmes as the Eaves Brook, about two miles from the centre of Preston, which Bull and Seed describe as being in a sharply sided cut.[77]

Hodgson's description shows that the cavalry were in the lane described by Cromwell as "very deep and ill," and with numerous hedged and enclosures either side it would have been difficult for the cavalry to take the defenders in the flank. This was done by Hodgson and his men coming upon the Scots from the shelter of a hedge.

During this action "an hot dispute was at the Bridge" and "Major Smithson had two horses shot under him," an indication of the fierceness of the fighting. On 1st September Parliament awarded Major Smithson £200 for "gallant service in the war, and especially in this late utter defeat of the whole Scots army."[78] The Diary, but not the *Relation*, implies that Sanderson was personally engaged with the Scottish lancers, who Hodgson says engaged the forlorn of horse. This may show that Sanderson was in the forlorn. But he also says that his regiment was in the rear of the foot, in the van of the left wing of horse, which may be a record of his own place in the battle.

The location of Lilburne's and Lambert's during this stage of the battle was previously uncertain except by elimination, as Cromwell merely refers to the "remaining horse". In his despatch of 20th August, he names all the full regiments present, including the Lancashire Militia, with the exception of Lambert's and Lilburne's and, despite the fact that both took a major part in the fighting over the following two days, he ignores them completely. An unnamed contemporary source gives "some disagreement betwixt him [Cromwell] and Lambert" at this time, which might explain the omission.[79]

During the fight from the Eaves Brook bridge into Preston the *Relation* says that for an hour no quarter was given except to Captain Salkeld of Rook, whose life Sanderson "saved with great difficulty." 'Rook' is Rock in Northumberland, where a branch of the Salkelds lived in the seventeenth century and where Sanderson had been quartered and had visited in February, March, and April. There must have been a very compelling reason for this action, as he would either have to stop himself short or prevent others from killing Salkeld while full of the heat of action. He would then have had to protect him from those coming up behind, and presumably to detail one or more troopers to escort him to the rear as a prisoner.[80] Salkeld had also been taken prisoner on 1st July.

The Diary makes no mention of the fight for the Ribble Bridge, although the *Relation* deals briefly with it, giving the Lancashire troops credit for taking it with the pike. Interestingly, two royalists, Turner and Burnet, see the attackers benefiting from the hedged enclosures,[81] while Sanderson gives the advantage to the defenders. No two men ever see a battle in the same light.

Cromwell notes that some of his horse chased the retreating royalist horse ten miles up the road to Lancaster "and had execution of them." Sanderson gives a description of the slain seen six miles towards Lancaster which he probably had from someone in Twistleton's with whom he was working two days later, as it was Twistleton's and Thornhaugh's which took part in this action.[82] The *Relation* wrongly says that Langdale fled north with his horse, whereas in fact he rejoined Hamilton.

During Friday 18th the pursuit to the south continued, during which Colonel Thornhaugh was killed. The fact that he was not wearing his armour was presumably quickly rumoured around the army as it was recorded by both Hodgson and Sanderson. The horse kept up the chase, fighting their way into Wigan at midnight, under a "bright moon" despite the weather, before pulling back to await the foot.[83]

The following day, Saturday 19th, Lilburne's was again in the van "because no other Regiment was neere." A party of 72 troopers under the command of Major Cholmley was drawn, as was normal, equally from all six troops, with Sanderson's quartermaster as one of the officers, and was clearly a forlorn hope. There was more slaughter in Wigan and the retreating Scots were pursued south by the cavalry, with more killed all along the road until they made a stand at Winwick Wood. The place, identified by Heath as Redbank, is a steep-sided valley giving a defensible position on the east side of the road from Wigan to Warrington just over a mile north of Winwick.

The royalists held for three hours (Cromwell says many hours) before breaking, and then resumed their retreat. Sanderson's and Capt. Lilburne's troops, with two of Twisleton's, "carreered up to Winwicke" about a mile away, where many Scots were killed beside the church and 1500 made prisoner inside. It is generally said that the Scots were pursued to Winwick, but the *Relation* makes it clear that the cavalry reached Winwick first and prevented the Scots from retreating further. Thereafter, as the Diary says, the horse charged on to Warrington three miles to the south. The whole sense of the day is a fast-moving, 12 mile running fight, interrupted only by the stand at Winwick, with the cavalry mostly used in what has always been one of their most successful roles, that of the cutting down from behind of near-defenceless infantry in retreat.

With the surrender of Lieutenant-General Baillie at Warrington Bridge, Sanderson's *Relation* of the battle ends. His graphic description of the "high wayes, Corne Fields, Meddows, Woods, and ditches strewed with dead bodies" tallies with Cromwell's estimate of 2,000 enemy dead. He gives precise figures for the dead of his regiment, only 12 troopers or 2%. This is very low, but not as low as Cromwell's figures for his army as a whole which he gives as under 100 out of 8,600, or less than 1%. A death which, significantly, Sanderson does not record is that of Major Cholmley, who may or may not be the one serving in Lilburne's (see Appendix 7a).

The three chief parliamentary accounts of Cromwell, Hodgson, and Sanderson concentrate on different aspects of the three day battle, as one might expect. What is surprising is the extent to which a general, a field officer of cavalry, and a junior infantry officer agree. Cromwell's and Sanderson's accounts were both written at Warrington on 20th August, when neither of them had had much time for research into events. Sanderson even knows the terms of surrender at Warrington ("the officers to be furnished with horses for their journey") which Cromwell does not mention in his despatch. Perhaps the horse had been hoping to acquire some of the horses. Hodgson's *Memoir* was written later and could have made use of other accounts.

What is not surprising is that Sanderson makes no mention of the weather, which seems to have been appalling. Turner describes "so very foule weather and, extremelie deepe way"[84] and Cromwell refers to Friday as "twelve miles of such ground as I never rode in all my life, the day being very wet."[85] Burnet's comments have already been noted in chapter 1, *Weather*, and he goes on to say that the rain "made the March very heavy both to Horse and Foot." Given the weather and the heavy ground, it is understandable that at the end of the three day running battle Cromwell bemoaned the lack of active cavalry.

Sanderson gives thanks that "both my Brothers and all my Officers are well, in health, and unhurt." This indicates that two of his brothers were in the battle. Henry was not there as John asks for a copy of the letter to be given to him, and the likeliest candidates are Samuel and Charles. Their status is discussed above, *Army careers of John Sanderson's brothers*, in chapter 2.

The *Relation* was written at Warrington when at least some of the army was resting. By the 23rd, Cromwell was in Wigan with the greater part of the army on his way back to Preston and thence to Skipton and northwards on the east side of the Pennines in pursuit of Munro, who eventually retreated through Berwick.[86]

Lambert was sent on to follow Hamilton, with 2,000 horse (including Lilburne's) and 1,400 foot, reaching Uttoxeter on 24th August. Both the *Relation* and the Diary record that the Scots horse were believed to have gone to Wales, something which may be related to an incident in the Diary. On 25th, the day the Duke of Hamilton surrendered, Sanderson "came to Roseter that night". This could be either a place or a person. There is a Colonel Rossiter known but Sanderson tends to give military men their ranks. In the Diary Sanderson uses precisely the same construction – I/we came to (place name) – 18 times, as well as a number of very similar phrases. When he "came to (a senior officer)" he invariably gives the place name as well. Also, as Rossiter had been wounded at Willoughby Field near Nottingham a month earlier, so seriously that Parliament sent a Surgeon, a Physician, and an Apothecary, he is most unlikely to have been with the army.[87] The only place which can be found resembling this name is Wroxeter in Shropshire, 5 miles south east of Shrewsbury.[88]

Hamilton and the cavalry had marched first to Malpas in Cheshire (SJ487473) and then Stone in Staffordshire (SJ900340) before being brought to bay at Uttoxeter.[89] Burnet (362) says "Our Cavalry rode divers miles towards Westchester"; Ogilby's maps show that Chester was also known as Westchester in the seventeenth century. Sanderson may have been sent off to get intelligence of any remaining royalists in the general area as Wroxeter is 30 miles south of Malpas.

Five days earlier, Cromwell bemoaned the lack of "a thousand horse that could but trot thirty miles . . . truly we are so harassed and haggled out in this business, that we are not able to do more than walk an easy pace after them."[90] Given this state of the pursuing army, the reason must have been important for Sanderson to ride 41 miles one day, and 56 the next to rejoin his troop at Thorpe.

Lambert was then ordered to assist in the campaign against Munro, and marched towards Carlisle with four regiments of horse, some dragoons, and 1,400 infantry.[91] Sanderson was not a part of this move, and he does not make clear whether his route northwards on the east side of the Pennines was as part of Lilburne's or indeed with any other troops or not. The fact that the daily mileage was between 11 and 17 miles might suggest that they were accompanying infantry, but they may have been allowing their horses to recover.

September

Sanderson and his troop moved slowly north until on 14th September they quartered at several places, including Chopwell which is only 15 miles north of Hedleyhope. It is somewhat strange that he does not call at his home, where he had not been since 21st April, although it was only a few miles out of his way. The point is discussed in chapter 7. From there they moved up to their old patrol grounds near Alnwick.

On 18th September, Sanderson was sent to Cheswick, a few miles south of Berwick-upon-Tweed, to Lt.-General Cromwell who was moving his army up towards Scotland, and stayed overnight. It may be Cromwell wished to take advantage of Sanderson's knowledge of the border area, or that the latter had some special qualities which made him useful to Cromwell, and even though it is not necessary to go as far as Oxberry, who pictured Cromwell and Sanderson seated together in front of the fire,[92] one may wonder. However, Sanderson was not necessarily a personal guest of Cromwell, but could simply have been delivering a message and have stayed over at his headquarters, a very different thing. It is worth pointing out that in the 14 regiments of horse in the New Model there were only 336 officers and Cromwell, as Lieutenant-General of Horse, probably knew of him by name at least.

As a sidelight, it is interesting to consider the effect on the countryside of the movements of the army, to say nothing of Monro's retreat through it to Berwick. Rushworth quotes a letter from Newcastle "Cromwell will come hither tomorrow, . . . not Meat for a Regiment being left in all Northumberland." Two days later he noted " the inhabitants of Carlisle Petition the Governour to let in no Soldiers, neither Scots nor English", and in a letter dated 20th from Cromwell's headquarters at Norham

"The Sad Condition of the County of Northumberland, and our Army in it, would make a Heart of Flint to melt. Neither Corn nor Cattel did the wretched Army of Monroe leave ...", and even "in the Head Quarters . . . only a little Biskit."[93]

Cromwell's forces began crossing the border on 19th September. Sanderson, probably with the rest of the regiment to judge by later entries, tried and failed to cross the swollen Tweed at Twizle, down river from Coldstream, on 22nd, perhaps at the Border Maid ford (*plate 23*). They had to spread out as much as 20 miles to find quarters over the next four days while they waited for the water level to fall. On 25th September he rode to Lambert's headquarters[94] at Mordington House north of Berwick, for orders, and the following day the regiment crossed at Coldstream, over the ford which was the only crossing there until Smeaton's seven-arched bridge was completed in 1766.

The day after that Sanderson was sent from Lauder to see Major-General Lambert, for unspecified reasons, and rode all night, returning to Lauder to find that Colonel Lilburne had moved, apparently with the regiment, to Abbey St Bathans and Garnett. The latter place is unidentified. Sanderson does not make it clear whether he rode straight on to Abbey St Bathans, but as his troop quartered there that night he probably did. Over the next few days he and the rest of the regiment, including Major Cholmley, moved their quarters westwards, with Sanderson ending up at Cockpen, close to Dalhousie to the south of Edinburgh.

October

Sanderson went to Edinburgh on 4th October, on the same day as Cromwell went there from his quarters at Seaton[95] to the east. There is no indication as to whether his visit was concerned with escort duties.

On 7th, "Leeuᵗ-genˡˡ, maior generall my Collo, &c. came to my qrters at my lord Dalhouseys", the phraseology almost suggesting that he graciously received his seniors, whereas they presumably simply quartered in the same place with Sanderson's presence in the area being incidental. Two days later Sanderson records that "my oune fine gray nag dyed at Arneston". This was perhaps the "grey nag" lame and unfit to race on 17th April. Given the amount of travelling he sometimes did, the loss of the horse is not altogether surprising (see Appendix 6).

Sanderson was then sent to Newcastle, with a body of horse of undisclosed size, to collect pay. The journey was probably down the Roman Dere Street (A68) as far as Lauder, then to Floors near Kelso where he could cross the Tweed, then to Wooler and south to Newcastle.

On the orders of Cromwell, who was now in Newcastle, he received £3700 for two months pay for two regiments, Lilburne's and Lambert's, plus £100 for Major-General Lambert. The discrepancy in the money which he records was perhaps due to Mr Bilton (see Appendix 7). When Sanderson met Cromwell in Newcastle the latter ordered him to collect more money, but the individual sums mentioned are 4d short of the total.

During this trip he found time to spend a night at Hedleyhope, the first recorded visit since 21st April, and took the opportunity to pay his servants.

The return journey took a different route, up the east coast through Berwick and on to Dunbar before turning west to Seton. Perhaps the route was chosen to avoid burdening the same area with quarters for his party.

On his return he began to pay the men at the rate of £200 a troop, which would come to £2,400. Two months' full pay for two regiments would amount to £6,720 for the troopers alone at the war establishment, but it was not unusual for the troops to be given a fortnight's wages instead of a month's. On this occasion they got rather less than that: at 100 per troop they received 20 days' pay instead of 56, or 25 days at 80 men per troop. Sanderson makes no mention of the officers. Perhaps the balance of £1,300 was shared out among them; the average would be just under £10, but no doubt the colonels received more than the saddlers.

In terms of purchasing power, £3,800 in 1648 would be worth £350,000 in 2006. Payment to 1200 modern troopers of the same proportion (about 57%) of their wages for two lunar months would be worth in the order of £1,800,000.[96] Direct comparisons such as this are not wholly realistic, but it is clear that he was entrusted with a very large sum of money indeed.

November

The comment that on 2nd November he "paid all the troopes" probably meant the completion of the process which he began on 25th October. With the troops spread out over the countryside it would take some time to get around them all.

After escorting Lambert to Edinburgh on 6th he returned to England, crossing the Tweed on 8th; it is not quite clear at what point he met up with his troop. Rushworth quotes a letter from Lambert's quarters saying that Lilburne's will cross the Tweed on 9th.[97] This could either show a change of timetable or indicate that Sanderson and his troop went over on their own.

It was a relatively slow progression south to take part in the siege of Pontefract with his troop covering between 5 and 16 miles a day. On the way he was approached about the release of the royalist Major Ord, a namesake of his "cousin" of Longridge. The outcome is not mentioned. Sanderson then headed off on his own to Capheaton for two days, for which he gives no reason.

In Newcastle he engaged a new servant, William Fletcher and loaned him 13s, presumably as an advance on his wages of £4 a year. He then made his last recorded visit of the year to his home at Hedleyhope.

On the 29th November "I came . . . to my Collo:" which sounds as though he had travelled independently from the rest of the regiment. In fact it is probable that all six troops travelled by different routes to avoid overwhelming small towns and villages by the descent on them of 600 horsemen. However, when Major-General Lambert travelled post from Newcastle to Pontefract he left Col. Lilburne in command of all the horse,[98] which shows that they were in contact even if widely spread.

On the same day Sanderson "Set Leeut generall onwards towards wentbridge" (probably through Stapleton Park as there is no direct road) but it is not clear whether he formed part of an escort or whether Cromwell wished to speak to him. The fact that he came back with the Major-General (Lambert) might indicate that he was in some senses a staff officer, a point discussed in chapter 7. On the following day he went with Lambert and Lilburne to Pontefract.

December

After some days of inaction he and his troop went to the guard at Pontefract, which did not surrender until 25th March 1649. Rushworth quotes from a letter "Major General Lambert is appointed to come in chief to the Leaguer: The line to be drawn three parts about the Castle".[99] When, on 1st December, the troop was sent to quarter near Leeds they were nine miles away. This was a long way from the siege, but an explanation may be seen in a letter from Cromwell which also emphasises the degree to which the army was in arrears. The county was "not able to bear free-quarter; nor well able to furnish provisions, if we had moneys."[100]

On 11th December Sanderson went to Pontefract "to Councell" which was held on the following day; he does not mention that Lambert was present. In the evening he helped "write a letter to my lord generall." This was a declaration to Fairfax in support of the Remonstrance of the army which called for an end to treaty with the king and demanded that he be brought to justice. The declaration was backed by a letter from Lambert, dated 12th December, which says that the meeting of officers "appointed Capt. Bayns with Capt. Bradford to wait upon your Excellency therewith."[101] Perhaps based on this, it has been generally reported that Baynes and Bradford went to London together.[102] The Diary, however, says only that "Captaine Baynes to be sent with it" and does not mention Bradford.

The explanation lies in the record of the Council following their meeting, in which "Captaine Baynes was appointed to carry the same and to joyne with Capt. Bradford now at London in the presenting thereof to his Ex^{cy} and the Gen^{ll}. Councell."[103] Furthermore, Thomas Margetts wrote to Capt. Adam Baynes, on 13th December 1648, Pontefract, telling him in a postscript that "You will find Capt Bradford at the Knight Head in Grays Inne Lane."[104] Captain Bradford attended the Council alone on 15th December 1648 and Captains Baynes and Bradford together on 21st December 1648.[105] The record of the council in Lambert's Order Book shows Sanderson as "Capt. Saunderson" in the list of those present and as "Major Saunderson" in the list of members of the standing council.

The council meeting was of all the officers in the besieging force, not just Lilburne's regiment. After the meeting on 12th Sanderson was one of six officers to form a Standing Council to meet every week. The five other officers mentioned by him in connection with the council were his colonel,

Major Rokesby and Captain Goodrick from Lambert's,[106] Major Smithson from Lilburne's and Major Catterell who is not known unless he is the later Lt Colonel Cotterell.

This list does not agree with the record made after the meeting, which reads: Coll. Lilburne, Maior Saunderson, Coll. Bright, Maior Pownall, Lt. Coll. Goodrick, Capt. Goodrick, Maior Rookeby, Maior cotterell, Maior Smythson. Any six of them were to form a quorum.[107] The time of the meeting is given as nine o'clock, rather than ten o'clock as in the Diary.

There had been a previous meeting, on 4th December, which Sanderson did not attend as he was quartered near Leeds, one of the "divers officers being absent by reason of their imployments somewhat remote" in the words of a subsequent letter to Fairfax.[108] This letter was signed by 29 officers, with John Lambert's name appearing twice.

On December 22nd 1648 Sanderson wrote to Captain Adam Baynes on two matters.[109] First, he asked Baynes to enquire of Mr Rushworth whether he had passed a letter on to his Excellencie, (Fairfax, to whom Rushworth was secretary), in a tone which suggests that he suspected Rushworth of dilatoriness. On the *verso* he passes on the thanks of the "officers appointed to meet every Friday" for the care Baynes and Bradford had had "of the businesses recomended to you." This sounds as though Pontefract had already had news from London about the presentation of the declaration from the council. The 22nd was a Friday, and it looks as though Sanderson were acting as secretary to the standing council (as opposed to the main Council, to which Thomas Margetts was secretary), writing after their weekly meeting. He takes the opportunity to send "harty and faithfull love" to Captain Bradford. The letter is in writing typical of the Diary: a round hand using a rather thick nib. The paper is thick, and clearly not an interleaf torn from the Almanac.

Most of December was a time of inactivity. On 20th Sanderson paid his servants, with a bonus equal to five days' full wages for a trooper. Not until 25th, 17 days after his troop had retired to Leeds, does he record military action other than paying the troops: "a party of seauen of a troope out of both Regimts: to meet mee at wakefeild to go with the maior generall to disband the militia horse." It would surely have been administratively simpler to take one troop rather than 84 men from 12 troops, but it may be that it was designed for political purposes. Perhaps the men were selected to avoid any risk of a preponderance of those who did not wish to see the army reduced, especially as their pay was often still in arrears. Whatever the reason, Sanderson was in charge of the troops under Lambert, another sign that he was a trusted man and perhaps as much a staff officer as a regimental officer. Cornet Baynes wrote to his brother from Pontefract on 30th December, saying that "the Ma: Gen: is now disbandinge daily of the Malitia's forces."[110] As late as July 1649 he refers to the "pestilent and turbulent militia,"[111] perhaps an indication that picked men were indeed necessary to oversee the work of disbanding.

Six troops were disbanded over the next few days, and more were to come when the Diary ended on 30th December 1648 at Appletreewick from where Major Sanderson rode out of direct history.

CHAPTER SIX

HIS LATER CAREER AND HIS END

From the end of the Diary to 8th June 1649 no reference can be found to Sanderson. On that date he wrote from York to Capt. Baynes, mainly on financial matters to do with the regiment[1] (see Appendix 4). He is concerned chiefly with the pay of the troopers and the apportionment of the levy on the Ridings of Yorkshire. The handwriting is recognisably Sanderson's, but is much neater than that of the Diary, the lines are straight, a finer pen has been used, and the ink is of more consistent density. He seems to be sitting at a desk or table with access to better equipment than was available in his campaign quarters, and it runs to well over 500 words, unlike the brevity of the Diary.

No other letters by Sanderson are known but there are references to him, all concerned with financial matters. On 23rd June 1649 Captain Bradford wrote to Baynes, largely about the Northern Brigade accounts, and refers to Major Sanderson having thoughts of going to London.[2] On 4th August 1649 he wrote again, in the hope that Major Sanderson's servant has delivered duplicates [of debentures?] and goes on to refer to "my Coll, maior Saunderson Capt Goodricke and the rest of that body . . ."[3] This could be a reference to the Standing Council set up on 12th December at Pontefract, and if so may be an indication that the Council was still in being. Captain Bradford's writing is always execrable and it is not easy to divine precisely what he is saying.

Firth says that in 1649 Sanderson claimed arrears of pay for service in Lilburne's regiment, but the papers he cites date to 1648[4] and the claim has not been found.

Thomas Margetts wrote from York to Captain Baynes in London on 4th December 1649,[5] and added in the left hand margin after his signature "Present my humble service to Col. Lilburne & Ma: Sanderson." Margetts and Sanderson were at least acquainted, through the Council of Officers of the Northern army, and the note shows that Col. Lilburne and Sanderson were in London.

On 5th January 1650 a Thomas Dickinson wrote to Captain Baynes complaining rather bitterly about Major Sanderson's actions over the former's accounts, which he explains he had properly presented. The substance of the problem was that Dickinson had paid over money to Major-General

Lambert in accordance with his orders, and if that money had not reached the regiments it was not his fault.[6]

On 27th March 1650 Lambert wrote to Baynes passing on Cromwell's authority for "Captaine Baynes, maior Sanderson, Captaine goodrick and Capt. Shepperson Attorneys for the Northern Brigade" to negotiate for the late king's land.[7]

In view of this it is not surprising that Sanderson spent at least some of the time between the end of 1648 and his death in property deals. Surtees called him "a great dabbler in the purchase of Crown-lands"[8] both for himself and on behalf of his regiment. He names much personal property in his Will: Leicester Castle, 30 acres of land in the forest of Leicester, the Manor of Oxton, houses and lands in Southwell, Huckling, Cropwell Bishop, Calverton, Blidworth, and Wood-Burrow, and the Park of Someborne. In addition he was involved with [Major] George Smithson and others in the purchase of Alburgh manor, Bolingbroke honor, Edlington manor and Lincoln castle (National Archives E 320/K3); Buckholt (E 320/P19); Nonsuch (E 320/R8); Pontefract honor (E 320/W15); Meux (Melsa) and Sutton (E 320/W33) (and see also Madge). All these last were probably bought on behalf of his regiment or the Northern Brigade.

A Phillip Gouldsmith referred in a letter of 2nd April 1650 to £300 left with him by Major Sanderson, but the reason for the deposit is not given.[9]

In June 1650 Major John Sanderson had a Warrant for "Like gratuity for the officers who conducted the reduced recruits of Col Lilburne's regiment"[10] (that is, men drawn from Lilburne's to serve in Ireland). He was thus still with the regiment.

On 10th August 1650 G. Baynes asked to be remembered to, among others, Major Sanderson,[11] and on 24th August writes "get out the Conveyance known of maior Sanderson."[12]

This seems to be the last reference to him in correspondence or official documents during his lifetime, but there is a posthumous reference in January 1651[2] (chapter 2, note 61).

On 19th September 1650 Sanderson made his Will[13] "before my goeing into Scotland". This journey would presumably have been to join Cromwell's army: his regiment was already there, Cromwell having crossed the border on 22nd July 1650. The will is the last historical record by Major Sanderson. No record has yet been found of the date, place, and cause of his death.

Probate was granted in Durham to his executors, brothers Samuel and Charles, Henry being absent in Scotland. A copy was made for PS (presumed to be Peter), dated 19 No[vember] 1650, and certified as true by Gabriel Jackson, the local notary on duty that day in the Durham Probate Court.[14] The probate act records that a bond was entered, but this does not survive. As he also owned property outside the county the Will was proved in the Prerogative Court of Canterbury on 10th February the following year.[15] No witnesses are recorded.

He made his Will in anticipation of going into Scotland not, as was a frequent reason for so doing, because he was suffering from some illness.

One may suspect a scrappy outpost skirmish somewhere in Scotland, of which no one took much account, or he could have caught some infection and died on his journey north. If the death were in Scotland, then a few days must be allowed for the news to reach the family, and may have taken place as early as the first week in November within six weeks of him making his will.

There is no reference in the Baynes correspondence to his death, although his brother Henry's death was mentioned by Robert Baynes in a letter from Edinburgh.[16] That no record of it has been found does not mean that the death was not considered noteworthy by his contemporaries. The letter of January 24th 1651[2] referred to above, appears to be the last reference to him, over a year after his death.

Previous commentaries and references

Sanderson's Diary has received surprisingly little attention in print. Firth has a reference,[17] including the account of Sanderson's activities in 1647, but that volume was not the place to pursue Sanderson in detail.

In 1895 Bates gave an account of the attack on the royalists in Tossons, Cartington and other places on 1st July; this seems to have been based on Sanderson's and Hesilrige's letters and the letter from 'a gentleman of quality,' rather than on the Diary.[18] Shortly after the transcript was first published, a brief comment appeared in the same journal,[19] wondering whether the phraseology indicated that Bates had already seen the Diary, but in fact any common usage seems to come from the various letters.

In the same year, Oxberry gave a good general background to Sanderson's activities, and also made some very pertinent comments on the man himself, albeit taking a somewhat romantic view.

Sanderson appears several times in the *Northumberland County History* and on the Northumberland National Park web site, and is mentioned by Bull and Seed in their excellent account of the battle of Preston.[20]

There is perhaps some indication that Sanderson's role was at times more important than his rank might suggest, but it is unfortunate that almost every reference from Bates onwards credits him with more than is justified. He may well have played a significant role in driving the royalists out of Chollerford and Simonburn on 9th June, and he certainly led the forlorn on 1st July, but he was not in command on either occasion. *Northumberland County History* even goes so far as to say that on 1st July "Sanderson turned back to Whittingham where he prevented an attempted rally by the royalists."[21] We have Sanderson's word for it that it was Colonel Lilburne who did this.

Major Sanderson was a competent and loyal officer who had an important part to play in keeping the Northumberland royalists in check in the first half of 1648, and who received the particular thanks of Parliament for his work on 1st July. He is already a man of some historical significance, without the need to invent roles for him in the absence of evidence.

PART III

CHAPTER 7

JOHN SANDERSON AND THE DIARY

John Sanderson the man

After following his career through his Diary and his five extant letters, what conclusions can be reached about him as a person? The answer must be: very little directly, but much more by inference. He is " a shadowy figure . . . who emerges . . . into the light of history for a brief period."[1] Slightly conflicting views emerge in the Diary, his Will, and his letters.

The terse entries in the Diary show him as a man who concentrated on essentials, recording what he saw as immediately relevant and not wasting time on peripheral matters. The state of the weather, the roads, his quarters, none of these actually *mattered* to him regardless of how frustrating it is for the modern reader. Others, from Major-General Lambert, commanding the Northern Army, to the more humble Samuel Birch, captain of militia foot, found time to expound on the weather and the quarters, and Lieut.-General Cromwell mentioned both the rain and the mud at Preston. Major Sanderson presumably saw them as part of the pattern of campaigning life and not worth spending time on.

Of his early life nothing is known. His writing is much better than that of Captains Bradford and Goodricke, and may be an indication that he had received a better education. Evidence is lacking as to whether he followed his father and elder brother to university. His Will shows that he had mathematical instruments[2] and books in both London and Hedleyhope, and to an extent that made them worth mentioning.

He comes across in the Diary as a man devoid of personal relationships, without friends or enemies. This view perhaps owes more to the military nature of the Diary than reality, but he certainly wasted little ink on people. His brothers Peter and Samuel make one appearance each related to army matters, and he records a loan to Samuel, but his family is otherwise absent. He visits Hedleyhope several times but without mentioning his parents, for he saw no need. In fact his *Relation* shows his father to be at Newcastle in August – was his mother with him, and were they living there rather than at Hedleyhope? If so, Sanderson makes no mention of visiting them when passing through Newcastle.

His letter to Captain Adam Baynes in December 1648 (Appendix 4) has a postscript "Remember my harty and faithfull love to honest Captaine Bradford." This is not an uncommon expression for the times, but it is no formality. He clearly had a liking for the fellow-officer with whom he had shared the boredom and dangers of endless patrolling. But it is interesting that the nearest he comes in the Diary to any personal note is when "my oune fine gray nag dyed at Arneston." This entry is divided from the more official record of the day by a short bold line as though to emphasise that this was a private matter. The theft in August of his "great white gelding" is more impersonal; the grey may have been his favourite, but this may be reading too much into the brief entry.

He certainly did have personal friends, as his Will shows. "To my much esteemed friend Mrs. Elizabeth Jennings, wife to Captaine James Jennings . . . my house in Cropwell" even if only for life, suggests a close friendship. Perhaps "much esteemed" indicates no more than a firm friendship of mutual respect.

It is both easier and more difficult when it comes to the other bequest to a lady, Jane Norton, only daughter and heiress of Toby Dudley of Chopwell:

"To my dear friend Mrs. Jane Norton, of Chopwell, I give my dyamond ring, with 9 dyamonds, and my little gold enameld picture case, with 8 rubyes sett in it; and I desire that my picture may be coppyed in little, and that little coppye putt into the case, and soe given to her to keepe in remembrance of mee."

"My dear friend" sounds more intimate than "esteemed", and yet it may mean no more. To order a miniature of his portrait, to be put into a locket for her to remember him by, certainly suggests a more than usually close friendship, but it is too easy to read into the few words meanings which are not there.

In fact, they must have known each other for many years. His father had had an interest in the Chopwell woods, 15 miles from Hedleyhope, and the Sandersons and Dudleys were at least acquainted over a long period even if they were not always on the best of terms (see Appendix 7). John took the Protestation in 1642 at the same time as Jane's father Toby, which might suggest an ongoing link between the families. Jane Norton was a widow for a year before Sanderson's death, and yet they did not marry.

The fact that he visited and possibly quartered at Chopwell, rather than Hedleyhope, on 14th September, may be significant, but Sanderson is not telling. The jury must remain out in the absence of further evidence. Of the diamond ring and ruby-set locket, more later.

As to Sanderson's character, Oxberry points out that he must have been a man of some personality, with the self confidence of a leader of men. He must also have been physically strong to withstand the rigours of campaigning in cold, wet weather. It may be that this hard life contributed to his early death at the age of about 34.

He was a man of some courage. In September 1647 when Capt. Lilburne's men were unfit to go on, he attacked the moss troopers with only his own troop. Saving the life of the royalist Salkeld at Preston, in the middle of a desperate fight with no quarter being given, must have been accomplished with considerable risk to himself.

He must have been a good horseman, not merely because he lived most of the year in the saddle but as evidenced by the long rides he was able to make. On more than 40 days he rode over 30 miles and 17 journeys were over 40 miles. He must also have had a care for horses, and made sure his men did the same, or these rides would not have been possible.

Sanderson was responsible at various times before and during 1648 for between one and two hundred men. There is no mention of any punishment meted out – were his men all so well-behaved that there was no cause for any hearing of a misdemeanour? Even when they "were like to mutiny" in June the resolution is not mentioned.

He probably maintained discipline with an easy firmness, he knowing when to look the other way, they knowing that beyond certain limits retribution would be swift and hard. Certainly it is difficult to see how such wide-ranging patrolling, independent of regimental organisation for weeks on end, could have been carried out any other way. Perhaps he followed the advice recorded 20 years later: "I would not have you spoil them with overmuch kindness . . .as you must take care of the pay and provision of your soldiers, so you ought to be very severe in your discipline . . . 'pay well and hang well, makes a good soldier.'"[3] There must have been mutual trust and understanding between him and his men, and there is an undertone of satisfaction when he recorded "every Soldyer a bottle under him."

As well as having a care for his men, he seems to have been conscientious in paying for quarters, as summarised above, chapter 3, *Parliamentary Army*. Apart from the matter of natural justice, a reputation for consideration towards those on whom his men were billeted would stand him and the troops in good stead for the future.

He also seems to have treated his servants well. Six men who were indisputably servants are mentioned; on half a dozen occasions he either paid them more than their wages or lent them money, and two of them were still with him when he made his Will. His parenthetical comment "I am obliged to remember them" had the meaning "grateful to." John Jackson was left £20 and Robert Taylor £15, respectively four times and three times their annual wages. For comparison, a trooper was paid £36 10s a year, but out of this had to pay quarters for himself and his horse, and was probably left with no more than £9 or £10 a year. Four other servants, including his two "new men," were remembered to the extent of between three quarters and two and a half times their annual wages.

The accounts on the back flyleaf of the Diary (Appendix 3a) do not mention servants but seem to be exclusively concerned with army personnel. The intriguing feature of them is that all the people who received money from him have their names recorded in code.

It is unlikely that this was done in case he were captured, as the advantage to royalists of knowing that Daniel Russell had nine weeks pay is difficult to see. It is much more likely that he was concealing the information from his friends and superiors. The fact that Lieutenant Strangeways, along with two men, was being paid by Sanderson is puzzling. He was certainly in the regiment in the late 50s: was he there in 1648 but in some capacity which required payment out of the regular course? He can hardly have been on official duties for Sanderson or he would have been mentioned in the Diary. Lieutenant Shepperson was paid for service "before he went" but this entry follows that of Strangeways who was paid up to a date in May. There is no satisfactory explanation of these payments.

In the previous chapter his purchase of land and property was mentioned. It is clear that some of the purchases were made with the aid of soldiers' debentures which many officers bought up very cheaply. This was in general a most reprehensible practice, but it did at least give the soldiers some immediate money whereas they could have waited long for the government to redeem their debentures. Also, Madge lists numerous purchases of land by officers acting on behalf of their regiments. There is no doubt that Sanderson had an entrepreneurial eye to the opportunities offered by the Civil War, but it is clear that he was an honourable man. His Will says that he bought a farm for Captain Stafford with "my owne souldiours bills", and was thus acting on their behalf, and that if Stafford could not pay up then the farm should go to them. In this case he was not merely acting for the regiment as a whole but for men in his own troop, whose interests must be preserved.

He was seen by his superiors as trustworthy in a personal as well as political sense, as exemplified by his being sent to fetch the equivalent of something like £350,000 from Newcastle. He was chosen to command Lambert's escort for the possibly difficult task of disbanding militia forces in December 1648. In 1649 he was one of those appointed by Lambert to carry out property deals on behalf of the Northern Brigade. All of these duties called for a man who could not only be trusted to act with honesty and loyalty but was intellectually capable of negotiating for the purchase of Crown lands.

In fact he had advantages when it came to selection for unusual jobs. He was probably well educated, he had been commanding two independent troops in 1647 and, although reduced in rank when he joined Lilburne's, he was a senior and experienced man who did not have the same regimental responsibilities as Major Smithson. He was therefore an ideal officer to use for special duties and probably a godsend to Lambert and other senior officers.

About Sanderson's political and religious convictions there is little evidence. He twice mentions attending a sermon, but whether this was an unusual occurrence or a regular event he happens to note only twice is simply unknown. He took the Protestation in 1642 but this may have been no more than the politic thing to do. He gives thanks to God for the various victories but only in his letters; God does not enter the private record of his Diary.

Sanderson clearly worked hard in the Parliament's cause but was not a fanatic or a Leveller. He makes no strong statement about the royalists, referring to them in his Diary as the "enemy", "Scots", and "cavaliers". These are all accurate and unexceptionable terms and his letter of 3rd July call them cabbs" [cavaliers] and "blades", hardly the usage of fervent crusader. He fought them but was not single-minded about their destruction, witness the saving of Thomas Salkeld at some risk to himself.

He was clearly no Puritan. The possession of a diamond ring and a ruby-set locket, together with his interest in horse racing, are sufficient to dispel any such thought. His personal loot of two hogsheads of French wine at Alnwick on 12th July shows that he was not averse to alcohol.

He was certainly keen to oppose any accommodation with the king, as his part in writing the letter to Fairfax from Pontefract shows. How far he wanted to go is unknown. If only his diary for 1649 had survived, there would have been some comment about the king's execution but we have no record of him between 30th December 1648 and 8th June 1649. He may have been a supporter of Cromwell and wanted the king dead to prevent further warfare, or he may have followed Lambert who wanted no king but was (possibly) not necessarily eager for his death. Perhaps, as Lambert appears to have been, he was somewhat equivocal about the matter.

Whether he would have supported Colonel Lilburne and General Lambert in 1659, or whether he would have followed Major Smithson with three other troop commanders in deserting to Fairfax cannot be judged from his writings.

This review of Sanderson the man shows him as something of a paragon of all the virtues. In fact, it is doubtful if he was particularly unusual. He was clearly a trusted, loyal, and competent officer but not necessarily more so than, say, Major Smithson. He was probably honest in his dealings, but awake to the possibilities of benefiting his own situation. He must have been serious about the cause for which he was fighting but he appears, like his Diary entries, to have been undramatic, understated, and dispassionate.

The significance of the Diary

Major Sanderson's Diary is important on a number of levels. First, diaries written by participants in the Civil War are very rare. Memoirs are more common, but were usually written after the passage of time, and tend to concentrate on what hindsight saw as important. Birch kept a diary not unlike Sanderson's but the latter's 270 entries, plus 10 missing days, for a single year is unrivalled. Sanderson's Diary provides a remarkable and unique glimpse into the second Civil War, although it is but one fine thread running through the lives of thousands of soldiers. It is impossible to read his manuscript without feeling close to the action.

Both Birch and Sanderson refer their readers to other accounts of the battle of Preston. This raises the question of who the intended readers were. Was it the case that every officer commanding a troop or company was obliged, or found it convenient, to record daily events in a way which could be used as the basis for reports which were placed – as Birch puts it – on the file? The present authors have not been able to find any evidence of this whatsoever, but the general similarity of content and the reference to other accounts does give an indication of this. It may be that there are more diaries to be discovered.

Although the Diary entries are terse, they do throw light both on events in the north of England in 1648 and on the way in which the parliamentary cavalry went about its business. Many of the points are very minor: it was known from elsewhere that Colonel Weldon's oats and rye were taken in by parliamentary troops, but only the Diary says which troops. Rushworth recorded the garrisoning of Cartington in May but only from the Diary is it known that fighting took place beforehand.

The account in the Diary of the battle of Preston adds a little to other accounts, but is perhaps chiefly valuable for its reference to his *Relation at Large*, which led to its rediscovery. Cromwell, Hamilton, Langdale, and Turner give a broad picture of the battle, but hitherto there were only two accounts extant which were by participants other than senior commanders. Captain Hodgson and Captain Birch were the only fighting soldiers in the battle known to have given their view: Major Sanderson can now be added to the list, and the *Relation* is the only detailed account from beginning to end, although even it has to be read in conjunction with the Diary to get the full picture as Sanderson saw it.

It is well known that after Preston Cromwell returned north through Skipton while Lambert went up to Carlisle. From the Diary it is clear that some of the horse went back through Bakewell and Leeds, not an earth-shaking fact but one of interest. And did Lambert send out other officers to gain information about the royalist cavalry after Preston, as Sanderson seems to have done?

Some of these details are of minor importance, but nonetheless interesting for that. As noted in chapter 1, the Diary not only adds to our existing knowledge but the need to explain its brief entries more fully has led to other discoveries and interpretations.

Perhaps the major, and unique, advantage of the Diary is that it provides a *day by day* insight into the tedium and monotony of patrolling which is not to be found in any other source. And from this detail, it is possible to recreate Sanderson's itinerary with remarkable accuracy. From nowhere else is it possible to calculate that a parliamentary (or any other) officer rode 4,360 miles in a year with an average journey of over 20 miles a day for those days on which he travelled.

Taking only the "To" column of the transcript, Appendix 3, he visited 215 places, 45 of them more than once. The shortest day was of two miles, the longest 80 miles including skirmishing. On 88 days he covered 20 miles or more a day, and 43 of these were of 30 miles or over. Seventeen journeys were of 40 miles or more. It is no great surprise that his "fine gray nag" died, and the wonder is that he did not lose more horses. When it is recalled that many journeys were not alone but with troops, it is clear that the humble troop horse, no less than the officer's mount, was of remarkable endurance.

This book has taken into account all known relevant sources, published and unpublished, which have a direct bearing on the Diary and on Sanderson's life. Much interesting material has had to be omitted as only marginally relevant to a book of this size, but there must be more undiscovered information which would throw further light on this interesting character. The authors would be grateful to hear of anything bearing on the life, friends, and family of Major John Sanderson.

APPENDIX 1

JULIAN STYLE CALENDAR FOR 1648

Saturday	1	January					1	July				
Sunday	2	January					2	July				
Monday	3	January			1	May	3	July				
Tuesday	4	January			2	May	4	July				
Wednesday	5	January	1	March	3	May	5	July			1	November
Thursday	6	January	2	March	4	May	6	July			2	November
Friday	7	January	3	March	5	May	7	July	1	September	3	November
Saturday	8	January	4	March	6	May	8	July	2	September	4	November
Sunday	9	January	5	March	7	May	9	July	3	September	5	November
Monday	10	January	6	March	8	May	10	July	4	September	6	November
Tuesday	11	January	7	March	9	May	11	July	5	September	7	November
Wednesday	12	January	8	March	10	May	12	July	6	September	8	November
Thursday	13	January	9	March	11	May	13	July	7	September	9	November
Friday	14	January	10	March	12	May	14	July	8	September	10	November
Saturday	15	January	11	March	13	May	15	July	9	September	11	November
Sunday	16	January	12	March	14	May	16	July	10	September	12	November
Monday	17	January	13	March	15	May	17	July	11	September	13	November
Tuesday	18	January	14	March	16	May	18	July	12	September	14	November
Wednesday	19	January	15	March	17	May	19	July	13	September	15	November
Thursday	20	January	16	March	18	May	20	July	14	September	16	November
Friday	21	January	17	March	19	May	21	July	15	September	17	November
Saturday	22	January	18	March	20	May	22	July	16	September	18	November
Sunday	23	January	19	March	21	May	23	July	17	September	19	November
Monday	24	January	20	March	22	May	24	July	18	September	20	November

Tuesday	25	January	21	March	23	May	25	July	19	September	21	November
Wednesday	26	January	22	March	24	May	26	July	20	September	22	November
Thursday	27	January	23	March	25	May	27	July	21	September	23	November
Friday	28	January	24	March	26	May	28	July	22	September	24	November
Saturday	29	January	25	March	27	May	29	July	23	September	25	November
Sunday	30	January	26	March	28	May	30	July	24	September	26	November
Monday	31	January	27	March	29	May	31	July	25	September	27	November
Tuesday	1	February	28	March	30	May	1	August	26	September	28	November
Wednesday	2	February	29	March	31	May	2	August	27	September	29	November
Thursday	3	February	30	March	1	June	3	August	28	September	30	November
Friday	4	February	31	March	2	June	4	August	29	September	1	December
Saturday	5	February	1	April	3	June	5	August	30	September	2	December
Sunday	6	February	2	April	4	June	6	August	1	October	3	December
Monday	7	February	3	April	5	June	7	August	2	October	4	December
Tuesday	8	February	4	April	6	June	8	August	3	October	5	December
Wednesday	9	February	5	April	7	June	9	August	4	October	6	December
Thursday	10	February	6	April	8	June	10	August	5	October	7	December
Friday	11	February	7	April	9	June	11	August	6	October	8	December
Saturday	12	February	8	April	10	June	12	August	7	October	9	December
Sunday	13	February	9	April	11	June	13	August	8	October	10	December
Monday	14	February	10	April	12	June	14	August	9	October	11	December
Tuesday	15	February	11	April	13	June	15	August	10	October	12	December
Wednesday	16	February	12	April	14	June	16	August	11	October	13	December
Thursday	17	February	13	April	15	June	17	August	12	October	14	December

Friday	18	February	14	April	16	June	18	August	13	October	15	December
Saturday	19	February	15	April	17	June	19	August	14	October	16	December
Sunday	20	February	16	April	18	June	20	August	15	October	17	December
Monday	21	February	17	April	19	June	21	August	16	October	18	December
Tuesday	22	February	18	April	20	June	22	August	17	October	19	December
Wednesday	23	February	19	April	21	June	23	August	18	October	20	December
Thursday	24	February	20	April	22	June	24	August	19	October	21	December
Friday	25	February	21	April	23	June	25	August	20	October	22	December
Saturday	26	February	22	April	24	June	26	August	21	October	23	December
Sunday	27	February	23	April	25	June	27	August	22	October	24	December
Monday	28	February	24	April	26	June	28	August	23	October	25	December
Tuesday	29	February	25	April	27	June	29	August	24	October	26	December
Wednesday			26	April	28	June	30	August	25	October	27	December
Thursday			27	April	29	June	31	August	26	October	28	December
Friday			28	April	30	June			27	October	29	December
Saturday			29	April					28	October	30	December
Sunday			30	April					29	October	31	December
Monday									30	October		
Tuesday									31	October		

APPENDIX 2

THE DIARY VOLUME AND ALMANACS

The Diary volume

The Diary is written on the blank pages of an interleaved edition, or "blank," of William Lilly's *Merlini Anglici Ephemeris* for 1648, published in November 1647, which is bound with the 1648 *Uranoscopia* by John Booker. The Almanac begins on 1st January, despite the fact that at that time the New Year began on 25th March in England. Scotland had already made the change, but the Almanac was printed in London for the Company of Stationers. It is clear from many contemporary documents that both systems were in use in England in the mid-seventeenth century.

The volume is bound in full calf, with the remains of two metal clasps on the back board. The front board is missing. The binding appears to be contemporary, and it is no surprise that Sanderson carried both works as Lilly and Booker supported the parliamentary side in the Civil War. Fairfax invited the two of them to his headquarters at Windsor in 1647 to further his cause, and they were both at the siege of Colchester the following year.[1]

The information given in each is to a certain extent complementary. On the calendar pages Lilly gives the rise and set times of the moon and the sun, and lists holy days, while his weather forecasts are given within the text of the monthly "Observations"; Booker, on the other hand, notes only the anniversaries of Civil War events and has much clearer weather forecasts in the right-hand margin of each calendar page. More importantly, he gives high tides for specific locations including Holy Isle, Hartlepool, Berwick, Newcastle and Dunbar, and the latitudes of notable towns and cities, the list again including places of relevance to Sanderson's movements, such as Berwick and York. Lilly refers the reader to Booker for the latitudes of the five planets other than the moon (which is to be found in his own almanac for 1646), and for his part, Booker advertises "Master Lillies Introduction to Astrology".

Interleaving of plain, unprinted, pages in the Lilly volume occurs between each signature in B, C and D, with a double leaf in the centre of each gathering. The paper is thin, which sometimes allows the writing to show on the other side. Although the binding is defective, it is not immediately obvious that anything is missing. A closer look at the collation, however, reveals that the blank leaf between B and B2 is lacking, which must explain why the text of the extant diary begins on 11th January. The second half of the centre leaf in D is also missing and there are further anomalies in E, but it is probably unlikely that any more of Sanderson's notes are lost as he does not use blank leaves in the almanac for accounts or other comments.

The use of almanacs as diaries was not uncommon in the seventeenth century, and several have survived in manuscript, some subsequently printed. However, none of those listed in Capp (61, 401) are similar to the military diary we have here. Most are much more discursive, and the almanac used is not always mentioned by the modern editor. The royalist lawyer John Greene wrote his own notes and comments on public events in the 1635 almanac published by Richard Allestree and in a Booker almanac for 1643, but the entries are on the whole less personal. Philip Henry, a nonconformist divine, used several editions of the almanac published by John Goldsmith for his diaries (1650-1684), but there are very few entries per month, some obviously written on the day and others later.

A Goldsmith almanac for 1682 was used by another minister, Samuel Angier, and apart from the subject matter this is the closest to Sanderson's, in that the entries are terse. Interleaved blank pages in the first part of the "small pocket diary"[2] are used for accounts and details of loans, while the majority of later entries concern the weather. Of particular interest is an undated entry suggesting that Angier's first cousin once removed, also Samuel, was in Newcastle "at Mr Jo: Emersons at cox close near new castle upon Tine Mr Peter Sanderson on the end of Tine bridge newcastle"[3]. Extracts quoted from the diary of Sir Richard Stapley, 1682 to 1724, concern money, accounts and the weather, with some national and local events noted. The earliest were written in a "clasped interleaved almanack" for six years, 1682-1687, published by Samuel Gilbert.[4] A copy of Lilly's *Merlini Anglici Ephemeris* for 1681 was used for accounts and notes, including the names of his wife's sitters, by Charles Beale, husband of the portrait painter Mary Beale (1633–1699) in the Archives of the National Portrait Gallery.[5]

Notes on the transcript of the Diary

The transcription on the following pages, in columns headed Day, Date, and Diary Transcription, is based partly on the original publication and corrigenda but includes amendments and some new readings based on a study of the manuscript. The names of the months were sometimes written against dates, as shown, but the month names centred in square brackets are insertions for clarity. Recognisable erasures are shown, but small, illegible changes, perhaps involving a single letter are not shown. Punctuation is given where this is clear, but there are many apparently random dots which are not clearly full stops. He kept some of his accounts on the flyleaves of the Diary, and these are transcribed in Appendix 3a.

The original transcription did not recognise Sanderson's use of planetary signs to indicate days of the week (*plate 1 and fig. 10*), referring to them instead as astrological symbols. Their true purpose has helped to separate some undated days from the previous ones, and in one case (14th June) makes a significant change to the reading. In the transcript the signs are indicated by the initial letters of the days of the week in black letter font. Where Sanderson omitted a date it has been added in square brackets, but planetary signs have not been added.

The columns of distances are derived from both computerised route planners

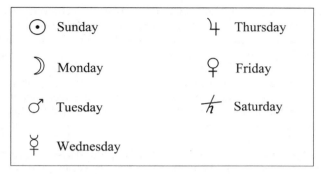

Fig. 10: Planetary symbols used in the Diary to indicate days of the week

and large scale maps, with care taken to use all minor roads when appropriate; modern roads which deviate from more ancient routes have been avoided. Where his troop quartered at several places the distance given is to the first place mentioned. At times, routes may have been a little shorter than shown if Sanderson went across country, although on the journeys where this can be determined he seems to have travelled on or very close to roads. Some distances may have been longer, if Sanderson himself did not stay in the first place shown for his troop's quarters, or he may have visited all the quarters before going into quarters himself. On balance, distances probably average out to what he did do over the year.

Mileage in the Subtotal column is entered in fractions of a mile, but displayed to the nearest whole mile, and may appear to disagree with the Total column which adds the fractions.

National Grid references are to the nearest 100m and refer to places in the 'To' column. The Notes column has glosses on place names where they are obscure or doubtful, and where explanation in the text seems unnecessary.

The writing of the Diary

It has not been convenient to make a detailed study of the graphology of the Diary, but it is possible to make a few comments on the time which elapsed between the events and their recording. However, it must be borne in mind that the sharpening of a quill or watering of thick ink in mid-task can show a false difference between entries all made on the same day.

The clearest indication of any delay occurs at the battle of Preston when his entries for 17th and 19th August refer to his Relation at Large which is itself dated 20th. It is no surprise that he had no time to attend to his Diary at the end of a day's fighting and it appears, although it is not certain, that all four entries for 17th-20th were made at the same time. Both Diary and *Relation* were written up during a day of rest at Warrington.

The entry for Monday 20th March includes a reference to Tho Whitfeild returning from York on Thursday 23rd. The handwriting, pen, and ink appear to be identical for that entry and for Thursday 23rd and Wednesday 22nd (in that order), suggesting that all three days were written up on Thursday, or even Friday for which there is no entry.

He says that his men were mutinous at Helm o' the Hill on 13th June, but the entry for 14th shows that it was only on that day that they went north of Morpeth and were thus in the area given for the mutiny. From the handwriting it appears that Sanderson wrote the entries for 14th and 15th on a single day, and this may have contributed to the error.

There are other small instances but these examples will serve to confirm what common sense would dictate: Sanderson did not always have the leisure or the energy to write his Diary every single day. In times of great stress and activity the delay could be as much as four days, but this does not detract from the value of the entries.

APPENDIX 3

TRANSCRIPT OF MAJOR SANDERSON'S DIARY

DAY	DATE	DIARY TRANSCRIPTION	FROM	TO	MILES		GRID REF	NOTES
					Sub Tot	Daily Tot	(for 'To' col)	
				[January]				
T	11	Janua: I went to Capheaton.		Capheaton			NZ 035803	Map 3
W	12	to morpeth to sessions. The Justices refused to grant any more sesses to our troopes but till Sa 15 January.	Capheaton	Morpeth		14	NZ200860	Map 3
F	14	I came to Capheaton.	Morpeth	Capheaton		14	NZ 035803	Map 3
Sa	15	to my quarters at Simonburne.	Capheaton	Simonburn		16	NY 873736	Map 3
Tu	18	I dispersed my troope to free quarter and came to west matfin myself reseruing standerton p'ish.	Simonburn	Matfen		13	NZ 031717	Map 3
W	19	to Newcastle.	Matfen	Newcastle		11	NZ 250640	Map 3
Th	20	I came back to matfin.	Newcastle	Matfen		11	NZ 031717	Map 3
F	21	I came to Cheesburne grange.	Haltwhistle	Cheeseburne grange		28	NZ 094713	Map 3 Cheeseburne Grange is near Stamfordham. For explanation of the route see Commentary
Tu	25	I went to Newcastle returned y' night.	Cheeseburne grange	Newcastle	13		NZ 250640	Map 3
			Newcastle	Cheeseburne grange	13		NZ 094713	Map 3
						26		
F	21[sic]	I payd Haltwizle quarters.	Matfen	Haltwhistle	24		NY705642	Map 2

90

DAY	DATE	DIARY TRANSCRIPTION	FROM	TO	MILES Sub Tot	MILES Daily Tot	GRID REF (for 'To' col)	NOTES
M	24 [sic]	payd woodburne q'ters.	Haltwhistle	Cheeseburne grange	28		NZ 094713	Map 3
			Cheeseburne grange	Woodburn	19	52	NY 892868	Map 3. If this is West Woodburn
			Woodburn	Cheeseburne grange	19		NZ 094713	
Th	27	payd my owne squadrˢ: assisting quarters.				39		The s of squadron is a straight slash with no attempt at a letter
Sa	29	I went Newcastle and returned.	Cheeseburne grange	Newcastle	13		NZ 250640	Map 3
			Newcastle	Cheeseburne grange	13	26	NZ 094713	Map 3
Su	30	I sent Dʳ Petty to yorke lent Jo: Jackson 6ˢ at Newcastle.						

DAY	DATE	DIARY TRANSCRIPTION	FROM	TO	MILES Sub Tot	Daily Tot	GRID REF (for 'To' col)	NOTES
M	31	I went to Newcastle to meet Sʳ Richard Bellasis and others about disbanding supernumeraries.	Cheeseburne grange	Newcastle		13	NZ 250640	Map 3
		[February]						
Tu	1	I came from Newcastle. Rec. order to quarter my troope about Alnwick and wooler.	Newcastle	Cheeseburne grange		13	NZ 094713	Map 3
W	2	Rendeuoused at Newton sent my Troope Northward, but came to hedlyhope my selfe.	Cheeseburne grange	Newton	7		NZ 035645	Map 3
			Newton	Hedleyhope	22	28	NZ 150405	
Th	3	I went to Durham, came back at night.	Hedleyhope	Durham	9		NZ 270420	Map 3
			Durham	Hedleyhope	9		NZ 150405	Map 3
F	4	my brother Peter & I drew certificates & debenters.				17		
S	[5]	I went to Durham & got my papers referd to Mr. Gilpin and Mr. Marchall to examine.	Hedleyhope	Durham		9	NZ 270420	Map 3. Assumed that he stayed in Durham
M	7°	the Comissioners signed the debentures for my supernumerary soldiers						
Tu	[8]	I receiued 175ˡ of Mr. Marchall to pay 2 monthes pay to Corpo. Racket & 30 priuate soldyers - & then disband them.	Durham	Hedleyhope		9	NZ 150405	Map 3. Assumed that he returned to Durham that night.
W	9°	I transcribed debenters & send 2 copies to mr. Gilpin.						

DAY	DATE	DIARY TRANSCRIPTION	FROM	TO	MILES Sub Tot	MILES Daily Tot	GRID REF (for 'To' col)	NOTES
W	9	I payd Corpo: Rackot & gaue him his debenter.						
F	11	I went from Hedlyhope to Newcastle.	Hedleyhope	Newcastle		20	NZ 250640	Map 3
Sa	12	to Anwick.	Newcastle	Alnwick		34	NU 186136	Map 3, 4
Su	13	after sermon to Rock where I quarter.	Alnwick	Rock		6	NU 204203	Map 4
M	14	I begun to disband my supermumaries. Lent Robert Somerside 2s 6d						
Tu	15	I disbanded all my sup'numerarie soldyers and payd them 5-12-0 a man. sent my Leeu't to gouernour of Newcastle for directions to qrter. Recd order from generall to march into Bishopprick.						
F	18	I marched from bambrough ward and quartered about Cramlinton that night.	Rock	Cramlington		32	NZ 270770	Map 3
Sa	19	marched through newcastle & quartered about Hilton. I got y't night to Hedly hope.	Cramlington	Hilton	17		NZ 270500	Map 3. Assumes Hilton is near Chester-le-Street, see Commentary
			Hilton	Hedleyhope	12		NZ 150405	Map 3
						30		
M	21	I quartered my troope in Barnard castle.	Hedleyhope	Hilton	12		NZ 270500	Map 3

DAY	DATE	DIARY TRANSCRIPTION	FROM	TO	MILES Sub Tot	MILES Daily Tot	GRID REF (for 'To' col)	NOTES
			Hilton	Barnard Castle	31		NZ 050160	Map 5
						43		
Tu	22	I went to Richmond.	Barnard Castle	Richmond		14	NZ 170010	Map 5
W	23	I got to yorke, ye generall poferd mee my troope, and gaue me 14 days pay for them & 7 days quarter being in all 161.1.2.	Richmond	York		46	SE 606520	Map 5
F	25	febr: I got to wil. Lees house neare Leeming.	York	Leeming		35	SE 293893	Map 5
Sa	[26]	to Barnard castle and payd my soldyers 14 days pay.	Leeming	Barnard Castle		24	NZ 050160	Map 5
M	28	in the morning all my soldyers payd their quarters in Barnard castle.						
Tu	29	I sent my brother sam to pay my troopes quarters about Chester for Sa & Su the 20 & 21 febr : I went towards yorke. Lay at Willm Lees.	Barnard Castle	Leeming		24	SE 293893	Map 5. Saturday and Sunday were 19 and 20th
		[March]						
W		At yorke I lent Jo: Jackson fiue shillings.						
W	1°	martij I got to yorke, and receiued order to dismiss my Leeueten^t & Chirurgion.	Leeming	York		35	SE 606520	Map 5
Th	2	I got order to receiue another fortnights pay for 80 soldiers and it was payd to me the next day.						

DAY	DATE	DIARY TRANSCRIPTION	FROM	TO	MILES		GRID REF	NOTES
					Sub Tot	Daily Tot	(for 'To' col)	
F	3	twenty of Capt: wilkinsons Troope ordered to Joine with mine &c. Leueten[t] Leuen appointed to be my Leeueten[t].						
Sa		I lay at Northaluerton.	York	Northallerton		33	SE 370940	Map 5
Su	5	I got to Barnard Castle.	Northal-lerton	Barnard Castle		29	NZ 050160	Map 5
Mo	6	I sent my qsterm[r] [quartermaster] to yorke for the 20 men &c. my Leeueten[t]: Chirurgion. Ro. Byerly, Ge: Taunton, An: Smith, mat. Tindall Cuth. Grey reduced.						
Tu	7	gaue Robert Taylor and Rob Somerset 9[s] 4[d] to diet themselues aweeke. And 17[s] 8[d] for a yard of hay. And 24[s] to by a y[e] q[r]ter of oats. I lay that night at Newburne.	Barnard Castle	Newburn		41	NZ 168664	Map 3
W	8	I came to Bedlington & payd all my soldyers quarters to the townes adiacent, for F 18 febr:	Newburn	Bedlington	14		NZ 255820	Map 3
W	8°	I went from Bedlington to morpeth from thence to Pegsworth from thence to Ellington where I lodged that night.	Bedlington	Morpeth	5		NZ 200860	Map 3
			Morpeth	Pegswood	3		NZ 225875	Map 3. Formerly Pegsworth (Eckwall).

DAY	DATE	DIARY TRANSCRIPTION	FROM	TO	MILES		GRID REF	NOTES
					Sub Tot	Daily Tot	(for 'To' col)	
			Pegswood	Ellington	5		NZ 270920	Map 3
Th	9	I dined at Lesbury, got to Rock at night	Ellington	Lesbury	14	27	NU 235116	Map 4
			Lesbury	Rock	14	33	NU 204203	Map 4
F	10	I payd euery towne in Bambrough ward for my soldyers quarters from 4 to 18 februa:	Rock	Bamburgh	11		NU 180350	Map 4
			Bamburgh	Rock	11	22		NU 204203
Sa	11	I went from Rock, cald at Newcastle, gott to Hedly hope.	Rock	Newcastle	38		NZ 250640	Map 3
			Newcastle	Hedleyhope	20	58	NZ 150405	Map 3
Su	12	I came to Barnard castle.	Hedleyhope	Barnard Castle		23	NZ 050160	Map 5
M	13	my troope was mustered at Staindropp, and consisted of 77 priuate soldyers besides ye Leeueten^{ts} men who are not com'd yet.	Barnard Castle	Staindrop	6		NZ 125205	Map 5. Between Barnard Castle and Bishop Auckland
			Staindrop	Barnard Castle	6	12		Map 5. assumes he returned to Barnard Castle
F	17	I went to Hunwick edge, & from thence to Hedlyhope.	Barnard Castle	Hunwick	17		NZ 192325	[Map 5] 4 miles N. of Bishop Auckland
			Hunwick	Hedleyhope	8	25	NZ 150405	Map 3

F. 1. wee marched to Sr Basils to gether
H. 2. wee marched to Darton.
O. 3. wee marched to Battley. (...
D. 4. wee marched to Horsforth new
Sr. 5. to killingall & stayd there till. 4.
H. 7. to Norton Hutton & marston.
Q. 8. to Bedall & Askew. Langtho...
H. 9. wee rested at Bedall & Askew
O. 10. to Gilling and Gilling wood
D. 11. to midridge grange Redworth New
biggen & rest thickly.
H. 12. lay still all day.
F. 13. to Durham.
H. 14. to Ryton pish winlaton Chopwe...
F. 15. to Bywell & wilam Stockfeild.
H. 16. to Capheaton Shortflat harnar...
O. 17. to Longhurst, Boggsworth, ougho...
D. 18. to Long houghton Lesbury &
I was sent to Chefwith to Leu.
genr: Cromwell and came back
to Rock the next morning. get of...
H. 19. quarter at fillingam.
F. 20. rested all day
H. 21. marched within a mile of
Barwick and went off to
at Barrinton Ancroft Skrimorsto...

1 A page from Major Sanderson's Diary, September 1648

2 Part of the Hedleyhope estate owned by the Sandersons in the seventeenth century, showing High Hedleyhope and Hedleyhope Hall Farm

3 Bewcastle, where Sanderson sent 40 men in October 1647 to apprehend moss troopers.

4 Thirlwall castle, arrowed, close to the dramatic line of Hadrian's Wall. It was taken by Sanderson from thieves in October 1647

5 Alnwick Castle which was garrisoned by Sanderson's troops at intervals from March and June

6 Morpeth Castle, the original Gatehouse with nineteenth century modifications

7 Barnard Castle, Lambert's base in July 1648. Sanderson's troops were quartered in the town in February, and he sent his race horses there in April

8 Bamburgh Castle. Sanderson's troops quartered in Bamburgh ward on several occasions

9 Warkworth Castle, to which Sanderson sent all the provisions from Alnwick on 1st June

10 Cartington Castle, which was assaulted unsuccessfully by Sanderson in May, and which held out for two hours on 1st July. The windows and some other features date from the nineteenth century

11 Holy Island, which Sanderson provisioned for six months early in June 1648

12 The river North Tyne at Chollerford where "wee ventured desperately to ride the water" on 9th June 1648

13 The Roman road now known as the Stanegate, along which the royalists were pursued to Haltwhistle and beyond on 9th June

14 The road between Forestburn Gate and Great Tosson at 3.55, just as the sun was rising

15 The tower at Great Tosson which the Forlorn Hope under Sanderson captured on 1st July

16 Typical countryside over which Sanderson and his troop operated in Northumberland. This view is between Chollerford and Herterton

17 View over Kirkharle from the road followed by Sanderson on 9th June and 1st July

18 The view from Tosson tower to Cartington Castle (arrowed

19 The valley of the river Coquet near Rothbury

20 Looking north to the village of Branton, the limit of operations on 1st July

21 Looking west to the summit of Stainmore pass. The modern road follows the line of the Roman road

22 Bowes Castle, which Lambert's army held to prevent the Scottish army invading over Stainmore

23 The swollen river Tweed at Twizle, which Lilburne's failed to cross in September 1648. A small flooded island is indicated by the reeds in the middle of the river

THE NORTH-PART OF
ENGLAND and
THE SOVTH-PART OF
SCOTLAND

Scala Miliarium

PE·RTHIA

STRATHERNE

FI

FA

MEN
TEITH

STRIVILINGIA

LENNOS

LENOXIA

CLIDES-

CVNING-

DAILL

HAM.

DOVGLASDAL

KYLE

CARRIKE

ANANDALE.

ESKE

GALLOWAY.

NYTHESD

ALE

AN

ANDIA

LAVDONIA

MARCIA

DALIA

GILSLANDE.

TIVIDALE

Rededale

NORTHVMBRIA

TYNDALE

THE BISHOP-RICKE OF DVRRAM
AND CVMBERLAND, WESTMORELAND,
YORKE-SHIRE, LANCAST-SHIRE, AND
PARTE OF LINCONSHIRE

The Scale of Myles

CVMBER
LAND

DVNELMENSIS

ANDIA

EPISCOPAT·

WESTMOR
LANDIA

CLEVELAND

Blakamore

E

BORA

CVM.

LANCAS

TRIA

LIN

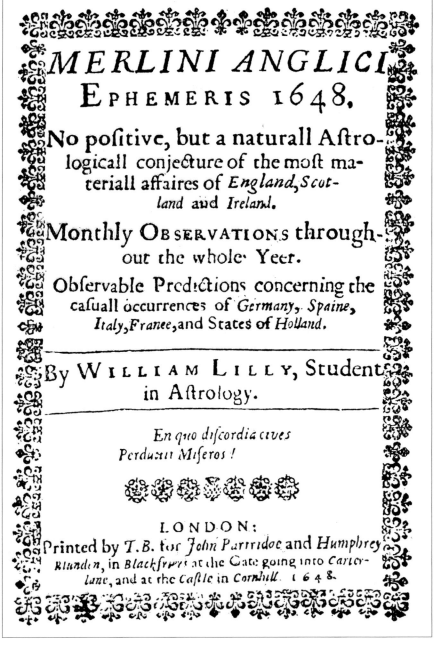

MERLINI ANGLICI

EPHEMERIS 1648,

No pofitive, but a naturall Aftro-
logicall conjecture of the moft ma-
teriall affaires of *England, Scotland* and *Ireland.*

Monthly OBSERVATIONS throughout the whole· Yeer.

Obfervable Predictions concerning the
cafuall occurrences of *Germany, Spaine,
Italy, France,* and States of *Holland.*

By WILLIAM LILLY, Student
in Aftrology.

*En quo difcordia cives
Perduant Miferos !*

LONDON:
Printed by *T. B.* for *John Partridge* and *Humphrey
Blunden,* in *Blackfryers* at the Gate going into *Carter-
lane,* and at the *Caftle* in *Cornhill.* 1648.

26 The title page of Lilly's almanac in which the Diary was written

Opposite above: 24 "The Quartermasters' Map" (SB-0915 N. England, reproduced
by permission of Durham University Library)

Opposite below: 25 "The Quartermasters' Map" (SB-0915 Durham, reproduced by
permission of Durham University Library)

27 Sir Thomas, afterwards Lord Fairfax, Lord General of Parliament's forces

28 Cavalry fight as depicted in Cruso's Militarie Instructions for the Cavallrie

DAY	DATE	DIARY TRANSCRIPTION	FROM	TO	MILES		GRID REF	NOTES
					Sub Tot	Daily Tot	(for 'To' col)	
Sa	18	I came to Barnard Castle.	Hedleyhope	Barnard Castle		23	NZ 050160	Map 5
Su	19	my Coronet came from yorke with three weekes pay.						
Tu	21	my Coron^t payd the soldyers. I went to woodam moore & came back at night.	Barnard Castle	Woodham	19		NZ 286267	[Map 5] NE of Newton Aycliffe
			Woodham	Barnard Castle	19		NZ 050160	Map 5
20 ma M	20	martij Sent Tho Whitfeild to yorke, he returned Th after.				38		
Th	23	orders came from the generall & Collo. Lilburne to march into Belford and woller.						
W	22	Richard Robeson came to mee. Since I came from to Barnard castle I bought other two yards of hay one at 17^s 8^d the other 21^s 9^d I gaue my men mony to dyet themselues till munday night the 27 martij.						

DAY	DATE	DIARY TRANSCRIPTION	FROM	TO	MILES Sub Tot	MILES Daily Tot	GRID REF (for 'To' col)	NOTES
Sa	25	Martij I payd Ro: Taylor, John Jackson & Robert Somerside their wages & gaue each 5ˢ more. For 4 pecke of peas 5ˢ4ᵈ) for rase / Wheat 7. 6.) / horses Sa 25⁰ / Candles, &c. 0. 3.) / Martij						
M	27	I left with Rich: Robinson and John Jackson fiue pounds for to keepe my Rase horses till I come to them. I marched with my troope from Barnard Castle. quartered that night in & about Lanchester.	Barnard Castle	Lanchester		29	NZ 165475	Map 3
Tu	28	I marched through Newcastle and quartered, at sighill, &c.	Lanchester	Newcastle	14		NZ 250640	Map 3
			Newcastle	Seghill	8		NZ 290743	Map 3
						21		
W	29	I marched through morpeth & quartered at Cockle parke &c.	Seghill	Morpeth	11		NZ 200860	Map 3
			Morpeth	Cockle Parke	5		NZ 202913	Map 3. About 1 mile south of Tritlington
						16		
Th	30	I came to Balmebrough ward & quartered my selfe at Rock.	Cockle Parke	Rock		20	NU 204203	Map 4
F	31	I rode to see mʳ Ogle of Eglingham.	Rock	Eglingham Hall	9		NU 104196	Map 4
			Eglingham Hall	Rock	9		NU 204203	Map 4

DAY	DATE	DIARY TRANSCRIPTION	FROM	TO	MILES		GRID REF	NOTES
					Sub Tot	Daily Tot	(for 'To' col)	
		[April]				18		
Su	2	Apr. I went to Alnwick; dined there. came back at night.	Rock	Alnwick	6		NU 186136	Map 4
			Alnwick	Rock	6		NU 204203	Map 4
						12		
M Tu	3	I sent my squadron to Chillingam, 2 Lilburnes & Hebron. Coronets Squadron to 2 Bewicks, Benely Roseden & woperton. Leeueten^ts squadron to Belford midleton and grange.					NU 062260	Map 4. Lilburn Tower (NU021241), East Lilburn (NU044236), Hepburn (NU069246), Old Bewick (NU066215), New Bewick (NU069203), Beanley (NU082183), Roseden (NU031215), Wooperton (NU039203), Belford (NUIIO339), Middleton (NU111356), ?Easington Grange (NU119358)
Tu	4	the troope payd all quarters.						
W	5	I went from Rock to Chillingam and quartered at Chatton.	Rock	Chillingham	12		NU 062260	Map 4
			Chillingham	Chatton	2		NU 055283	Map 4
						14		

DAY	DATE	DIARY TRANSCRIPTION	FROM	TO	MILES		GRID REF	NOTES
					Sub Tot	Daily Tot	(for 'To' col)	
M	10	By ten of the Clock I payd mr Swinoe for all my quarters till that morning 1.3.00 but he would take onely xs for oates.						
Tu	11	my quartermr payd the troope 14 days pay Recd from the Comittee of Northumberland 156.16.00. I went to grindon Rigg, came back at night.	Chatton	Grindonrigg	15		NT 925430	Map 4. Grindonrigg, closer to Duddo than to Grindon
			Grindonrigg	Chatton	15	29	NU 055283	Map 4
Th	13	I went to Rock came back at night, my Coronet went to see Barwick.	Chatton	Rock	14		NU 204203	Map 4
			Rock	Chatton	14	27	NU 055283	Map 4
F	14	I came from Chatton, lodged at Capheaton.	Chatton	Capheaton		37	NZ 035803	Map 3
Sa	15	I got to Hedlyhope.	Capheaton	Hedleyhope		36	NZ 150405	Map 3
Su	16	my brother sent Robert Bell to me with an order from generall Lambert to march with my troope into newcastle.						
F	14	I payd mr Swinho of Chatton for all my quarters euer since I came thither, as well what he before refused as that due since. Lent my brother Sam~ 4li 00 00 . Lent Robert Somerside 0.06.00.						The amount for Samuel is possibly crossed through with three rough diagonals, but this is not uncertain]
F	14	I came from						Day, date, and text crossed through

DAY	DATE	DIARY TRANSCRIPTION	FROM	TO	MILES Sub Tot	MILES Daily Tot	GRID REF (for 'To' col)	NOTES
M	17	I got to Cawdwell where my running horses were kept, and I founde my gray nag lame, so that he could not run the next day as I did intend, therefore on	Hedleyhope	Caldwell	24		NZ 162135	Map 5
			Caldwell	Gatherley Moor	2		NZ 190070	Map 5 Gatherley Moor, about 1.5 miles NW of Scotch Corner.
						26		
Tu	18	I tooke my meare and let her Ride at gatherley: maior Smithson wone the plate, & my meare came second; after the race I rode to Cawdwell againe. before I went to the Course I payd John Jackson his bill & the 7ˢ 3ᵈ in full of all charges till my returne; And after I came from the race I gaue Richard Robinson 5ˡⁱ 00.00 upon account; to keepe my horses, &c. I gaue him 5ˢ to pay for ye stable. I gaue Richard 5ˢ to himselfe & John 2ˢ I haue not yet payd for the running Saddles nor Richard riding sute.	Gatherley Moor	Caldwell	2		NZ 162135	Map 5. The sense seems to be that he went back to Caldwell
Tu	18	after I had clered all with my seruants at Cadwell I rode to will'm Lees in Leeming loning; & the next day to yorke. but the generall being gone to Colonell Brights I sent mathew Allyson with a letter to him on Th	Caldwell	Leeming	18		SE 293893	Map 5. A house in the Leeming area on the The Great North Road (A1) (see chapter 5 and Inglis R8)

DAY	DATE	DIARY TRANSCRIPTION	FROM	TO	MILES		GRID REF	NOTES
					Sub Tot	Daily Tot	(for 'To' col)	
	[19]	[see previous entry]	Leeming	York		35	SE 606520	Map 5
Th	20	I came from yorke to Burniston.	York	Burneston		34	SE 30850	[Map 5] Near Bedale
F	21	I cald at Cawdwell and came to Hedlyhope that night.	Burneston	Caldwell	22		NZ 162135	Map 5
			Caldwell	Hedleyhope	24		NZ 150405	Map 5
Sa	[22]	my Race horses were to go to Barnard castle.				46		
M	24	I went to Durham where I receiued 100li for ye Troope and from thence to Newcastle.	Hedleyhope	Durham	9		NZ 270420	Map 3
			Durham	Newcastle	16		NZ 250640	Map 3
Tu	25	I went to my quarters at Rodberry.	Newcastle	Rothbury		24	NU 057017	Map 3, 4
We	26	I went to Alwick with my Troope.	Rothbury	Alnwick		30	NU 186136	Map 4
						12		
Th	27	Sr Arthure heslerig came to Alnewick, and went away to morpeth that night capt: lilburnes Troope came & returned with him. and my & my troope came back to quarter at Shilbottle, 2 bustons, grange, &c.	Alnwick	Shilbottle		4	NU 195086	Map 4
F	[28]	my troope marched to morpeth I sent partyes from felton brige & hebron; my selfe went to Simonburne and on Sa 29. to wilmotswike came back that night to Hexam and from thence to Belseye	Shilbottle	Simonburn		43	NU 200085	Map 3, 2

DAY	DATE	DIARY TRANSCRIPTION	FROM	TO	MILES		GRID REF	NOTES
					Sub Tot	Daily Tot	(for 'To' col)	
Sa	29	[see previous entry]	Simonburn	Willmontswick	10		NY 770636	Map 2
			Willmontswick	Hexham	11		NY 930640	Map 2
			Hexham	Belsay	19		NZ 085785	Map 3
						40		
Su	30	I came to morpeth and heard that the Cavileers surprised Barwik on fryday night last. Captaine Lilburnes Troope came to meldon.	Belsay	Morpeth		9	NZ 200860	Map 3
				[May]				
M	1°	maij; Captaine Lilburne and I mett to aduise how and where to quarter neare unto Newcastle but wee drew into morpeth.						
M	1°	maij Sr. Art: Heslerig sent 30 dragoones to us and desired us to march with our two Troopes to warkeworth Castle & posses it.						
Tu	2	wee got thither: possest it without opposition; brought in victualls for 14 days. tooke 2 men & 2 horses of Coll: greys going to Barwick.	Morpeth	Warkworth		16	NU 248060	Map 4
W	3	wee left my Corpor: John Nichols and nine of my horse with nine of Capt: Lilburnes in warkeworth and marched with the rest to morpeth, and quartered there that night.	Warkworth	Morpeth		16	NZ 200860	Map 3

DAY	DATE	DIARY TRANSCRIPTION	FROM	TO	MILES		GRID REF	NOTES
					Sub Tot	Daily Tot	(for 'To' col)	
F	5	notice being giuen to me yᵗ maior Errington was Labouring to plant a garrison at Cartington I marched imediately with 120 horse, and sumoned it; he refused to yeald it. I caused 50 horse to dismount and assalt the outhouses. they tooke the barne the kilne, graynery, washouse and Chappell in fiue houres time yet when night came on I drew of my men and marched away to morpeth againe.	Morpeth	Cartington	19		NU 038045	Map 4
			Cartington	Morpeth	19	39	NZ 200860	Map 3
Su	7	information being brought that Errington marched from Cartington on Satterday about noone, I sent to Newcastle for 40 dragoones to aduance with us unto the place.						
M	8	Capt: Rogers with 40 foot came to us at morpeth I got horses in the Country for the foot; wee possest Cartington that day.	Morpeth	Cartington	19		NU 038045	Map 4
W	10	I aduanced with 80 horse to glanton Pike, Benely &c. & returned.	Cartington	Glanton Pyke.	7		NU 058143	[Map 4] 1m west of Glanton
			Glanton Pyke.	Beanley	4		NU 082183	[Map 4] Between Powburn and Eglingham

DAY	DATE	DIARY TRANSCRIPTION	FROM	TO	MILES		GRID REF	NOTES
					Sub Tot	Daily Tot	(for 'To' col)	
			Beanley	Cartington	11		NU 038045	Map 4
						22		
Th	11	maior Smithson with his & Coll Lilburnes Troope came to us, wee dyned at Eslington & Callilee. quartered that night at whittingham.	Cartington	Whittingham		7	NU 070119	Map 4. Eslington and Callaly were probably in reverse order.
F	12	wee sent a Corporall of maior Smithsons and one man from each squadron to remaine with the garison of Cartington.						
Sa	13	wee came to quarter at Alnewick where Coll brights reg' were before us my Troope had the guard. wee brought 17 loade of hay from m' Ramseys of litle Bewick.	Whittingham	Alnwick		8	NU 186136	Map 4
Su	14	wee left 50 horse and my Coronett at Alnewick and marched with 5 troopes to Chillingam. got thither about ten a clock at night.	Alnwick	Chillingham		13	NU 062260	Map 4
M	15	wee brought 100 Country horse loade of hay from Chillingam and euery Soldyer a bottle under him. I was sent post to Newcastle.	Chillingham	Newcastle		44	NZ 250640	Map 3

DAY	DATE	DIARY TRANSCRIPTION	FROM	TO	MILES		GRID REF	NOTES
					Sub Tot	Daily Tot	(for 'To' col)	
Tu	16	I came back to Alnewick. Captaine goodrick and Lilburnes Troope marched from us towards generall Lambert. I sent my man Robert Somerside wth my two horses to Newcastle. I sent him 20ˢ by John Gibson and I gaue him 10ˢ my selfe this day to account for my horses. wee receued a weekes pay.	Newcastle	Alnwick		33	NU 186136	Map 4
Th	18	maior Smithsons and Coll: Lilburnes Troope with 6 Companyes of Coll Brights Regimᵗ marched from us & left onely my Troop & Cap: Bradfords with maior Legards & Capt: Challenors foot Companyes.						
Su	21	our two Troopes aduanced so far as Belford and lay in Etherston feild all night wee had 5 bowles of Coll: weldons oates that night.	Alnwick	Belford		15	NU IIO339	Map 4. Etherston field - location not known, probably very close to Belford.
M	22	wee sent 3 bowles of Rye and 34 bowles of oates from Coll. weldons to Alnewick.						
Sa	27	my Coronet with 30 horse went out and tooke mᵣ Grey of howick and Mᵣ Reed of Titlington.						
Su	28	Ralfe Nicholson brought a trumpet prissoner.						

DAY	DATE	DIARY TRANSCRIPTION	FROM	TO	MILES Sub Tot	MILES Daily Tot	GRID REF (for 'To' col)	NOTES
Tu	30	I marched with my Troope Capt: Bradfords Capt: John Ogles and 40 draggoones through woller and beyond Ewart & Copeland wee came back supped in woller & Turuelawes at m^r Greys. lay in midleton hall feild that night.	Belford	Wooler	17		NT 990280	Map 4. Turvelaws, about 1 mile north of Wooler
			Wooler	Coupland	5		NT 937310	Map 4
			Coupland	Middleton Hall	6		NT 990255	Map 4
						29		
W	31	wee marched by woller through Chatton, to Chillingam where wee stayed till 2 a clock afternoone then came to Bewick. where wee bated and then came to Alnewick to muster.	Middleton Hall	Wooler	2		NT 990280	Map 4
			Wooler	Chatton	5		NU 055283	Map 4
			Chatton	Chillingham	2		NU 062260	Map 4
			Chillingham	Old Bewick	2		NU 066214	Map 4
			Old Bewick	Alnwick	10		NU 186136	Map 4
						20		

DAY	DATE	DIARY TRANSCRIPTION	FROM	TO	MILES Sub Tot	MILES Daily Tot	GRID REF (for To' col)	NOTES
		[June]						
Th	1°	Junij Comissary Baynes mustered our Troopes at Alnewick. orders came to mee to send all our prouisions to Warkeworth Castle & march with horse & foot to Newcastle; wee marched by nine that night came to felton by one of the Clock where wee met an order that left it to me to come on or stay (as I would:)	Alnwick	Felton		9	NU 185005	Map 4, 3
F	2	I came to morpeth.	Felton	Morpeth		11	NZ 200860	Map 3
Sa	3	the foot marched to Newcastle I gaue Tho: whitfeild 20ˢ more, so rests unpayd 8ˡⁱ 0-00. I drew out our Troopes and marched 3 miles north of morpeth, the next day wee fell vpon a party of the enimy beat them to Alnewick took 3, kild 2. and they tooke two of mine; (will Mʳ Baynes & will. windsore). Coll: Grey sent to exchange them I sent his two, he sent me but one back, kept Mʳ Baynes. at night I aduanced through Lesbury & so to Alnewick.	Morpeth	Hebron		3	NZ 195896	Map 3
			Hebron	Lesbury	17		NU 235116	Map 4
			Lesbury	Alnwick	4		NU 186136	Map 4
						21		

DAY	DATE	DIARY TRANSCRIPTION	FROM	TO	MILES Sub Tot	MILES Daily Tot	GRID REF (for 'To' col)	NOTES
M	5	I marched to Tuggil more to preuent their musters And quarter in vtch-ester feeld.	Alnwick	Tughall	11		NU 210264	Map 4
			Tughall	Outchester	9	19	NU 140334	[Map 4] A house between Belford and Bamburgh
T	[6]	wee lay still, untill I sent for prouisions for holy Island						
W	7	I put corne and fat beasts into holy Island, which being done I aduanced to gosewick from thence through Buckton fenwick and to sams house, came back to dine at ditchen afterwards marched to Chillinga'.	Outchester	Holy Island	13		NU 125420	Map 4. Probably down the coast, inland to Buckton, then north to Fenwick
			Holy Island	Gosewick	6		NU 056452	Map 4
			Gosewick	Buckton	5		NU 083384	Map 4
			Buckton	Fenwick	2		NU 066401	Map 4
			Fenwick	Samshouse	4		NU 015397	[Map 4] Part of or very close to Lowick
			Samshouse	Detchant	5		NU087366	Map 4
			Detchant	Chillingham	10	44	NU 062260	Map 4
Th	8	I marched from Chillingam to Cartington. I sent mr Baynes 12s by To: Atkinson.	Chillingham	Cartington		16	NU 038045	Map 4

109

DAY	DATE	DIARY TRANSCRIPTION	FROM	TO	MILES Sub Tot	MILES Daily Tot	GRID REF (for 'To' col)	NOTES
F	9	wee came to Cartington west harle bated there marched through Chollerford. the enimy fled from Simonburne Newbrough &c. wee pursued to Haltwizle. lay that night in the feild.	Cartington	West Harle	19		NY 990820	[Map 3] Just west of Kirkharle.
			West Harle	Chollerford	12		NY 919706	Map 3, 2
			Chollerford	Simonburn	4		NY 873736	Map 2
			Simonburn	Newbrough	5		NY 876679	Map 2
			Newbrough	Haltwhistle	11		NY 710642	Map 2
			Haltwhistle	Low Row	7		NY 585640	Map 2. Grid reference is north of Low Row (see Commentary)
						58		
Sa	10	wee came to Hexam where wee stayed till munday.	Low Row	Hexham		21	NY 930640	Map 2
M	12	wee quartered at Pruddo.	Hexham	Pruddoe		11	NZ 095630	Map 3
Tu	13	wee came to morpeth but dined at Corbridge.	Pruddoe	Corbridge	9		NY 995643	Map 3
			Corbridge	Morpeth	25		NZ 200860	Map 3
						33		
W	14	wee came to Akelington where mr Baynes came to us from Berwick. memorandum that Tu 13 my troope and Capt: Bradfords would needs go back and were like to mutinie at helme oth hill.	Morpeth	Acklington	15		NU 230020	Map 3. Helm o' the Hill, about 2m S of Felton

DAY	DATE	DIARY TRANSCRIPTION	FROM	TO	MILES		GRID REF	NOTES
					Sub Tot	Daily Tot	(for 'To' col)	
Th	15	wee marched by warkeworth and so to doxford sent a party to fleetham; returned to quarter in Alnewick. I sent a man of mine & one of Capt Bradfords troope with leters to the generall.	Acklington	Warkworth	3		NU 248060	Map 4
			Warkworth	Doxford Hall	14		NU 187242	[Map 4] Taken as Doxford Hall, SE of Ellingham.
			Doxford Hall	Alnwick	9		NU 186136	Map 3
						26		
Sa	17	Capt: Bradford came to us to Alnewick.						
M	19	wee came from Alnewick to Brenkeley, and thence to gosford.	Alnwick	Brenkeley	27		NZ 219751	Map 3
			Brenkeley	Gosforth	6		NZ 245681	Map 3. Formerly Goseford (Ekwall).
						33		

DAY	DATE	DIARY TRANSCRIPTION	FROM	TO	MILES		GRID REF	NOTES
					Sub Tot	Daily Tot	(for 'To' col)	
20	Tu	wee remoued by reason of raine at night to Longbenton. li. s. I payd Richard Robinson for his wages 2. 0 Robert Taylor } qrter wages { 1. 5 John Jackson } { 1. 5 li. lent Rob: Hedly 01. 00. 00 lent Vall. Apleby 0. 2. 06 lent Robert hogsen 0. 5. 00 lent harry Lodge 0. 10. 00	Gosforth	Longbenton		3	NZ 270685	Map 3
23	F Th	wee marched to high Collerton.	Longbenton	High Callerton		9	NZ 161705	Map 3
24	Sa-F	to Nafferton.	High Callerton	Old Nafferton		9	NZ 057655	[Map 3] Some 4 miles east of Corbridge
25	Su	to Thropley, after sermon to Newborne. That night Collonell wrens Reg^t came to us.	Old Nafferton	Throckley	7		NZ 157669	Map 3
			Throckley	Newburn	2		NZ 168664	Map 3
						8		
26	M	wee marched to Chipchase preuented the Rendeuous at Cholerton.	Newburn	Chollerton	19		NY932720	Map 3

DAY	DATE	DIARY TRANSCRIPTION	FROM	TO	MILES Sub Tot	MILES Daily Tot	GRID REF (for 'To' col)	NOTES
			Chollerton	Chipchase	4		NY 880755	Map 3
						23		
Tu	27	wee marched by Harloe hill to blackheddon.	Chipchase	Harlow Hill	16		NZ 078683	[Map 3] 5 miles W of Throckley
			Harlow Hill	Blackheddon	7		NZ 079760	Map 3
						23		
W	28	to Capheaton.	Blackheddon	Capheaton	4		NZ 035803	Map 3
Th	29	to Hexam; I sent to Coll: Lilburne at Heydon bridge to meet us in the morning by nine at Chollerford.	Capheaton	Hexham	17		NY 930640	Map 6
F	30	wee mett at Chollerforde marched to harterton . that night about eleaven a Clock wee aduanced I had the forlorne hope.	Hexham	Chollerford	6		NY 919706	Map 6
			Chollerford	Harterton	16		NZ 023881	Map 6
		[July]						
Sa	1°	July. I tooke at Tossons a leue' of draggoones & sixe of his men the rest of the forlorne tooke at Lurbottle 60 horse & 60 men. our army and forlorne hope toke at Callelee Whittingam Eslington glanton &c. 50 grand officers and 400 prissoners troopers, wee came to morpeth that night.	Harterton	Great Tosson	10		NU 029005	Map 6

DAY	DATE	DIARY TRANSCRIPTION	FROM	TO	MILES		GRID REF	NOTES
					Sub Tot	Daily Tot	(for 'To' col)	
			Great Tosson	Cartington	3		NU 038045	Map 6
			Cartington	Lorbottle	1		NU 034066	Map 6
			Lorbottle	Callaly	3		NU 053099	Map 6
			Callaly	Eslington	2		NU 042121	Map 6
			Eslington	Branton	4		NU 046160	Map 6. Just short of Branton
			Branton	Whittingham	3		NU 070120	Map 6
			Whittingham	Newtown	9		NU 036007	Map 6. Near Great Tosson
			Newtown	Morpeth	17		NZ 200860	Map 6. via Netherwitton
						79.6		
Su	2	I conducted them to Newcastle. Sr Rich. Tempest got away from morpeth.	Morpeth	Newcastle		15	NZ 250640	Map 6
Tu	4	I marched my troope to duddo. I lay at Belsy.	Newcastle	Belsay (Park/Castle)		14	NZ 085785	Map 6. Belsay. Newcastle to Duddo is 57 miles, so this must be an error. See Commentary.
W	5	wee all marched to Swinburne the southerne horse to Hexam.	Belsay (Park/Castle)	Swinburne		12	NY 935755	Map 3
Th	6	the southerne horse to Allenton our horse Rendeuoused at heydon bridge. Coll: Lilburne with 3 of his Troopes marched after the southerne horse; Capt. Bradfords mine and the dragoons marched to Dilston.	Swinburne	Dilston		9	NY 975634	Map 3
F	7	we marched to Bywell Bearle ouingam ouington Newton &c.	Dilston	Bywell	5		NZ 048615	Map 3. Across the Tyne from Stocksfield

DAY	DATE	DIARY TRANSCRIPTION	FROM	TO	MILES Sub Tot	MILES Daily Tot	GRID REF (for 'To' col)	NOTES
			Bywell	Bearle	2		NZ 055642	Map 3
			Bearle	Ovingham	2		NZ 085637	Map 3
			Ovingham	Newton	2	9	NZ 035645	Map 3
Sa	8	wee came to Collerton & Prestwick at night to Pont Island.	Newton	Callerton	10		NZ 161705	Map 3
			Callerton	Prestwick	3		NZ 184725	Map 3
			Prestwick	Ponteland	2	16	NZ 165730	Map 3
Su	[9]	to Bolam gallow hill & whawton - at night to Thorneton but returnd to meldon.	Ponteland	Bolam	9		NZ 807825	[Map 3]
			Bolam	Gallow Hill	1		NZ 107819	[Map 3]
			Gallow Hill	Whalton	2		NZ 130815	Map 3. Or Whalton Park, 1.5 miles to west
			Whalton	Temple Thornton	5		NZ 113856	[Map 3]
			Temple Thornton	Meldon	3	19	NZ 118839	Map 3
M	10	wee came North to morpeth. stayd there till weddensday.	Meldon	Morpeth		7	NZ 200860	Map 3. This is Monday
W	12	wee marched to Alnewick, got in the Castle 8 musketts one fowling peece & the barrell of a fowling pece. I likewise got 2 hogsheads of french wine, that was coming in carts from Capt: Scott of Barwick.	Morpeth	Alnwick		20	NU 186136	Map 4

DAY	DATE	DIARY TRANSCRIPTION	FROM	TO	MILES			GRID REF	NOTES
					Sub Tot	Daily Tot		(for 'To' col)	
Th	13	orders came from Collo: Lilburne for us to march to the army, wee got to morpeth that night.	Alnwick	Morpeth		20		NZ 200860	Map 3
F	14	we came through newcastle quartered at heyworths & Vsworths.	Morpeth	Usworth Hall		21		NZ 315588	[Map 3] Great Usworth, Little Usworth, Usworth Common, Usworth House, Usworth Hall, now all part of Washington, Tyne and Wear. Taken as Usworth Hall. Heyworth may be Heworth about 2.5 miles north, now part of Gateshead,
Sa	15	gott to Durham; sent before to Coll:	Usworth	Durham		12		NZ 270420	Map 3
Su	16	wee lay still. but the scots advanced to Appleby: skirmished with our Army on munday till 9 at night.							
M	17	wee quartered at headlam.	Durham	Headlam		18		NZ 180190	Map 5
Tu	18	wee mett our Army at Bowes my troope lay all night at Bolxan	Headlam	Bowes	15			NY 995135	Map 5
			Bowes	Bolam	16			NZ 196215	Map 5
							30		
We	19	my Troope and captaine Bradfords came to Peercbrigg.	Bolam	Piercebridge		5		NZ 210159	Map 5
Su	23	wee, with the Collo: Troope and maior Smithsons went to the guard at Bowes.	Piercebridge	Bowes		7		NY 995135	Map 5
M	24	wee had a generall Rendeuous at wicliff moore.	Bowes	Wycliffe	9			NZ 116143	Map 5

DAY	DATE	DIARY TRANSCRIPTION	FROM	TO	MILES Sub Tot	MILES Daily Tot	GRID REF (for 'To' col)	NOTES
			Wycliffe	Piercebridge	8		NZ 210159	[Map 5] He was in Piercebridge the next day
						17		
Tu	25	2 Troopes of Coll: harisons Regim^t came to Peercbrig and my Troope went to Cleasby Capt: Bradfords to Stapleton.	Piercebridge	Cleasby		4	NZ 250130	Map 5
F	28	Capt: Bradfords troope and mine came to quarter at Bolam.	Cleasby	Bolam		8	NZ 196215	Map 5
Sa	29	I lent the william Charleton of Lee hall xx^s.						
M	31	went to the guard at Egleston.	Bolam	Eggleston Abbey		15	NZ 061150	[Map 5] Probably Eggleston Abbey about 1 mile SE of Barnard Castle rather than Eggleston 6 miles to the NW.
		[August]						
Tu	1	came from the guarde to Bolam. my Leeuet^t brought me 50^{li} from the generall that was owing to mee; and six case of pistolls and holsters.	Eggleston Abbey	Bolam		15	NZ 196215	Map 5
W	2	I payd Leeueten^t 35^{li} 9^s 4^d vizt for him selfe 29. 17. 4. for his men 05. 12. 00. wee Rendeuoused neare Peercebrig. marched to Richmond my quarter was at m^r Nortons, my troope at Brunton.	Bolam	Piercebridge	4		NZ 210159	Map 5

DAY	DATE	DIARY TRANSCRIPTION	FROM	TO	MILES Sub Tot	MILES Daily Tot	GRID REF (for 'To' col)	NOTES
			Piercebridge	Richmond	10		NZ 170010	[Map 5] Location of Brunton not known, but it appears on a contemporary map, colour plate 21, NW of Bedale.
						14		
Th	3	Rendeuoused at horneby castle marched to Rippon. my quarters were at Audfeild. I payd each Corporal Trump: and Soldyer 12ˢ I came to quarter at mʳ Smiths in Awdfeild.	Richmond	Hornby Castle	7		SE 222938	[Map 5] SSE of Richmond
			Hornby Castle	Ripon	20		SE 315710	Map 5
			Ripon	Aldfield	4		SE 263694	Map 5, 7
						30		
M	7	the Army marched beyond Knaresborough but our Regimᵗ lay still. I sent Robert Taylor to yorke to buy some things I gaue him 4ˡⁱ 10ˢ 00 upon accompt.						
W	9°	My great white gelding my Cornetts black horse & mich Dicksons meare stolne from oldfeild in the night.						
Sa	12	wee came to quarter in Sawly. my troope & capt: Bradfords kept guard at sawly & Pately bridge.	Aldfield	Sawley	3		SE 249677	Map 7. Very close to Aldfield
			Sawley	Pately Bridge	7		SE 160655	Map 7
						9		

DAY	DATE	DIARY TRANSCRIPTION	FROM	TO	MILES Sub Tot	MILES Daily Tot	GRID REF (for 'To' col)	NOTES
Su	13	wee Rendeuoused at Linlye neare otly where Leeuten¹ generall Crumwel met us with 3 Reg^ts of foot 1 Reg' horse wee quartered at Rigton the Army about otley.	Pately Bridge	Lindley	14		SE 225490	Map 7
			Lindley	North Rigton	2	16	SE 280492	[Map 7]
M	14	wee Rendeuoused at Romell moore betwixt Skipton & long Addingam. Lay y' night about Skipton. ye Rest of our Reg' and Coll. Twizletons kept guard about gargraue.	North Rigton	Skipton		19	SD 990520	Map 7. Romell Moore not identified, but probably close to or part of Addingham Low Moor, around SE 055505
Tu	15	wee Rendeuoused in Broughton pasture, quartered about gisburne wee at Pathorne. that night our forlorne hope to Collo: Tempest of Crauen & some others.	Skipton	Broughton	3		SD 942512	Map 7
			Broughton	Gisburne	8		SD 830489	Map 7
			Gisburne	Paythorne	2	13	SD 830519	Map 7
W	16	wee Rendeuoused at Clethero. q^tered in the feilds about m^r Sherburns great house two miles north of Ribchestr that day our forlorne tooke the Earle of Cornewath and his lady & some others.	Paythorne	Clithero	10		SD 744421	Map 7
			Clithero	Stoneyhurst	9	19	SD 691391	Map 7

DAY	DATE	DIARY TRANSCRIPTION	FROM	TO	MILES		GRID REF	NOTES
					Sub Tot	Daily Tot	(for 'To' col)	
Th	17	wee marched streight towards Preston maior Smithson had the forlorne hope, engaged there nere about Langrige Chappell, slew & tooke many Langdales Army and Leeut gen: Baylyes Brigade with some Lancers fought us near Preston were rooted &c as in my Relation at large &c.	Stoneyhurst	Longridge	6		SD600370	[Map 1] A small settlement, now the town of Longridge (Smith)
			Longridge	Preston	8	14	SD530290	Map 1
F	18	Coll Thoring slaine at Charly our Regm' orderd to the van our forlorne hope rooted and slew many till wee came at wigan, wee tooke maior gen^ll von druske & another Collo: 2 foot Coulours.	Preston	Chorley	9		SD 586185	[Map 1]
			Chorley	Wigan	8	17	SD 586050	Map 1
Sa	19	our Regiment tooke the van againe maior Cholmley comanded the Party. in wigan wee ooke 4 Leeueten' Collo: slew many all the way to winwick wood where the enymy fought us; wee lost some men but won the day (as in my relation, &c.) wee charged on to warrington brige where Leeu' generall Bayley seemed to opose but parlyed, and yealded himselfe all his officers and soldyers prisoners with all arms amunition and horses. The Scotts horse gone to wales.	Wigan	Winwick wood	8		SJ 598941	[Map 1] Redbank, between Newton-le-Willows and Winwick (see Heath's Chronicle 323)

DAY	DATE	DIARY TRANSCRIPTION	FROM	TO	MILES Sub Tot	MILES Daily Tot	GRID REF (for 'To' col)	NOTES
			Winwick wood	Winwick	1		SJ 610880	Map 1
			Winwick	Warrington	3			
						12		
Su	20	we rested about warington my quarters & Bradfords & farneworths.						
M	21	we marched & quartered at Norton at Lady Brookes.	Warrington	Norton		8	SJ 550820	[Map 1] Near Runcorn
Tu	22	wee quartered at All Lostock nere Knotsworth. left Ro: Ta: sick.	Norton	Lostock Gralam		12	SJ 693750	[Map 1] Taken as Lostock Gralam, 4.5 miles from. Knutsford (formerly Knotsford, Ekwall)
W	23	wee quartered at Rushon neare Leeke.	Lostock Gralam	Rushton Spencer		20	SJ 940623	[Map 1]
Th	24	wee lay in the feilds nere utoxceter: treated wᵗʰ yᵉ Scots.	Rushton Spencer	Uttoxeter		24	SK 090330	[Map 1]
F	25	Duke hamleton & all the Scots horse yealded themselues. I came to Roseter that night.	Uttoxeter	Wroxeter?		41	SJ 563083	Map 1. Wroxeter? see Commentary
Sa	26	I came to my troope at Thorpe.	Wroxeter?	Thorpe		56	SK 155501	[Map 1]
Tu	29	wee marched to Bakewell to qrter.	Thorpe	Bakewell		15	SK 218683	Map 1
Th	31	wee marched to Barlo to qrter.	Bakewell	Barlow		11	SK 345746	[Map 1]
			[September.]					
F	1°	wee marched to Ecclesfeild to qrter.	Barlow	Ecclesfield		15	SE 355946	[Map 1] North side of Sheffield
Sa	2	wee marched to Darton.	Ecclesfield	Darton		13	SE 315100	[Map 1]
Su	3	wee marched to Battley.	Darton	Batley		12	SE 235245	Map 7

DAY	DATE	DIARY TRANSCRIPTION	FROM	TO	MILES		GRID REF	NOTES
					Sub Tot	Daily Tot	(for 'To' col)	
M	4	wee marched to Horsforth nere Leeds.	Batley	Horsforth		12	SE 235384	Map 7
Tu	5	to Killingall & stayd there till Th.	Horsforth	Killinghall		15	SE 285586	Map 5
Th	7	to Norton Hutton & marton.	Killinghall	Norton-le-Clay		13	SE 401711	Map 5. Norton-le-Clay, Hutton Conyers, Marton-le-Moor
F	8	to Bedall & Askew, Langthorn.	Norton-le-Clay	Bedale.		16	SE 267881	
Sa	9	wee rested at Beedall & Askew.						
Su	10	to Gilling and Gilling wood.	Bedale.	Gilling West		14	NZ 182052	Map 5
M	11	to midridge grange Redworth Newbiggen & west thickly.	Gilling West	Middridge Grange		17	NZ 252260	[Map 5] All between Newton Aycliffe and Bishop Auckland.
Tu	12	lay still all day.						
W	13	to Durham.	Middridge Grange	Durham		12	NZ 270420	Map 3
Th	14	to Ryton p'ish winlaton Chopwell.	Durham	Ryton		19	NZ 153643	Map 3
F	15	to Bywell & wilem Stockfeild.	Ryton	Bywell		8	NZ 048615	[Map 3] Wylam, Stocksfield.
Sa	16	to Capheaton Shortflat harnam.	Bywell	Capheaton		16	NZ 035803	Map 3
Su	17	to Longhurst, Pegsworth, ougham.	Capheaton	Longhirst		17	NZ225892	[Map 3] Longhirst, Pegswood, Ulgham
M	18	to Longhoughton Lesbury, &c. I was sent to Cheswick to Leeu' gen[l] Crumwell and came back to Rock the next morning. pt of his horse marcht into Scotland.	Longhirst	Longhoughton	19		NU 243152	Map 4
			Longhoughton	Lesbury	3		NU 235116	Map 4
			Lesbury	Cheswick House	28		NU 029464	Map 4
						47		

DAY	DATE	DIARY TRANSCRIPTION	FROM	TO	MILES Sub Tot	MILES Daily Tot	GRID REF (for 'To' col)	NOTES
Tu	19	quarter at Ellingam, &c.	Cheswick House	Rock	22		NU 204203	Map 4
			Rock	Ellingham	5		NU 175257	Map 4
						27		
W	20	rested all day.						
Th	21	marched within a mile of Barwick and went off to qrter at Berrinton Ancroft Skrimerston, &c.	Ellingham	Nr Berwick-upon-Tweed		20	NT 000500	Map 4. Berrington, Ancroft, Scremerston
F	22	were ordered to march into Scotland ouer Twizle ford; but when wee came there we could not ride the water; but sent ye troopes to qrter in grindon Tilmouth Cornell, Heeton, &c. till ye waters fall againe.	Nr Berwick-upon-Tweed	Twizle	12		NT 870430	Map 4. A ford, 2.5 miles downstream from Coldstream (approximate location). cornell=Cornhill-on-Tweed
			Twizle	Grindon	4		NT 915448	Map 4
						16		
Sa	23	Lay still all day.						
Su	24	back to Berrington haggerston &c. so farr as Ross.	Grindon	Berrington	7		NU 007432	Map 4
			Berrington	Haggerston	3		NU 040437	[Map 4]
			Haggerston	Ross	8		NU 132370	Map 4
						17		
M	25	I went to mordinton for orders.	Ross	Mordington House	18		NT 950560	Map 4
			Mordington House	Ross	18		NU 135370	Map 4
						35		

DAY	DATE	DIARY TRANSCRIPTION	FROM	TO	MILES Sub Tot	MILES Daily Tot	GRID REF (for 'To' col)	NOTES
Tu	26	our Reg^t Rendeuouzed at Duddo marcht over at Cawdstreeme & qrterd in Eccles pish Kelsy parish. my Collonell & I quartered at ye Earle Roxboroughs house ye ffleures. I lay still W & Th.	Ross	Duddo	12		NT 936427	Map 4
			Duddo	Coldstream	8		NT843397	Map 4, 8
			Coldstream	Floors	10		NT 710347	[1] Close to Kelso
						29		
Th	28	wee marched to Lawther where m^r Alexander Hume of St Leon^{rds} refused to let us in to the lord Lauderdales house. my Coll: sent mee to maior generall Lambert. I rode all night. first to haddington then to Dunbar then to Brocksmouth.	Floors	Lauder	18		NT 528477	Map 8
			Lauder	Haddington	21		NT 510740	Map 8
			Haddington	Dunbar	12		NT 680790	Map 8
			Dunbar	Broxmouth	2		NT 696776	Map 8
						51		
F	29	mr. Hume sufferd us to quarter in his lords house. I came back to my Coll. he was gone Bothoms to quarter.	Broxmouth	Lauder	32		NT 528477	Map 8
			Lauder	Abbey St Bathans	26		NT 760623	Map 8
						58		
Sa	30							

DAY	DATE	DIARY TRANSCRIPTION	FROM	TO	MILES Sub Tot	MILES Daily Tot	GRID REF (for 'To' col)	NOTES
F	29	7 br. my Collonell with all his officers came to the lord Twedall yesters house at Bothomes. Capt: Lilburnes & Capt: Bradfords Troopes quarterd in garnett p'ish. ye other foure troopes in Bothoms p'ish.						Twedall is an insertion, by Sanderson. Garnett = ??Grantshouse, see Commentary.
Sa	30	my troope remoued to Barow p'ish and Cholmleys to moram p'ish.	Abbey St Bathans	Bara		18	NT 590709	[Map 8] ?Bara. Ancient parish of Haddingtonshire now annexed to Garvald. Moram=Morham (4) centred 4 miles ESE of Haddington NT 550710)
				[October.]				
Su	1	my Coll^s & m^r Smithons troopes remoued to Salton pish, the offic^{rs} quarterd in the Lord Endenpeffers house. I stayd at the lord yesters house all night.	Bara	Yester House		4	NT 543672	[Map 8] E. and W. Saltoun are 6m SW of Haddington.
M	2	I went to the lady Chesters.						Unknown
Tu	3	I went to Cockpen to qu^{r}ter in m^r Cass his house.	Yester House	Cockpen		17	NT 325638	[Map 8] Very close to Dalhousie. This mileage is from Yester.
W	4	I went to Edenbrough and at Night came to Dalhousey. stayd in my lords house.	Cockpen	Edinburgh	9		NT 250730	Map 8
			Edinburgh	Dalhousie	8	16	NT 323636	Map 8
Th	5	maior Smithsons troope went to Borthick pish wth m^r Chomly.						

DAY	DATE	DIARY TRANSCRIPTION	FROM	TO	MILES		GRID REF	NOTES
					Sub Tot	Daily Tot	(for 'To' col)	
Sa	7	Leut: genll, maior generall my Collo, &c. came to my qrters at my lord Dalhouseys and I sent my horses to Arneston.						
M	9	Leeutent generall marched away towards Carlile with all his Regts of horse except maior generalls and Coll: Lilburnes with 2 troopes of draggoones who were to stay in Scotland.						
		my oune fine gray nag dyed at Arneston.						
M	9°	I set forward with a party of horse towards Newcastle for pay. lay at Lauther.	Dalhousie	Lauder		20	NT 528477	Map 8
Tu	10	Cald at a fflewers butt and came to woller to mr Greys of Turvilaws.	Lauder	Floors	17		NT 710347	
			Floors	Wooler	20		NT 990280	Map 4
			Wooler	Turvelaws	1		NT 996293	[Map 4] North of Wooler
						38		
W	11	quarterd at Bockenfeild but my party lay at ffelton & Thrustons. Carlile was deliuered to Leut genll Crumwell.	Turvelaws	Bockenfield		26	NZ 179979	Map 3
Th	12	I came to Newcastle and qrtered my party at kenton and long Benton.	Bockenfield	Longbenton		22	NZ 270685	Map 3
F	13	receiued from mr Bilton 3725li 12s 8d for 2 monthes pay to 2 Regts and 100li for mr genll Lamberts incident charg.						

DAY	DATE	DIARY TRANSCRIPTION	FROM	TO	MILES		GRID REF	NOTES
					Sub Tot	Daily Tot	(for 'To' col)	
Sa	14	I went to hedlyhope. payd my seruants wages.	Longbenton	Hedleyhope		22	NZ 150405	Map 3
Su	15	I came back to Newcastle.	Hedleyhope	Newcastle		19	NZ 250640	Map 3
M	16	I desired mr Bilton to change tell ouer the mony because some bags fell not right. Leeut: generall came to Newcastle.						
Tu	17	I got order from Leeut: general to rec so much of mr Bilton as would make 3800li.						
W	18	Recd the same 74li 7s 00d and came with my party to morpeth yt night.	Newcastle	Morpeth		14	NZ 200860	Map 3
Th	19th	I came to Alnwick.	Morpeth	Alnwick		19	NU 186136	Map 4
F	20	quartered my party at Buckton and fenwick & Dichen.	Alnwick	Buckton		19	NU 083384	Map 4. Detchant
Sa	21	I marched through Barwik and quartered at Heymouth.	Buckton	Berwick-upon-Tweed	12		NT 995535	Map 4
			Berwick-upon-Tweed	Eyemouth	8		NT 940640	Map 8
						20		
Su	22	I came to Dunbarr.	Eyemouth	Dunbar		21	NT 680790	Map 8
M	23	I got to Haddington with my party.	Dunbar	Haddington		12	NT 510740	Map 8
Tu	24	I came to maior generall at my lord winters house at Seaton.	Haddington	Seton		7	NT 416751	Map 8
W	25	I begun to pay 200li to each Troope.						
F	27	our Two Regimts mustered.						
M	30	I counted over the mony and pickt out the Clipt mony.						

DAY	DATE	DIARY TRANSCRIPTION	FROM	TO	MILES		GRID REF (for 'To' col)	NOTES
					Sub Tot	Daily Tot		
		[November.]						
Th	2ᵈ	I payd all the Troopes.						
F	3°	I came from Seaton to the Lord Ellibankes at Baukrith.	Seaton	Ballencrieff		12	NT 485780	Map 8. A seat of Lord Elibank
Sa	4	I came to Brocksmouth to my lord Roxboroughs. my Troope to Ennerwick & old hamstock.	Ballencrieff	Broxmouth		27	NT 696776	Map 8. Innerwick, 14m SE of Dunbar, on coast NT 7273. Oldhamstocks NT 7470
M	6	I wated on the maior generall to Edenborough and came back to Seaton that night.	Broxmouth	Edinburgh	29		NT250730	Map 8
			Edinburgh	Seton	10		NT 416751	Map 8
						39		
Tu	7°	wee came to Broxmouth my Troope marched from old hamstock and Ennerwick to Noram.	Seton	Broxmouth		19	NT 696776	Map 8
W	8	I came from Broxmouth through Dunce to grindon Rigg.	Broxmouth	Duns	21		NT 786535	Map 8
			Duns	Grindonridge	13		NT 925431	Map 4
						34		
Th	9	my Troope came to Chatton and my selfe & officers to Horton.	Grindonridge	Horton		13	NU 029309	Map 4
F	10	to the two Lilburnes; mʳˢ Grey of Bradford and my Cozin Ord of Longridge came to us thither about release of maior Ord.	Horton	East Lilburn Lilburn Tower		7	NU 044236 NU021241	Map 4
Sa	11	we quartered at Eslington.	East Lilburn Lilburn Tower	Eslington		7	NU 041121	Map 4

DAY	DATE	DIARY TRANSCRIPTION	FROM	TO	MILES		GRID REF	NOTES
					Sub Tot	Daily Tot	(for 'To' col)	
Su	12	lay still there.						
M	13	my Troope came to long horsley and nunriding but I went to Capheaton and stayed till wedensday.	Eslington	Longhorsley	15		NZ 148945	Map 3
			Longhorsley	Nunriding	5		NZ 133876	[Map 3] Half way between Morpeth and Netherwhitton, one mile south of the road.
			Nunriding	Capheaton	15		NZ 035803	Map 3
						35		Assuming he saw his troops to their quarters. If he went direct to Capheaton, then his journey was only 25.3 miles
Tu	14	my Troop came to Belsey Blackheddon Shortflatt harnam Bitchfeild Bradford kirke harle.						
W	15	I went to Newcastle but my Troope to newborne, Throckley east hedon.	Capheaton	Newcastle	20		NZ 250640	Map 3
Th	[16]	lay still in those quarters						
Sa	18	I intertained willm ffletcher to be my seruant; for 4^{li} p'an and lent him aforehand 13^{s} 0						
F	17	Troope qrterd about Chester. I went to hedlyhope.	Newcastle	Hedleyhope	20		NZ 150405	Map 3. Chester-le-Street
Sa	18	my Troope came to Durham I quarterd at the maiors house.	Hedleyhope	Durham	9		NZ 270420	Map 3. This is the Mayor of Durham, Richard Man
Su	19	lay still.						
M	20	quarterd at Shadford.	Durham	Shadford	5		NZ 344410	[Map 3] ESE of Durham.

DAY	DATE	DIARY TRANSCRIPTION	FROM	TO	MILES		GRID REF	NOTES
					Sub Tot	Daily Tot	(for 'To' col)	
Tu	21	at great Akley.	Shadford	Aycliffe		18	NZ 285225	Map 3. Acle in 1254 (Ekwall)
W	22	at Hurworth & nesam.	Aycliffe	Hurworth		8	NZ 305092	Map 3. Hurworth-on-Tees, Neasham
Th	23	at Danby wiske & Smeetons.	Hurworth	Danby Wiske		11	SE 337986	
F	24	rested all day.						
Sa	25	quarterd at Thorntons & 2 ottringtons.	Danby Wiske	Thornton-le-Moor		8	SE 394883	Map 5. Thornton-le-Moor and Thornton-le-Beans, North and South Ottrington
Su	26	at skelton & 2 hewicks.	Thornton-le-Moor	Skelton		16	SE 361685	[Map 5] Skelton on Ure, Copt Hewick and Bridge Hewick, nr Ripon
M	27	at Spawford, follyfoot & Plumton.	Skelton	Spofforth		14	SE 363510	[Map 5] Spofforth (5 miles SE of Harrogate), Follifoot, Plumpton Square/Plumpton Hall)
Tu	28	at Aberford mickleton.	Spofforth	Aberford		10	SE 433372	[Map 1] 8 miles N of Pontefract. Micklefield, 2.6 miles SSE of Aberford, or Mickeltown, 6 miles SSW of Aberford.
W	29	at Rodwell & olton.	Aberford	Rothwell	9		SE43283	Map 7 Rothwell and Oulton are SE of Leeds.

DAY	DATE	DIARY TRANSCRIPTION	FROM	TO	MILES Sub Tot	Daily Tot	GRID REF (for 'To' col)	NOTES
W	29	I came to kipax parke to my Collo: & went with him to Knottingley. Set Leeut: generall onwards towards wentbridge. I came back wth mar: genll to Knottingley. and quarterd yt night at fferrybrige.	Rothwell	Kippax	5		SE 416303	[Map 1] 7 miles N of Pontefract
			Kippax	Knottingley	7		SE 500240	[Map 1] 4 miles E of Pontefract
			Knottingley	Stapleton Park	2		SE 505195	[Map 1] say, half way to Wentbridge
			Stapleton Park	Knottingley	2		SE 500240	[Map 1]
			Knottingley	Ferrybridge	1		SE 481241	[Map 1]
						26		
Th	30	I came with mr genll and my Collo: to Pontefract; went to Castleford to mr murreys that night.	Ferrybridge	Pontefract	3		SE 461225	Map 1
			Pontefract	Castleford	3		SE 420253	[Map 1] 4 miles N of Pontefract
						6		
				[December, 1648]				
F	1°	my Troope quarterd in Rodwell Rodes, Rodwell hague Loftus, Carleton & wood lesworth. [I think S was there as well - see Order Book]	Castleford	Rothwell		6	SE343283	Map 7. Rothwell, ?Royds Green Lower/Royds Green Upper, ?Bothwell Haigh, Lofthouse, Carlton,, all on the south side of Leeds. S. seems to have been with them as he was not at the Council meeting on 4th December.

DAY	DATE	DIARY TRANSCRIPTION	FROM	TO	MILES		GRID REF	NOTES
					Sub Tot	Daily Tot	(for 'To' col)	
Tu	5°	I gaue my seruant Andrew Tomson 30s in pt of his halfe yeares wages which shall be due at the 25 day of march next.						
W	6	my Troope to the guard at Pontefract.	Rothwell	Pontefract	10	3	SE 461225	Map 1
F	8	my owne Squadron went to quarter (with others) at midleton cum Thorpe and quiet olton.	Pontefract	Middleton cum Thorpe		13	SE 300280	Map 7. Middleton is 1 mile north of Thorpe on the Hill. Quiet Olton not located. Oulton is 3m east of Middleton.
M	11	wee went to Councell at Pontefract. and I stayd that night there with maior Rookesby maior Smithson & Captain Baynes to write a letter to my lord generall.	Middleton cum Thorpe	Pontefract		8	SE 461225	Map 1
Tu	12	The officers all mett and agreed upon a declaration to be sent to the lo: generall and Captaine Baynes to be sent with it & to remaine with the southerne Army. to give us aduertisement of their proceedings from time to time. And this Councell likewise chose a standing Councell to meet every fryday by ten of the Clock at Pontefract. viz': Coll: Lilburne maior Rookesby maior Smithson my selfe Captaine Goodrick maior Catterell.						

DAY	DATE	DIARY TRANSCRIPTION	FROM	TO	MILES Sub Tot	MILES Daily Tot	GRID REF (for 'To' col)	NOTES
W	20	I payd my seruants Robert Taylor & Jo: Jackson their wages and gaue each of them ten shillings more.						
Th	21	Rec' to Comissiond officers 14 days pay. And to non Comissiond officers and soldyers 15 days pay.						
M	25	a party of seauen of a troope out of both Regim'ts: to meet mee at wake-feild to go with the maior generall to disband the melitia horse.	Pontefract	Wakefield	9		SE 330200	Map 7
M	25	maior generall disbanded S' Edw: Rhodes his Troope at Barnesdale my Party lay at Wakefeild that night.	Wakefield	Barnesdale	13		SE 510137	[Map 1] Barnsdale Bar, junction of A1 and A639
			Barnesdale	Wakefield	13	35	SE 330200	Map 7
Tu	26	Capt: Byards Troope was disbanded at wakefeild outwood. my party qrterd at Leeds. maior gen'll at S' Ar: Ingrams.	Wakefield	Wakefield Outwood	1		SE 333235	Map 7. Northern part of Wakefield
			Wakefield Outwood	Leeds	8	9	SE 300330	Map 7
W	27	Capt: wentworths Troope dis-banded at Temple Newsom, I lay at Newbiggen y' night my pty at, &c.	Leeds	Temple Newsam	4		SE 365322	Map 7

DAY	DATE	DIARY TRANSCRIPTION	FROM	TO	MILES Sub Tot	MILES Daily Tot	GRID REF (for 'To' col)	NOTES
			Temple Newsam	Newbiggen	14		SE 545348	Not certainly located. The nearest Newbiggen is almost 60 miles away. Biggin, 3 miles east of Sherburn in Elmet is the only possible location found, 14 miles from Temple Newsam, 26 miles from Otley, and has been used here for mileage.
						18		
Th	28	Captaine Cookes & maior Persons Troopes disbanded about Otley. my party qrterd in otley & Burley.	Newbiggen	Otley		26	SE200450	Map 7. Mileage is from Biggen near Sherburn
F	29	Capt: Currers & Capt: Gudricks Troopes disbanded at Long Addingam. my pty quarterd (my selfe) at Haughton) Beemesley Bolton Emsay Eastby maior gen[ll] at Skipton.	Otley	Addingham	10		SE 075500	Map 7
			Addingham	Halton	6		SE 043540	Map 7. Haughton=Halton East, between Bolton Abbey and Embsay, Eastby, and Skipton. Beamsley 1.5m south of Bolton Abbey.
						16		

DAY	DATE	DIARY TRANSCRIPTION	FROM	TO	MILES		GRID REF	NOTES
					Sub Tot	Daily Tot	(for 'To' col)	
Sa	30	my pty quarterd at Linton Threshfeild girsington Burnesall Thorpe Hebden Hartlington & Appletreewick.	Halton	Linton Appletreewick		9	SD 995625 SE 055601	Map 7. Grassington
						4360		Total mileage
						20.6		Average miles per travelling day

SANDERSON'S ACCOUNTS

On the front fly leaf of the Diary

first Rec[d] from. the 14th day
of february — 14 days pay
from 28. febr: to
12 martij. 14 days pay more
from 13. march to the second
of Aprill three weekes pay more
From the 3[d] of April to the
sixteenth other 14. days more
From the 17th of April to the [30th] day. rec[d] 14. days pay more
From the first of maij to the
7th day. rec[d] seauen days pay more
Rec[d] 2[d] Aug: for euery Corporall Trumpet and Trouper 12[s]
Rec[d] 20° 8br 28. days pay more
Rec[d] 20 xbr   {to officers Comiss [?]days
                      {to soldyers & non Com [?] days

On the back fly leaves of the Diary

The clere account of Kddtsdmzms [Leeutenant][1]
Rsqzmfvzxr cdt enq ozx [Strangways due for pay]
eqnl [from] 14. febr. to 7° maij 1648.
being sgqd lnmsgdr.[thre monthes] at 9[s.] 4[d] p day
which is 13[t.] 1[s.] 4. p month
comes to   39. 04. 00
But payd Kddtsdmzms Rgdoodqvnm [Leeutenant Shepperson]
before he went   9. 6. 8
For Kddtsdmzms [Leeutenant]   }
Rsqzmf: [Strang:] debenter =   }-   0. 9. 4
for orders   0. 6. 8
              10 2.8   𝕾a   [odd symbol]
     Then will rest clere 29. 01. 4
of three monthes pay eeqzmbhr [ffrancis] }

qtrrdk² [russel] eekdsbgdq [ffletcher] receiued of }
Captain uzsihmrnm [watkinson] 7 weekes}
Pay. So rest due for 5 weekes   3.10.00
Czmhdk qtrrdkk [Daniel russell] receiued }
nine weekes pay so rests }—   2. 02. 00
due to him }

        totall   34: 13: 4
payd Leeue^t 2° August

18. Aprillis 1648. The race
at gatherley for the plate
brought in by Capt: Wilkinson.

Remaines for Leeu. [partly erased] Kddt.qdmzms. [Leeutenant]
Rsqzmfdvzxdr & ghr svn ldm [Strangeways & his two men]
first 28.   28. 13. 00
[Illeg] for 14 days expired }9. 6. 08
30. Aprill   }
And for 7 days due } -   4. 13. 04
7° maij 1648   }

Sum   42. 13. 00

APPENDIX 3B

SANDERSON'S CLAIM FOR EXPENSES

From Calendar of State Papers, Domestic 1648-1649, 136-137, 20 June, 1648

Accomt of money laid out by Major Saunderson for intelligence in May and June, 1648. Amongst others are the following items:—To Thos. Gooley, Mr. Ogle's man, for going into the enemy's quarters near Berwick presently after the taking of it 5s. For sending post to the Governor of Newcastle for procuring dragoons to take Cartington, in Northumberland, 6s. 4d. To another messenger to discover what Scotch troops were about Twizell 5s. To one to go to Alnwick and from thence to Ford Castle, when the enemy first settled a garrison there 6s. To one to lie at Tweedmouth three days to give me timely notice of the enemy's drawing out of Berwick 12s. Upon report of four Scotch troops coming I sent a man by Belford to go to Norham, and so up the Tweed to Learmouth 6s. 8d. When our troops were commanded back from Alnwick a man met us from Felton with a letter from the Governor of Newcastle which required us to stay, we sent the same messenger back and he took post horses at Morpeth upon my score 5s 4d. Upon 2 June Mr. Marshall's man of Morpeth to go up to Ryall and Wall for intelligence upon the report of [Sir Marmaduke] Langdale's coming thither 5s. June 3 my Quartermaster riding post to the Governor of Newcastle and comiing [*sic*] back again 10s 8d. Total 4l. 10s. 4d.

There is also a receipt for the money: This is a true accompt, John Saunderson.

LETTERS AND OTHER DOCUMENTS WRITTEN BY MAJOR SANDERSON

1

John Sanderson to Peter Denton of Lanchester, 13th May 1648

(Quoted in Fawcett 1921, 47)

Sir, When I was at Hedleyhope last I received from my brother the letter you had sent there for me. I am sorry I could not meet you at Lanchester. As I had to hurry back to my troop I came straight to Durham by way of Ashe [Esh]. I hope when next I come to Hedleyhope I may be able to advise you so that you can make it convenient to ride over there and meet me. Pray give my best respects to [names gone]. I am [sending] this by my man Somerside to Newcastle with orders to send it on with my messages to Hedleyhope, to be delivered to you from thence. In the middest of many duties.

I am, yours etc., John Sanderson.

Alnewicke 13 may 1648
P.S. Since I saw you at Lanchester I have been constantly on the move.

2

John Sanderson to an unknown recipient, 3rd July 1648

(From *Skirmish in Northumberland*)

Deare Sir,—I received your letter by the last post, for which I thank you. You may remember, that I left my last intelligence at the comming of a strong party of horse from Langdale into Northumberland, &c.; and at Lambert's withdrawing from Carlile, to joyn with the Lancashire forces. We sent to Generall Lambert, for assistance. On Sunday, June 25, the Lancashire forces joyned with Lambert, who fell upon the cabbs [cavaliers], beat their foot into Carlile, and their horse into Scotland; which being done, Lambert lay his horse and foot in three quarters, to straiten the town. Whilst this was acting in the west, wee bestirred our selves for assistance. On Sunday night. Col. Wren, with 220 Bishoprick new raised horse, came to Newburn. The next day, June 26, we advanced to Cholerton edge, to prevent the enemies randezvouse, and hoped to meet ayd from the west; but the next day we marched eastward again, to Blackheddon. The 27 day, we marched to Capheaton (50 dragoones came to us from Newcastle): then were we within 4 miles of the enemies body, who advanced within a mile of us, to fall on us, but declined to attempt us. We being truly informed of their great strength, resolved, after serious consultation, that, for two reasons, we ought to retire towards Hexam, viz. that we might joyn with the forces expected, and draw the enemy into security, who would perswade himselfe we were run away: these two respects hit right.

Thursday, 29, we came to Hexam, viz. Col. Fenwick, and our two old troops. Col. Lilburne came to Heydon Bridge, with three troops. Friday, 30 Junii, according to agreement, we randevouzed, about eleven of the clocke, at Chollerford, three miles north of Hexam. We hasted away that night, and marched sixteen miles, from Hexam to Harterton; bated our horses two houres; then mounted again, and marched from thence. I had the command of the forlorne hope. The first towne we fell into was Tossons, where wee tooke a lieutenant and six of his dragoons, all in bed: the next town was Lurbottle, where we took 60 horse, and 60 men, all in bed. The next quarter was Carlile, [Callaly] where Col Grey, Lieu. Col. Salkeld, and many others, were taken, with 80 horse. The next quarter was Whittingham, where Lieu. Col. Millet, and many considerable men, with 200 horse. The next was, at one time, an engagement upon Eslington, where were 100 horse, at Glanton: in Glanton, were 180 horse, most of them taken, with the officers and souldiers in that quarter. At Eslington was taken Sir Richard Tempest, Major Troulop, [Trollop] and many others. Wee advanced on towards Branton, but finding that wee were cloyed with prisoners and horse, and booty, we retyred towards Whittingham, where Col. Lilburne was labouring to rally into a firme body; for there appeared about Shawton four bodies of the enemies horse, who had taken the alarme, and got together: but all the rest we tooke before they could mount.

The victory was beyond all expectation, God working it for us. We had but one horse shot dead, and one man shot through the thigh: and of the enemy there was five slaine, and Cap. Smith run through the body, and some others wounded. The enemies bodies of horse that appeared at Shawton, retyred from us northward; and when they were gone out of sight, two miles, we drew off to Newtown, staid two houres; withdrew to Morpeth, disposed of our prisoners as well as we could. We brought to Morpeth 309, that were droven a foot, because we wanted horses to carry them on; there were many officers and gentlemen amongst them; and we brought 42 of them on horseback: so that we had 359 prisoners, besides many that escaped. We took about 600 horse, but the soulders drove them away towards Newcastle, and sold them at high rates. Sunday, July second, we brought our prisoners to Newcastle; but Sir Richard Tempest escaped from Morpeth, after he had brok his fast on Sunday morning. We have received information that the enemies forelorne hope are advancing, now about Long Framlington. We are drawing our horse together, and shall advance so soone as we can. We have ten troopes of horse come to us this night, under Col. Harrison; they are to meet us at Meldon.

The enemy hath about 600 horse left yet, and 3 troopes of dragoones: they brag of the Scots comming in to-morrow into England. If the Scots come not in, we shall, by God's helpe, free this country of these blades.

Yours,
John Sanderson.

Newcastle, July 3,1648.

Col. Ed. Grey, Col. Rich. Tempest, Sir Fran. Ratcliffe, Bar. Ratcliffe's son. Sir Jer. Lucas, M. Geo. Bellassis, M. Geo. Collinwood, M. Jo. Collinwood, Lieu. Col. Jo. Salkel, Lieu. Col. Ra. Millet. Lieu. Jo. Thornon, Ma. Tho. Saukel [Salkeld], M. Trowlop, Cap. Fran. Braulin, Cap. T. Shaftree, Ca. Hugh James, Cap. Smith, Cap. Fetherston, Cap. Fran. Carlton, Cap. Askne, Cap. Am. Carlton, M. Geo. Ratcliffe, M. Jo. Wright, M Cham.Wright, M. Jo. Thornton, M. Rich. Hodg, M. Char. Selby, M. Jo. Thurwell, M.Will. Lampton. M. Shaw, M. Ro. Ratcliffe, M. Lan. Selby, M. Woodhouse, M Ant. Trowlop, M. Jo. Sissons, M. Th. Hardin, M. Jo. Watson, M. Ra. Claxtra, Co. Jo. Tempest, Co. Ogle, M. Jo. Collinwood, junior, Ra. Comp, Wil. Hochton, Jo. Wegden, Wil. Fregrin, Wil. Porte, Ro. Hardin, Gilb.Rennek, Tho. Ilea, Hump. Marchald, Ri. Emerson, Tho. Jopson, Hum Terling, Jo. Wil. And. Jobler, Ra. Wood, Hen. Calliday, Rob. Vickel, Ra. Eodon, Tho. Thomson, Hen. Meriam, Ri. Rakler.

And many other gentlemen, as Lieu. and other officers, and 300 souldiers, and 600 horse, and many arms, &c. There are many captaines, which are not named in this note, which I have seen in another list; the reason is, many at first past for common souldiers, which are now knowne to be officers. Col. Sir Rich. Tempest, as he was brought toward Newcastle, slipt away, and so hath made an escape. This list was given me, and I had not time to write it over. There are 24 Cap. taken, at the least, with reformade captains.

3

John Sanderson to his father, 20th August 1648

(Worcester College Library, Wing S578A)
Reproduced by permission of the Provost and Fellows of Worcester College Oxford:

A full, exact, & particular
RELATION
of the chiefe passages of the
Parliaments army in
Lancashire,
against the Scots Army, for five
days together.
As was signified in a Letter (of the
20 August,) to his Father at
Newcastle, by Major *John*

Sanderson
Printed *Anno Domini.* 1648
A full, exact, and particular Relation of the
chiefe passages of the Parliaments Army
in Lancashire, against the Scots Army, for five dayes together

Deare Father,
We desire that all our friends may prayse and glorifie our gracious God, who hath
wonderfully wrought for us and the whole Kingdom these five dayes together.
I shall give you a full Relation of the chiefe particulars. *Saturday* 12 *of August,*
our Regiment (Collonell Lilburnes) had the guard at *Sawley* and *Pately* Bridge.
Sunday 13. we rendevouzed neere *Otley,* where Lieutenant Generall *Cromwell*
met us with three Regiments of foot and one of horse; we left all the new raised
Forces in *Yorkshire* except the *Lancashire* horse and foot. *Munday* 14. we rendevouzed at *Romell Moore,* neere *Skipton,* our Regiment, and Collonell *Twizletons,*
had the Guard at *Gargrave Tuesday* 15. we rendevouzed in *Broughton Pasture,*
and marched to *Gisburne* (for the *Scots and Cavaleers* were marching Southward.)
Our Forlorne hope tooke Collonell *Tempest* of *Craven,* and divers other Prisoners
in a Towne called *Whalley. Wednesday* 16. we rendevouzed at *Clethero,* and lay
in the Field all night, two miles North of *Ribchester* neere to Master *Sherburnes*
great house; this day was the Lord *Cornewath* and his Lady, with divers others
taken Prisoners, the *Scots* had so many foot in *Ribchester* that our For[np]lorne
hope thought it not fit to *engage,* till the Army came up. *Thursday* 17. we marched
directly towards *Preston,* our Forlorne hope commanded by Major *Smithson,* who
engaged part of the enemies reare, about *Langrige Chappell,* took divers prisoners, and killed some (amongst who was a *Scots* Quartermaster shot in the Face
and as he was dying, spoke these his last words, *Oh how can we prosper that have
broken our Covenant with God and the poor English*) Major *Smithson* took Prisoners
all the way from the *engagement,* till he came neere a Bridge that is within a mile
of *Preston,* and there was forced to stay till more ayd came to him; our Army
marched with all possible speed (our Regiments place of marching that day,
was in the reare of the foot, in the Van of the left wing of horse) an hot dispute
was at the Bridge, where the Scots joyned Lieutenant Generall *Bayles Brigade* to
ayd *Langdale,* whose whole Force was *engaged.* The *Scots* Body was drawne over
Ribble Bridge about Noon. By Gods blessing our party prevailed, won the Passe,
beat the *Scots* and *English* horse and foot from *hedge to hedge. Langdale* had six
thousand foot there, they were all routed and the *Scots Brigade.* Major *Smithson*
had two horses shot under him. Collonell *Brights* Regiment of foot did very gallant service that day. *Langdale* left the Field so soon as he saw his foot routed;
he fled towards *Lancaster,* with the horse that escaped, his foot were most slain
and taken; for about an houre we gave no quarter to any, but to Captain *Thomas
Salkeld,* the youngest sonne of *Rook,* whose life I saved, with great difficulty: We
tooke about two thousand Prisoners, three hundred Barrells of Powder, two
thousand Beasts (provision for the Army) seven thousand Armes, and their
Magazine of Victualls valued at five thousand pound. At the South end of *Preston*
towards *Wiggon* is a Brige, called *Rible Bridge,* which the *Scots* stoutly kept,
being much secured from our shot by flanking hedges; but *Lancashire* foot drew
out their Pikes and charged over the Bridge [np] and by push of Pike gallantly

vanquished the resolute opposers, and made way for our horse, who did great execution for two miles, tooke *Duke Hamiltons* trunkes and plate, but the night made us all draw back to *Preston*.

Fryday the 18. we marched from *Preston*, our Forlorne hope soon *engaged* the enemies reareguard, routed and chased them till they came to the *Scots* Reserves; then were forced to retreat to *Charley*, where Major Generall *Lamberts* Regiment of horse were marching, and by hard fortune Collonell *Thorney* was before them, wanting defensive Armes; yet seeing our Forlorne hope retreat, and the enemy charge furiously, he led on Generall *Lamberts* Troop, routed the *Scots*, but was runne through the heart with a lance. About two miles from thence, the enemy drew up all their Army; our Regiment was ordered to take the Van: we sent out a Forlorne hope, and followed close: next our Regiment were three Troops of Dragoones and three Troops of Horse, and a commanded party of three hundred foot; other Regiments of horse did follow as close as they could; all the enemies parties were beaten at every Passe, slain and taken in abundance, threw downe their Arms daintly; neer *Wiggon* we took Major Generall *Vandurst* and another Collonell, with two foot Colours of the Marquesse of *Argiles* old regiment; we beat the enemy into the Townes end, and made it good till about midnight. But because our foot army was not come up, we drew back a mile, and there kept Guard all night; so soon as it was day, we drew out twelve men out of each of the six Troopes of our Regiment, and sent Major *Cholmeley* to command them, with Lieutenant *Wheatley*, and my Quartermaster.

Saterday 19 of *August*, our Regiment tooke the Van again, because no other Regiment was neere, we advanced to *Wiggon*, where we tooke foure Collonells, *viz.* Collonell *Hamelton* of *Gateside*, Collonell *Urrey*, Collonell *Innes*, and another; we slew many men in *Wiggon* and abundance all the way, till we *engaged* the reare of their foot at a Wood neer *Winwicke*; The Earle of *Roxbroughs Brigade*, commanded by Collonell *Dowglas*, *Buckleughs Regiment*, General Adjutant *Turners Regiment* (who was *Sinclers* Major) the Lord *Humes Regiment*, and some of other regiments, they stood stoutly to it for three houres; vve lost some men, every Troop of our Regiment lost two; but at length, by Gods goodnesse to us, the *Scots* run, and my Troop and Captain *Lilburnes* vvere placed outmost; on the left Wing next to us vvas Collonell *Twizletons Regiment*, two of their Troops, and our two, carreered up to *Winwicke* Towne, got before the *Scots*, and stopt them, so that many hundreds of them were slaine there.

In the Field and Towne was slain in that three houres about 1600 men, and a whole Church full of Prisoners taken, vve think there could be no lesse than fifteen hundred Prisoners in the Church.

We pursued to *Warrington Bridge*, which the *Scots* kept till our body came up. It is wonderful to see how many are slaine all the way from *Langrige* Chappell to *Preston*, and from *Preston* six miles towards *Lancaster*, and all along the way from *Preston* to *Wiggon*, and in the Field neer *Wiggon*; and from *Wiggon* to *Warrington*, all the high wayes, Corne Fields, Meddows, Woods, and ditches strewed with dead bodies.

So soon as our Army drew up neer *Warrington*, Lieutenant Generall *Bayly*, and the rest of the *Scots* Officers sent to treat with Lieutenant Generall *Cromwell*, and have yeelded themselves and all their foot army Prisoners, and are now in safe custody; they are the remainder of one and twenty Regiments; they yeelded all

Armes, Horses, Colours, and Ammunition, 19 *August*. They are onely to have their lives and their goods saved, and the officers to be furnished with horses for their journey. I prayse God both my Brothers and all my Officers are well, in health, and unhurt.

We heare that the *Scots* and *Langdale* have a party now about *Kerdale*, the Lieutenant General hath ordered horse and foot thither. I think Collonell *Wren* will be called up thither to joyne with others.

There are some horse gone in pursuit of the *Scots* horse. The Country men in *Cheshire* tooke five hundred *Scots* horse yesterday, and will take every day more and more; they endeavour to get to *Wales*, as we think.

To God be all glory and prayse, and may we be truely thankfull. I present my humble duty to you and my Mother, my love to all my friends; and you may give Coppies of this to my Brother *Henry*, or any other friends, for this is as particular and exact, as any can be at present procured, and I know it to be true.

Warrington, August 20   *Your obedient Sonne,*
1648   John Sanderson
                              Postscript
I Pray you be pleased to present my humble service to Sir Arthur Haslerige and let him see this Letter, I would have written to him, but time will not let me write to you both. I must ever honour him, and heartily present my humble thanks amongst many other English, for his excellent act of regaining Tynmouth Castle.

                              FINIS

                                 4

John Sanderson to Captain Adam Baynes, 22nd December 1648

                    (British Library Add. Mss 21,417 f. 22)
RECTO
Major Sanderson December 22 [1648]
Captaine Baynes
I sent a letter about three weekes since to Mr Rushworth the generalls secritary, and one inclosed directed to his Excellencie. as yet I have not had any notice whether it came to his Excellencies hand or no. I earnestly intreat you to deliver this inclosed to Mr Rushworth and aske him if he received my former letter and whether he were pleased to deliver myne to his Excellencie. good sr procure mee an answere from Mr Rushworth in Writing and send it to mee With what speed you can./ which will much oblige yo assured freind and servant

                                                         John Sanderson
Pontefract 22th
xbris 1648
Remember my harty and faithfull love to honest Captaine Bradford./

                                                         Turn over
VERSO
Captain Baynes

The officers appointed to meet every friday etc, have mett this day and have taken notice of the great care you and Captaine Bradford have had of the businesses recomended to your./ ~~care~~

I am comanded in the name of the regt to give you both harty thanks, and to intreat you to continue your former care for these three regiment[s]: in those matter within your instructions, and y[t] you will not fayle to advertise us of every thing that is or may be done in relation to us or by us for the Publique good; and by gods blessing ~~will~~ wee shall to the utmost of our powers really answer ~~your~~ the expectations of the Army; I rest

yrs assured freind
John Sanderson

Pontefract 22th
xbris 1648

5

John Sanderson to Captain Adam Baynes 8th June 1649

(British Library Add. Mss 21,417 f. 168)

Captaine Baynes
In your letter in may last you wrote that some Assignations y[t] are unsatisfyed could not be exchanged untill the treasurers give in their Accompts. vizt
2° may <u>1648</u> on Mr Dickinson for the horse __1900[i]
 ditt. more on him for the 5 loose companyes_0500
16 may more on him for the horse__0950
Mr Dickinson is now at London therefore you are desired (by the officers) to get them said Assignations Exchanged. wee doubt not but you have those Assignations, or else the maior gene:[ll] hath them, for they are not in any officers hands that is now in the North. And the maior generall being now at London it is hoped that he will be pleased to be a good helper to us and in the procuring an exchange for them;

This day the officers have taken into consideration the great inconvenience that the soldyers have suffered in their pay because when Assignations were granted it was not mentioned from and to what day that pay assigned was to be unto them./ But for the future you are desired to solicite the Comittee of the Armye that they will be pleased to add one line more that may demonstrate from and to what day the Assigned pay shall be accompted by the soldyer. And if they will not do it constantly, yet if they will do it once we shall be able both to reckon from that time forward and likewise finde what may be duly arreere unto us for the time by past.

Your are likewise desired to do what you can to procure Recruits to our severall Troopes according to the Certificates that were sent to you.

It will be very necessary to procure an order from the Parliam[t] or Comittee of State to direct this Countyes Comissioners how to devide the Assesments amongst the 3 Rydings./ the West Ryding would have the Citie to be part of their 12·parts; and the North & East Ryding would have the Citie a 20th pt of the whole county and then the rest to be divided by 12·10: & 8 – By this Controversie , there happens an arreer of 1300[l]·or more, and no ryding will assess it; so the Army suffers Preiudice thereby.

145

The Assignations for 1290^{l} on yorkshire 24th febru: last will not be payd, therefore it must be charged; Sr Edward rodes goes for London the next weeke to Accompt.

[Written top to bottom in left hand margin] York 8 June 1649 my Collonell sent us some letters about 10 days since to the Trea^{rs}: of Lincolnshire, Nottingham and Darbyshires for severall sums and we have sent partyes out to levy the mony; but we have not the Assignations yet; so that the receipts will be retarded if my Collonell do not send the Assignations speedily. I am humbly to intreat you to desire my Collonell to send them to us without the first. / Sr the officers here have taken into consideration the great paines you have taken for us and the many good offices you have done us, and have comanded me to give you thankes; your charges will be thankfully considered by them. Sr, I remaine your very faithfull freind John Sanderson.

6

Major Sanderson's Will

From Skirmish in Northumberland
In the name of God, Amen. I John Sanderson, being of perfect minde and memory att the makeing hereof, (praysed be God) have thought fitt to make my last Will and Testament before my goeing into Scotland, that the estate which God hath blessed mee with, may be disposed according to my minde.

Whereas I lent my father, in his lifetime, the sum of one hundred and seaventy pounds, for which hee made a lease of some part of Hedley-hope to mee for fourscore and nineteene yeares, if the said sum were not payd, I doe give my deare mother all that £170 and the lease till the money be payd.

I doe give to my brother Thomas all my sheepe at Hedley-hope, all my bookes and mathematicall instruments att Hedley-hope, and att London, and my roane mare, and stoned colt of two yeares old.

I doe give to my sister Mary and my sister Elizabeth, to each of them, the sum of three hundred pounds, to be raysid out of the rents of my whole lands, my debts being first payd, soe soone as possibly the sayd portions can be raysed to advance in maryage, first the one and then the other.

For all my other horses I desire they may be sold to rayse moneys to pay my debts.

To my much esteemed friend Mrs. Elizabeth Jennings, wife to Captaine James Jennings, and daughter of Sr. Arthur Smithees, Knt. att London, I doe give her dureing the tearme of her naturall life, and not otherwise, my house in Cropwell, in wch. Mr. Hugh Lowe now liveth, and six oskin of land that lyes to it, in the occupation of the said Hugh Lowe, to have, hold and enjoy the same during [the] tearme of her naturall life, and then to returne to the uses hereafter specifyed.

To my deare brother Henry I give him in his bond for forty pounds that he owes mee, and I quitt him of the said debt; and I give unto him and his heires for ever, all that the honor and Castle of Leicester, with the lands, houses, gardens, rents, royaltyes, profitts, and comodityes whatsoever thereunto belonging, and all that thirty acres of land, in the fforrest of Leicester, in the County of Leicester, which I have given order to inclose and improve to a better vallue then att present.

But it is my will, that my debts, and my sister's portions, shall first be payd, before that any of my brothers, or theire heires shall stand seized of any of my lands, according to this my last will.

And I doe give unto my deare and loveing brother Samuell, all that the Mannor of Oxton, secunda pars, in the County of Nottingham, with my houses and lands in Southwell, in Huckling and Cropwell Bishop; and revertion of that house and six oskin of lands in Cropwell, after the death of Mrs. Elizabeth Jennings aforesaid, and all those quitt rents in Calverton, Blidworth, and Wood-Burrow, with all rights, profitts, and comodities, whatsoever to the said Mannor belonging, my debts and sisters portions being first payd as aforesaid.

And I doe give to my deare brothers Peter and Charles all that Park of Someborne, in the County of Southampton, with the Conney Warren and meadowes thereunto belonging. And it is my will that my brother Peter shall have six parts of eleven, and my brother Charles shall have five parts of eleven, viz., the parke is valewed at 225 li. p. ann.; viz. to my brother Peter the value of 122li. 14s. p. ann.; and to my brother Charles one hundred and two pounds six shillings. And in case there should be some short time in the present tennents lease (if it be not expired) for I bought the land in possession, then my said two brothers to have their shares att present during that tearme, according to this said rule.

To my dear friend Mrs. Jane Norton, of Chopwell, I give my dyamond ring, with 9 dyamonds, and my little gold enameld picture case, with 8 rubyes sett in it; and I desire that my picture may be coppyed in little, and that little coppye putt into the case, and soe given to her to keepe in remembrance of mee.

And to my servants (I am obliged to remember them), John Jackson hath served mee faithfully and carefully, therefore soe soone as my horses and mares are sold, I desire, and it is my will, that my brothers give unto John Jackson twenty pounds, to Robt. Tayler fifteene pounds, to Tho. Jackson tenn pounds, to Jo Crawford six pounds, and to my two new men each of them three pounds.

I am likewise in conscience bound to write a little concerning the Manner of Thwing, in Yorkshire. I have bought it in my name, and past the convayances in mine own name, but the mannor, and all that land and tenements that are in possession, by the survey are vallued to 47li. p. annum, these I bought for Capt. Geo. Grey, of Sudwick, in Bprick, and for his officers and soldiers, I had debenters of theires amounting to 830li. I bought his 47li. 6s. 8d. att 16 yeares purchase, wch. came to 757lb. 6s. 8d., but because I was forced to give above 20 yeares purchase for some other lands for the Regement, it would be unequall that some should buy 4 yeares cheepar then others; therefore Capt. Grey must allow 18 yeares purchase for this, and then it will be 852 pounds; but on the whole hee may be abated soe much as this *surmounts*[1] the sum in his debenters.

And Capt. Staffords farme, in that mannor, I bought it, and payd for it (with) my owne souldiours bills, it being 23li. and some odd shillings p. ann. present, and 13l. more p. ann. after the death of Sr. John Savile, of Yorkshire, which cost in all about 490li. or thereabouts. I promised Capt. Stafford that if hee would purchase soe much land of this vallue p. ann. and a cleere title, I would exchainge with him; or if he would before Christmas next, procure for mee soe many good warrantable originall bills as his farme cost, and I would accept of them, and the purchase should be to him; and then I would convey the 47li. 6s. 8d. p. ann. to Capt. Grey, and Capt. Stafford's farme I must then convey to Capt. Stafford. But if Capt. Stafford neither procure good bills nor land, valuable to exchaing as afforesaid, that farm of Staffords must goe to soe many of my soldiers or the regiment, as these debenters will equall it in the accompt. Therefore it is my will, and therefore I desire that my brother Henry, Samuell, and Charles, or any two of them, doe convey the said manner of Thwing as aforesaid, to Capt. Greyes officers and soldiers; and the other part either to Capt. Stafford or my soldiers, as is before directed. But considering that the *particulers* and the convayances of this mannor cost me above 30li., my executors must receive the Martinmas rent fully, besides 4d. per li. from Capt. Grey; for his mens debenters.

Thus desireing my brothers, and it is my will, that my sister Curwen and sister Jenison shall have, each of them, the sum of one hundred pounds paid unto them, out of the rents of the whole lands aforesaid, soe soone as the debts, my sister Mary's and my sister Elizabeth's portions are payd.

I earnestly desire my brothers to live loveingly together, and give all helpe and assistance to each other; and for this great charge that I have laid upon the lands, I could not helpe, haveing much to doe and many to releive : and I will that the charge be equally laid on the whole lands, viz. the honor and castle of Leicester, with its appurtenances, the parke of Someborne, and the manor of Oxton, excepting Mrs. Elizabeth Jennings, her legacy, wch. is to be freed, as aforesaid, during her life. And the God of Mercy who loves mee in my Saviour Christ, be ever good and gracious to you all, my deare brothers and sisters, and bless you in all *things* that ever you undertake. I desire that my brother Henry, my brother Samuell, and my brother Charles wil be my Executors; and I hereby authorize them so to be; witness my hand and seale this 19th day of Septembr. 1650.

JOHN SANDERSON.

MEMORANDUM.—That if my brothel Samuell and my brother Charles, both or either of them, shall dye without issue, then it is my will that such of my lands as by my will I have given to either of them shall then come and be to my brother Thomas Sanderson, and his heires for ever. But, nevertheless, it shall and may be lawfull for my brother Samuell and brother Charles, both or either of them, to make theire wives joynters in any or all parts of the said lands, and theire wives to enjoye the same during there naturall lives. Witness my hand this 19th of 7ber, 1650.

JOHN SANDERSON

All my conveyances for my owne Land are in my Trunck att Mr. Dowsetts house, at Charing Cross, in London; viz. :—

{OXTON
{LEICESTER.
And alsoe the Conveyance for THWING.   {SOMEBORNE.

APPENDIX 5

SEVENTEENTH CENTURY ROADS AND MAPS

Roads

During the latter half of the sixteenth century a number of Acts were passed which laid the responsibility for highway maintenance on the parishes. The system was generally unsatisfactory and standards deteriorated, a situation exacerbated by the increasing use of wheeled transport from the beginning of the seventeenth century. Such roads as had a metalled surface were damaged by wheels for which they had not been designed, and unmetalled roads became muddy quagmires in wet weather. Parkes refers to riders being "up to their saddle girths in mud . . . the foot soldier would think it no uncommon hardship to walk in mud to the ankles." The only properly engineered roads in England were those left by the Romans, and without proper and regular maintenance even these were not necessarily easy for travellers. Given the appallingly wet weather in 1648, travel can never have been a simple matter. On the return from Scotland in November 1648 Lilburne brought on the cavalry to join Lambert at Pontefract "so soon as . . . the bad ways will give leave."[1]

Maps

In the mid-seventeenth century maps were very different from those of the modern Ordnance Survey. The nature of the landscape is indicated by pictorial representations of hills rather than shading or contour lines, and rivers are boldly shown but roads tend to be few and far between. It was not until 1675, with the publication of John Ogilby's atlas *Britannia* which showed roads in detail, with distances and inclines, to a scale of one inch to one mile, that seriously useful maps were available.

The maps reproduced in *plates 24* and *25* are by Hollar and dated 1676 although, as that edition had more roads added to it, it was probably a reprint of an earlier edition. It is known as the Quartermasters Map, presumably because it was found useful in billeting troops on the move, although to modern eyes the lack of roads would reduce its utility markedly.

The scale is small, about 20 miles to one inch. Sanderson would certainly have had access to a map like this, and perhaps to something better. The accuracy of his 16 miles from Chollerford to Herterton suggests that he had some sort of road book which gave distances.

Those roads which are shown are something of a surprise as very few Roman routes are given, even though many of them are still in use today. The road shown running north from York is approximately the modern A19 as far as Thirsk, then the A167 to Darlington and A1 to Newcastle. The Roman road through Boroughbridge, Leeming, Catterick, Scotch Corner (A1 to this point), and on to Piercebridge, and Corbridge is not shown, although Sanderson clearly used it on his journeys between Barnard Castle and York, as he stayed near Leeming. The continuation of this road north of Corbridge (A68) is also omitted, as are places on it. The modern A1 is shown running north to Tadcaster but then joins the road east to York. Numerous river bridges are shown, or at least crossing points, but rarely in conjunction with roads.

On 9th June the pursuit of fleeing royalists must have been largely on the Stanegate, the Roman road between Corbridge and Carlisle. The northern sheet of the Quartermaster's map shows a road from Newcastle to Carlisle approximating in part to the Stanegate, but the overlapping southern sheet shows no such road.

The (partly Roman) route used by Cromwell through Otley, Ilkley, Skipton, and Clithero to Preston does not appear although there is a road shown from Wetherby to Skipton. The Roman road over the Pennines through Bowes, Brough, Penrith and Carlisle (A66) is not shown, although it was certainly in use and defended by Lambert in July.

But clearly, the Quartermasters' map was satisfactory enough as it was sufficiently in use to acquire a nickname. Presumably one merely asked a local for the road to the next place one wished to reach. Over 100 years later the plot of Oliver Goldsmith's *She Stoops to Conquer* relied to a large extent on travellers having to ask their way from place to place.

APPENDIX 6

HORSES

The cavalry of the period had moved away from the mediaeval great horse to a lighter, faster animal. Tylden sees the typical troop horse as probably about 15 hands, not markedly either coarse or of Eastern type, and perhaps with a little of the Arab or Barb blood.[1] Edwards in his detailed reviews of Civil War cavalry, points out that many of the nobility and gentry had been importing Arabs to improve the stock to the point where, before the war, English horses were being exported in some numbers.[2] Sir John Fenwick of Hexham, to take one example from Sanderson's area, had a famous stud of Arab horses, and the Arab and Barb blood was beginning to appear in the general population, including some troop horses.[3] There is no doubt that Sanderson would have used some animals of this quality.

Macdonald Fraser, in discussing the horses available to the Border Reivers in the late sixteenth century, notes that the Stuart kings imported horses to improve the local breeds, and produced a swift and unusually hardy mount.[4] Operating in the Border area Lilburne's and other regiments would have had access to such horses.

Pease quotes Froissart's statement that the Border Reivers travelled 20 to 24 leagues (60 to 80 miles) a day, and argues that Froissart was well aware of the difference between leagues and miles.[5] Some have doubted that these distances were possible, but the fact that the Diary shows that large numbers of troopers (and not just better-mounted officers) could cover these distances bears out his statement.

And these were not necessarily the best mounts to be had. A report on enemy movements leading up to 1st July mentions " two troops of Gent. excellent well mounted,"[6] presumably better horses than the regimental average and perhaps with more than a little Arab blood.

The cavalry did not rely on the weight of their horses, but more on their speed and flexibility. Apart from Hesilrige's fully armoured regiment ("lobsters") the riders were lightly armed and armoured, and had no need of a heavy horse. Speed and endurance were much more vital elements in the use of cavalry.

Sanderson mentions the death of one of his horses, but one would expect there to have been a need for replacement of troop horses as they became broken down by endless hard work. His failure to mention the purchase of new troopers is surprising, given that he records details of hay and oats, but it is difficult to know what to read into this omission. Perhaps all the troop horses were of some quality and withstood the rigours of endless patrol and skirmish. But Edwards points out that in action horse

151

casualties were higher than those of men.[7] At Preston, Major Smithson had two killed under him, and it would be surprising if the attack on the position at Winwick did not involve further loss of horses. Inevitably there will have been losses on patrol as well, due to sickness or injury. It was presumably not Sanderson's direct responsibility to obtain fresh mounts, and so he ignored the subject. This is most unfortunate as, with his attention to detail, some hard figures about turnover in horses on patrol would have been available.

The distances covered by the cavalry in the Diary and elsewhere are considerable by any standard; it is worth looking at a few examples. In March 1648 a Captain Wogan and his troop were covering 40 miles a day as they deserted to Scotland,[8] but it could be argued that the fear of capture spurred them on.

On 4th July a letter out of Lancashire to London reported the victory on 1st.[9] The news cannot have been sent earlier than late on 1st, perhaps from Morpeth, reaching London no more than three and half days later. It may have travelled by Lancaster and Preston, or Manchester, a total of about 370 miles or just over 100 miles a day. Hesilrige's official despatch from Newcastle was dated 2nd July and was read in the Commons on 5th.[10] Allowing time for the news to reach Newcastle (?perhaps with Sanderson) and assuming that it was not read until late on 5th, again it took about three and a half days to travel 280 miles, or 80 miles a day.

A letter from Lambert's headquarters at Barnard Castle, dated 28th July, was in London on 31st. At the most it took four days for the 250 miles, a minimum of over 60 miles a day.[11] Cromwell's despatch to the Speaker after the battle of Preston, dated Warrington 20th August, was read to Parliament on 23rd. Warrington to London is 200 miles, and on the reasonable assumption that the letter was written on the day it was dated it cannot have taken more than about three and a half days, an average of almost 60 miles a day.

Messenger services no doubt included changes of horses, but the Diary is explicit that large bodies of horsemen rode nearly 60 miles on 9th June and over 80 miles on 1st July. Clearly the horses of the period were capable of considerable feats of endurance, and that while carrying fully armed troopers, their equipment, and at least some rations for horse and man.

Sanderson himself seems to have ridden large horses, perhaps rather better bred than the average trooper. The use of such phrases as " my fine gray nag" and "my great white gelding" certainly suggests this but he gives no details of either his own or the troop horses. His Will shows that he owned both mares and geldings, but makes no mention of stallions.

APPENDIX 7

BRIEF BIOGRAPHIES

See chapter 1 for explanation of the entries, which are listed in alphabetical order under the name used in the Diary, the *Relation at Large*, and Sanderson's will.

William Baillie (Bayley)

(d. 1653) having served in armies abroad, was appointed Major-General in the covenanter army when it went into England in 1640. He was Lieutenant General of Foot under Leven at Marston Moor, the siege of York and the capture of Newcastle, and was then sent in pursuit of Montrose with Urry (*q.v.*) as his second in command. He was MP for Lanarkshire 1645-7 and again in 1648 when he was appointed Lieutenant-General of Foot in Hamilton's army. He surrendered at Warrington only after his officers promised to sign a document exonerating him of any blame for the defeat.

Cornet John Baynes

was a Commissary in the parliamentary army during the Diary period, and took the muster of Lilburne's regiment in June 1648 and July 1649. His cousin **Adam Baynes** was a captain in Lambert's and also acted as an agent for the northern regiments, in the course of which duties he amassed a great deal of correspondence including two letters from Sanderson.

Sir Richard Bellasis

of Ludworth (d.1651) served Durham county as deputy lieutenant, high sheriff, and commissioner in the Northern Association, but refused to raise troops against Langdale in June of that year.

Mr Bilton

George Bilton was working for the Treasury in 1645, delivering to the Commissioners of Parliament £1333 borrowed from the Treasury to pay a 6s gratuity promised to the foot regiments. By March 1652 he was the Deputy Treasurer at Leith, receiving fines paid by the Scottish nobility and making payments to the army and the late King's creditors and servants. For this service he was to be allowed 2d in the pound of all the fines received by him. While working in Scotland he was involved in a serious case of corruption but references in Sanderson's diary may indicate earlier dishonesty. Aylmer suggests that Bilton was the only Treasurer guilty of fraud.

Lady Brooke

(1611-1664), on whom S. was quartered, is assumed to be Mary, daughter of Timothy Pusey of Selston, Nottinghamshire, and wife of Henry Brooke, although he was not created Baronet until 1662. Henry, son of Sir Richard Brooke, was a colonel in the parliamentary army in 1643 who held out with only 80 men, losing none, when besieged by a party of cavaliers. From 1644–47 he was a sheriff of Cheshire, and M.P. for the county 1654–56.

Earl of Carnwath

Robert Dalzell was created earl in April 1639, in recognition of his loyalty in joining the King at York during the first Bishops' War. According to Clarendon, he caused the defeat at Naseby in 1645 by dissuading Charles from charging at the head of the cavalry reserve. Because of his support for the royalists, he was forfeited and his lands and title were transferred to his son Gavin in February 1645, but he was still known as the Earl of Carnwath. Following the defeat of Lord Digby's forces at Sherborne in Yorkshire, Carnwath is said to have fled to Ireland and nothing more was known of his movements until he landed in Scotland with the King in June 1650. From the Diary and the *Relation* we now know that he fought at Preston and he and his wife, Christian, daughter of Sir William Douglas of Hawick, were captured there.

Mr Cass

Mark Cass of Cockpen was factor to the Earl of Lothian. It is thought that he was 'The Laird of Cockpen' in Lady Nairne's poem of the same name.

William Charle[s]ton

of Lee Hall was son of William Charleton whose will was proved in 1635. Another son, John, held Lee Hall in 1638, but by 1663 the ratepayers were Cuthbert and James.

Sir William Clarke

(1623/4-1666) assisted *Rushworth* (they both could do the same shorthand or Tachygraphy) and was secretary to the Council of Officers 1647-1650, Senior Secretary to Fairfax from1649 until the latter's resignation, then Secretary to Monck in Scotland 1650-1660.

Earl of Dalhousie

William Ramsay (d.1672) served as a colonel of horse in the covenanting army in the Bishops' Wars. He again commanded a horse regiment in the 1644 campaign in England, at the sieges of York and Newcastle, and at Marston Moor. The regiment disbanded in February 1647, but in May the following year the Estates appointed William or his son George as colonel of an Edinburghshire horse troop. William refused the commission but supported the Engagement and the troop was known by his name. It fought at Preston, probably as part of the cavalry under Middleton, and George was taken prisoner at Warrington Bridge.

Peter Denton

It has not been possible to trace either the man or the letter which John Sanderson wrote to him on 13th May 1648 (see Appendix 4). However the date tallies with entries in the Diary: Sanderson is in Alnwick on 13th May, and Somerside was sent to Newcastle with two horses on 16th when he could also have carried letters to be forwarded to Hedleyhope.

A Mr Peter Denton took the Protestation at Lanchester at the same time as members of the Sanderson family, but as his daughter Anne inherited Stobbilees in Co. Durham on her father's death in 1643, this cannot be Sanderson's correspondent.

Richard Douglas

is said by the *Relation* to have commanded the Earl of Roxburgh's brigade, presumably an *ad hoc* grouping of regiments including Douglas's own regiment of foot. His father William was one of the officers who later signed Lt.-Gen. Baillie's vindication of the surrender at Warrington bridge.

Lord Elibank

Patrick Murray was appointed Sheriff Principal of the constabulary of Haddington, and convenor of the Justices of the Peace in the same sheriffdom in 1633. He supported the king's policy throughout the civil war, and was created Lord Elibank in March 1643 for his own services and that of his father, Sir Gideon, who died in 1621, having refused food and drink for a fortnight following an accusation of financial mismanagement when acting as Treasurer-Depute in Scotland. Patrick died in November 1649.

Lord [Endenpeffer] Innerpeffer

Sir Andrew Fletcher held various judicial and parliamentary offices in Scotland, and was one of 13 MPs who voted against the parliamentary decision of January 1647 that Charles I should be left in Newcastle under the jurisdiction of the English parliament. In 1643 he acquired the Saltoun estate, where Lilburne's officers were quartered in October 1648.

Major (Gilbert) Errington

of West Denton in Northumberland, was a royalist major of horse. He compounded in 1649 for his delinquency the previous year.

Isaac Gilpin

having fought for Parliament, became Clerk to the Standing Committee of the Northern Association, to which Samuel Sanderson and his son Thomas were appointed. In July 1665 Elias Smyth, Minor Canon and Precentor of Durham Cathedral, accused Gilpin of embezzling "the rich velvet pulpit cloth, with the Church's arms fairly embossed upon it in gold and silver, and divers other ornaments and utensils of the Church", and of lending "Gerard's Herball (which cost ten pounds) to Coll. Robert Lilburn, who is now in the Tower, and still detaine the sayd book from the Library".

Grey

Several of the Greys mentioned in the Diary were descended from Sir Ralph Grey of Chillingham (d. 1565) and his wife Isabel (d. 1581), eldest daughter and co-heiress of Sir Thomas Grey of Horton.

Mr [Edward] Grey of Howick (d. 1653) was his great-grandson. His father, Sir Edward Grey of Howick and Morpeth Castle was the youngest son of Sir Ralph. The second son, also Sir Ralph, was father, by his second wife, of the royalist **Colonel Edward Grey** (1611-1675). Having petitioned to compound he was fined in January 1647, but returned to arms the following year as commander of royalist forces in Northumberland. Hesilrige, reporting to Speaker Lenthall in July 1648 that Grey had been taken prisoner, commented "there is not a man in the north of England that hath done you more mischief than Col. Grey".

Mrs Grey of Bradford was Mary, daughter of Thomas Lewen of Amble and Hauxley, and widow of John Grey, inheritor of the Bradford estate from his father Sir Ralph who had bought it just before his death in 1624. John matriculated at Christ's College Cambridge in 1618[9], and having been appointed Colonel in the parliamentary army, was killed in Ireland in February 1646[7]. His will was administered by John Orde. A servant of the same name, who received more from the will than the other servants, may be the same man.

Robert Grey of Turvelaws was probably from the same family although the descent is unclear. The Tankerville family, descended from the Greys of Wark (the first Lord Grey of Wark was William, brother of John Grey *q.v.*) owned estates at Wooler which included the farm of Turvelaws. Robert died in 1651 and was to be buried in the church at Wooler, leaving money in his will for its repair. Among the church plate is a silver chalice with the following inscription: *Robert Grey of Turve Law, his gift to Wooller Church 1642*. A man of the same name, perhaps his son, was present when Andrew Carr killed James Swinhoe *q.v.* at Chillingham in February 1672.

George Grey of Southwick

(born 1617) was not connected to the above family. He served as a captain of foot in the Northern Association Army and was disbanded in January 1647[8]. According to the short biography written by his grandson and transcribed in Surtees II, he lost 700 'broad pieces of gold' when Tynemouth Castle was plundered following the revolt in August 1648.

Sir Arthur Hesilrige

was one of the five Members of Parliament whom Charles I tried to arrest in January 1642. In December 1647 he was appointed governor of Newcastle with overall charge of the forces in north east England. It may have been him to whom Sanderson was reporting at intervals.

The orthography of the name is very varied in both primary and secondary sources. The form used here, other than in direct quotations, is that found in the pamphlet describing the retaking of Tynemouth in August 1648, Hesilrige's signature on the letter therein, and his letter of 2nd July.

James, Earl of Home

was active on the Covenanter side in the Bishops' Wars. In 1645 he was fined by the Estates for flirting with Montrose. On 4 May 1648 he was appointed colonel of the Berwickshire foot which fought at Winwick He was a signatory to Baillie's vindication for surrendering at Warrington, and escaped to Scotland thereafter.

Mr Alexander Home

of St Leonards had succeeded his father Alexander by 1623 when he became a JP for the bailiary of Lauder. He was a commissioner to Parliament in 1639, and on the Committee of War 1643-4 and 1646-8. As well as St Leonards he held land at

Barro, where Sanderson's troop quartered on 30th September. Why he should have denied Sanderson and his troops quarter at Lord Lauderdale's house is not clear.

Sir Arthur Ingram

husband of Eleanor, sister of Sir Henry Slingsby whose *Life* was published with the *Memoirs* of Capt Hodgson, had the manor and estate of Temple Newsam settled on him by his father (d. 1642). He deputised for his father as Secretary to the Council in the North in York from 1623.

Robert Innes

served as quartermaster general to Callendar's army and was with it in England on the side of Parliament from 1644. In May 1648 he was appointed colonel of Innes's horse, and was part of Hamilton's army of invasion. The *Relation* confirms Cromwell's note of his capture before Wigan.

Major-General John Lambert

came from a minor Yorkshire land-owning family, and joined the parliamentary army at the start of the Civil War. He rose rapidly in rank and influence and in July 1647 became Major-General of the Northern Association following a mutiny against Poyntz, the previous holder of the post. His mediation skills calmed the northern regiments. During 1648 he balanced his small forces against the larger numbers from Scotland in July and August, and prevented Hamilton from crossing the Pennines to the easier ground in Yorkshire.

Sir Marmaduke Langdale

fought for the royalists at Naseby, seized Berwick at the end of April 1648, and captured Pontefract castle in June of the same year. He led the English troops at Preston and was captured, but escaped to the continent.

Duke of Lauderdale

James Maitland (1616-1682) best known as a member of the Cabal, joined the covenanters and was a commissioner for the Church to the Assembly of Divines at Westminster in 1643, and from the Scottish Estates to Charles I in 1644 and 1647. He was one of the principal figures in the alliance between the Covenanters and the English parliamentarians, but his negotiations broke down when Cromwell defeated the Scots at Preston. Having been appointed colonel of 80 horse from Haddington in May 1648, he went to the Netherlands after the defeat, and accompanied Charles from there to Scotland in 1650.

Thomas Margetts

was Judge-Advocate for Major-General Lambert's forces in the north. He was Secretary to Lambert, and also acted as Secretary to the Council of the Officers of the Northern army in December 1648.

Gilbert Marshall

was a receiver of the late bishopric of Durham by 1652, and represented the county on the committees for militia and assessment in 1659 and 1660. He was said in July 1665 to be the person who could give the best account of 'the lead and timber of the 2 great broaches at the west end of the Church, how they were employed' when Isaac Gilpin (*q.v.*) was implicated in the destruction of the spires of the two western towers of Durham Cathedral.

Mr Norton

For being in arms against Parliament and an assessor of his neighbours for taxes and loans made for that purpose, **Maulger Norton** (c.1593-1673), of St Nicholas juxta Richmond in Yorkshire, compounded, with his eldest son Edmund, for their estates in February 1644, and was fined £756.

Edmund (bapt. 1622) matriculated at Pembroke College Cambridge in 1639 and was admitted to Gray's Inn on 11 February 1645/6. A year later he married Jane Dudley 'an excellent, fine and good gentlewoman' daughter and sole heir of Toby Dudley of Chopwell. But Edmund, 'a gentleman of a sweete good disposition to all, obedient and dutifull to his parents, and true friend in time of adversity, a religious young man, a faithfull subject of his majestie, for whom he suffered much' (he served as a colonel of dragoons in the Skipton garrison of Sir John Mallory) died 'of a plurisie' in York on 30 November 1648. (Thornton, 55)

Jane Norton née Dudley

widow of Edmund Norton (*q.v.*) married Robert Clavering at Ebchester on 15 July 1651, and had a family by him. (See below) She was the "dear friend" in John Sanderson's Will, and is discussed in chapter 7.

The Sanderson and Dudley families would have known each other as John's grandfather Henry received orders in November 1615 to take care of Chopwell Woods. However, they may not have been on the best of terms as Henry reported in June 1620 to Sir Robert Naunton on the neglect and misconduct of the Bailiff of Chopwell who had cut down and sold wood for his own advantage; in December 1632 a grant for 300*l* was set against Jane's grandfather, Ambrose, 'late keeper of his Majesty's wood at the manor of Chopwell' for putting timber to his own use.

Robert Clavering and Jane Norton had a son John (1655-1702) who married twice. His first wife was Anne Thompson, and they had two daughters: Mary (1685-1724) the diarist, who was the second wife of William 1st Earl Cowper (1665-1723), Lord

Chancellor; and Ann the political commentator who married Henry, 3rd son of Henry Liddell of Ravensworth. Spencer Cowper (1713-1774), second son of William and Mary, was Dean of Durham. By his second wife, Elizabeth Hardwick (d. 1703) John Clavering had a son John (1698-1759) who was MP for Marlow (1727-1731) and for Penry (1734-1741).

Mr Ogle of Eglingham

Henry Ogle (1600-c.1673) a strong supporter of parliament, was one of the seques-trators for Northumberland, deputy lieutenant, and a commissioner for raising forces in 1645. He is said to have entertained Cromwell at Eglingham in 1650, and served in his parliaments in 1653 and 1654. **John Ogle** (d. before 11 June 1686) son of the above, was appointed captain of militia for the four Northern counties, and served as a commissioner for sequestration in Northumberland in 1650.

Ord[e]s

A Major Orde was present at the surrender of Lichfield in July 1646, but nothing more is known about him. Thomas Orde of Longridge, lieutenant colonel of foot in James Swinhoe's regiment *q.v.*, begged to compound in April 1647 for being in arms against Parliament, but was in arms again the following year and was fined a second time in 1649. His cousin Francis is said to have held the same rank.

The relationship between the Ordes, Greys, and Sandersons has not been estab-lished. Mary Grey's father, Thomas Lewen, was related to the Sandersons, but no link to the Ordes has been discovered which would explain why Major John referred to the Orde of Longridge as "cosin".

However the Ordes belonged to such a large and complex family, with branches in Weetwood, Samshouse, Newbiggen, Longridge, and Berwick, that Raine in his *North Durham* apologised for omitting many from his pedigree.

Dr Petty

It is tempting to suggest that this is a reference to Dr William Petty (1623-1687) who qualified as a Doctor of Physic at Oxford in 1650, and was then appointed physician to the army in Ireland where he became Surveyor General. There is no hint in his correspondence that he visited the north of England but serving as Sanderson's surgeon for however short a period would have given him valuable experience for his later career.

John Ramsey

of "Berwick" compounded for his delinquency "during the last war" according to the report by Sir Arthur Hesilrige's secretary, Anthony Pearson, of the fines set in the northern counties by the commissioners appointed by Act of Parliament March 2 1649. There is no trace of any Ramseys at this period in Berwick, but the Eglingham registers have several entries under Ramsey of Bewick, and it is therefore safe to assume that there is a misprint in the report.

William Reed

of Titlington was probably a major in the foot regiment of Col. Sir Robert Clavering. In June 1636 he married Margaret, daughter of Henry Grey of Kyloe, in right of whom he held an estate in fee, for which he compounded in 1649 because of his delinquency in the war. He is then referred to as William Reed of Kyloe, a chapelry facing the Holy Island and the Farnes. He was allowed, amongst others, a rent charge payable to Mrs Grey of Bradford, *q.v.*

Lord Roxborough

Robert Ker, 1st Earl of Roxburgh (1669[70]-1650) was an active politician in Scotland and regular attender at the English court, being awarded a peerage on the baptism of Prince Charles in 1600. In the 1640s he was on the Committee of War for Roxburghshire and the constabularies of Haddington and Lauderdale. Stripped of all public offices in 1649 for his support of the Engagement, he died at Floors Castle the following year.

John Rushworth

(c.1612-1690) born in Northumberland and appointed solicitor to the town of Berwick in 1638, became Clerk-Assistant to the House of Commons and was used as a messenger between Westminster and the army in the north. When Sir Thomas Fairfax was appointed general of the New Model Army, Rushworth became Secretary to him and to the General Council of the Army. In 1641 he had started to collect newsbooks and his position gave him access to many official documents which he used to write a history of the period.

Thomas Salkeld

and his eldest brother **John** (1616-1705), who were taken prisoner in the 'Skirmish in Northumberland' (1 July 1648), were sons of John Salkeld of Rock. Having been rescued by Sanderson in August 1648, Thomas went overseas from Berwick in September. He later served as a captain in the Jamaican expedition 1654-6. John, an ensign in 1640, was described as a captain when he murdered John Swinburne of Capheaton in February 1643, and became a lieutenant colonel of horse in the royalist regiment of Col. Edward Grey *q.v.*

161

Adam Shipperson or Shepperdson

was the second son of William of Monkwearmouth, and took the Protestation at Dalton-le Dale in co. Durham. In May 1646 he, and his younger brother Edward (a lieutenant) in the company of Capt. Thomas Lilburne, gave evidence to the Committee of Estates on the King's march northward. A request was made in October 1649 for arrears for his troop of horse which was disbanding, but the following August there was a claim for 14 days pay for the three 'new-raised' troops commanded by Major [Henry] Sanderson, Captain Hutton, and Capt Shepperson. Adam acted with John Sanderson and others as attorney for the Northern Brigade, and in March 1659[60] he was on the committee for settling the militia with Thomas Sanderson. His will is dated October 1660.

Richard [Shireburn] Sherburn

(c.1591-1667) inherited Stonyhurst on the death of his father Richard in 1628. He supported the royalist cause in the civil wars, and was sequestered twice.

Mr Smith of Oldfield/Awdfield/Aldfield

A John Smith of Audfield, yeoman, is listed as forfeiting his estate to the Commonwealth for treason, 18th November 1652. This may or may not be the man Sanderson was quartered on.

Capt. Robert Stafford

Nothing is known about his army career, but he is probably the Stafford who became a surveryor of Royal property in Cumberland and was recommended as a commissioner for sequestrations in York in February 1653[4]. In November 1660 he was granted a lease of a messuage (a dwelling house, its outbuildings and land, from Old French mesnage) in Thwing, and two years later was described as the farmer of excise in the area.

Lieutenant Strangeways

is one of those named in simple code in Sanderson's accounts. No mention of him has been found in any capacity in 1648, let alone as a member of Lilburne's. In November 1656 Capt. Thomas Strangways, Major George Smithson and Capt. George Watkinson (the last two both of Lilburne's) were added to the Commission for Securing the Peace in county Durham. He is recorded as being in the regiment in the late 1650s, and for a brief time in February 1660 was major of the regiment, of which Smithson was then colonel.

James Swinhoe

was colonel of a royalist regiment of foot originally commanded by Robert Clavering . Having fought in both civil wars, he petitioned to compound in 1649 and paid his fine two years later. He was killed in a duel at Chillingham in 1672, witnessed by his brother, the dramatist Gilbert Swinhoe, and Robert Grey of Turvelaws.

Richard Tempest

captured by the parliamentary Forlorn on 15th August 1648, was of Bracewell in Craven. He compounded for being in the service of Charles I in the early 1640s and was fined again in 1649, after being in arms the previous year. His sister Troth was mother of Sir Richard Tempest of Stella *q.v.*, with whom he has sometimes been confused. His will, dated 10 days before he died a prisoner in the King's bench in November 1657, divised the manors of Bracewell and Stock to John Rushworth, *q.v.*

Sir Richard Tempest of Stella

Co. Durham (1610-1662), royalist colonel of horse and leader of the English forces during Langdale's insurrection, was captured on 1st July 1648. The following year he forfeited the estate of Stella for being a royalist.

Sir James Turner

(c.1615-c.1689) a mercenary, served in the Swedish army in the 1630s before joining the covenanter army in September 1640. When it was disbanded the following year, he was appointed major in Lord Sinclair's regiment in Ireland. After the return to England in 1644 he was present at the storming of Newcastle that year, and at the siege of Newark in 1647. The alliance of royalists and moderate covenanters in 1648 gave him an opportunity to fight for the king, and he served at Preston, being wounded by his own pikemen. After surrendering at Uttoxeter and being imprisoned at Hull, he fled to the continent, but returned to Scotland in 1650.

Sir John Urry

(d.1650) was noted for changing sides in the civil wars. Having been a mercenary abroad, he returned to Scotland in 1639 and was appointed lieutenant colonel in the covenanting army, then joined the parliamentarians at the outbreak of the civil war. He deserted to the royalists after Edgehill and fought at Marston Moor on the royalist right flank. At Shrewsbury he fled to Waller but later joined the covenanters under the Earl of Leven in north east England. In February 1645 he was appointed major general of horse and foot in Scotland and colonel of dragoons. He was sent north in March and took Aberdeen from the royalists but abandoned it next day and went in pursuit of Montrose whom he later joined. 1648 saw him in England with Hamilton and he was wounded and imprisoned at Wigan. He escaped to the continent where he joined Montrose again, but was beheaded in 1650 after his return to Scotland.

Jonas [Von Druske; Vandurst] van Druschke,

a Dutchman, was colonel of a regiment of horse in the Army of the Solemn League and Covenant. In 1646 it was in Yorkshire where it provoked many complaints about its behaviour, including its oppressive style of quartering and imposition of cess. It was said to consist of Roman Catholics, Irish, Scots, Dutch, French and English, with one in four ex-royalist officers, and a German major, Hans Georg van Sobell. By June the Council of the Army had made the decision to disband the regiment and Van Druschke was to leave the country. But it seems he remained fighting in England until his capture at Preston. He was also taken prisoner at Worcester.

Capt. George Watkinson

is recorded in Lilburne's regiment after 1648, and gave the alarm when the Scots advanced on the English camp at Musselburgh in the early hours of 31st July 1650, "a person of great worth for conduct and valour" (Hodgson). Together with Capt. Thomas Strangways, Watkinson was appointed to the Committee for Securing the Peace in co. Durham in November 1656, but was cashiered by Monck a year later for being a Quaker. He should not be confused with Captain Wilkinson who served with Sanderson and remained in the regiment until at least 1659.

Lord Winton [Winter]

George Seton, 1st Earl of Winton, (1584-1650) sworn for the Scottish Privy Council in 1607, took an active part in its proceedings during the reign of Charles I, and entertained the king twice, in 1633 and 1641, at Seton Palace. On the outbreak of war in 1639, Winton joined the King at Berwick, and his estates were thereupon sequestered by the Covenanters. Physically unfit, he was not able to join the fighting in 1642, but sent his sons, George and Alexander. In 1648 he was made colonel of foot and horse for Haddingtonshire and commissioner of war for that county and Linlithgow, and contributed £1000 to the Duke of Hamilton for the war in England. Alexander served as lieutenant colonel of horse in the army defeated by Cromwell at Preston. George senior joined Charles II on his arrival back in Scotland in 1650, but died at Seton just two weeks before the coronation.

Lord Yester

John Hay, 8th Lord Hay of Yester and 1st Earl of Tweeddale, took an active part in public and business affairs in Scotland and was a member of various committees of parliament. He signed the Solemn League and Covenant, and is said to have led an *ad hoc* force in co. Durham in 1640. In February 1642 he contributed £500 for the army in Ireland, and in March gave £3600 for the relief of Scottish forces there. His son John, 1st Marquess of Tweeddale, raised a foot regiment in 1648 and entered England with Hamilton but was not himself present at Preston.

Soldiers and Servants

Several servants, members of his troop, and messengers are mentioned in the Diary. It is unlikely that many of these can be identified, particularly as most have common names. However, some names occur in other sources and a connection might be made.

If one assumes that they were recruited locally, the Protestation of 1641[2] may indicate where they came from. For example, the William Fletcher listed in Lamesley, which is near Chester-le-Street, could well be the man of that name 'intertained' as a servant on 18th November when Sanderson's troop was quartered in the area. Of the 'reduced' soldiers, Matthew Tindell is listed under Norton with Stockton; Geo. Tanton (Taunton in the Diary) and An. Smith under Dalton-le-Dale; and Robert Byerly is mentioned twice in the Lanchester list. Thomas Whitfield may have come from Lanchester, and Cuth Grey could be from Lanchester or Ryton. Michaell Dixon is included in the Stanhope list, and only one Vall [Valentine] Appleby is listed, under Easington, while Ralfe Nicholson may have been from Barnard Castle. There are Rackets recorded in Brancepeth and Durham, but only one Richard Robeson, listed in Durham. Over 30 John Jacksons are noted, but the names of John and Thomas Jackson are adjacent in the Brancepeth list which would indicate that they are related (cf. Sandersons listed under Lanchester) and probably the servants mentioned in the Diary and Will.

Most of the other names are found in the list from Ryton where Sanderson himself took the protestation: Robert Hedly, Robert Hodgson (Hogsen), Richard Robinson, Thomas Atkinson, Robert Bell, John Gibson, and Robert Taylor. The last named was left sick at Lostock on 22nd August, but must have recovered as he was remembered in Sanderson's will.

No Allyson is listed but the person mentioned on 18th April might be Matthew Allenson from Witton-le-Wear. Other names are not recorded in the lists: John Nichols, Harry Lodge, Robert Somerside /Somerset, and Andrew Tomson. This may be because they came from elsewhere, or more probably, because they were not old enough to take the protestation.

Lieutenent Leven was appointed to Sanderson's troop on 3rd March 1648. Richard Robinson was paid on several occasions for the care of horses, and may have been Sanderson's jockey. Three years later these names appear in the Clarke accounts for Scotland: on 28th May 1651 £12 is given to "Lt Levins" for mounting Richard Robinson of Capt. Baynes Troop.

APPENDIX 7A

THE PROBLEM OF MAJOR CHOLMLEY

The Diary, and other evidence given in chapter 3, shows that a Major Cholmley served in Lilburne's regiment in 1648. It has been generally assumed that this is John Cholmley who appears in the register at Winwick as having been buried there on 3rd September.[1]

John Cholmley was the son of Colonel Thomas Cholmley of Carlisle, who asked for John's position as Custom Master of the town to be given to his younger son Richard, who had been in the Parliament's service, but it appears that it was Thomas himself who became the customs official.[2] Perhaps Thomas tried to get a civilian job for his surviving son, who did not want it. By the time Thomas wrote his will on 1st July 1654,[3] Richard was also dead but the date of death is not known.

Major-General Lambert, in a letter supporting Colonel Cholmley's application, refers to "Captain Cholmley, late of Col. Lilburne's regiment of horse, who commanded the forlorn hope in the late engagement at Winwick and was slain."[4]

This would be conclusive if it were not for Sanderson. In the *Relation* Sanderson records the death of two men from each troop of his regiment but does not mention Cholmley. He was writing his account on the following day, and would have known of the death of any officer in his regiment. It seems inconceivable that he would not record the death, or the serious wounding, of a fellow troop commander; he did, after all, trouble to mention that Major Smithson had two horses shot under him. Not only does he ignore Cholmley's death, but in the Diary he goes on to refer to Cholmley in Scotland on 30th September and 5th October, the first time naming his troop but the second naming him personally as Major Cholmley.

Hodgson, describing the third day of the battle of Preston, says of Cholmley "A great loss we had of such a youth, who was grown so expert, valiant, and faithful." This reads as though the man was known personally to him and probably in his own foot regiment, rather than a cavalryman. In a fight against a fixed position, as at Winnick, there will certainly have been a forlorn of foot as well as of horse. It may well be that the foot was also commanded by a Cholmley, serving in the infantry, and this could have led to the confusion. The presumption must be that Lambert (or his clerk) made an error in assigning the dead Cholmley to Lilburne's. Cromwell writes a letter not unlike Lambert's but refers to "Major Cholmley who was killed in the fight against the Scots at Winnick"[5] without mention of his regiment.

166

It is important to note that, although Cholmley led the commanded party at the beginning of the day, Sanderson nowhere says that he took the lead at Winwick.

The evidence is contradictory, but on balance it is more likely that the dead Cholmley was an infantry officer, whether or not related to the cavalryman. Sanderson's evidence for the continued existence of Major [?Richard] Cholmley of Lilburne's cannot be ignored. Bull and Seed, page 84, note 8, point out that more than one member of the family was serving. Further evidence is needed to settle the question.

BIBLIOGRAPHY

Abbreviations

AA	*Archaeologia Aeliana.*
CWAAS	Cumberland and Westmoreland Antiquarian and Archaeological Society.
DULASC	Durham University Library Archives and Special Collections.
HMC	Historical Manuscripts Commission.
PSAN	*Proceedings of the Society of Antiquaries of Newcastle upon Tyne.*

Abergavenny	*The manuscripts of the Marquess of Abergavenny, Lord Braye, G.F. Luttrell, Esq, etc.* (HMC, 10th Report, Appendix VI) (1887).
Abbott	Wilbur Cortez Abbott, *The Writings and Speeches of Oliver Cromwell* 4v. (Cambridge, Mass., 1937-47).
'Advice'	'Advice to a Soldier' *The Harleian Miscellany* ed. J. Malham v. VIII (1810) 353-361.
Akerman LFRO	J. Y. Akerman, *Letters from Roundhead Officers in Scotland* (Bannatyne Club) (Edinburgh 1856).
Akerman 1856	J.Y. Akerman, [Baynes letters] *Proceedings of the Society of Antiquaries of London* 3, (1856) 144-149.
Atkinson	J.A. Atkinson, *Tracts relating to the Civil War in Cheshire 1641-1659* (Chetham Society New Series 65) (Manchester, 1909).
Atkyns and Gwyn	Richard Atkyns and John Gwyn, *The Civil War* ed. Peter Young and Norman Tucker (1967).
Aylmer 1979	G.E. Aylmer, *Sir William Clarke Manuscripts 1640-1664* (1979).
Aylmer 1973	G.E. Aylmer, *The State's Servants* (1973).
Baillie	*The Letters and Journals of Robert Baillie . . .* ed. David Laing 3v. (Bannatyne Club) (Edinburgh, 1841-41).
Barnes	*Memoirs of the life of Mr Ambrose Barnes* ed. W.H.D. Longstaffe (Surtees Society 50) (Durham, 1867).
Bates 1891	Cadwallader J. Bates 'Border Holds 1' AA^2 xiv (1891).
Bates 1895	Cadwallader J. Bates *History of Northumberland* (1895).
Beaumont	William Beaumont ed. *A discourse on the War in Lancashire* (Chetham Society 62) (Manchester, 1865).

Birch   'A true and perfect account of the receipts and disbursements of Captaine Samuel Birch . . .' Portland Papers v. III (HMC 14th Report, Appendix, Part 11), 173-186.

BPR   Transcript of Brancepeth Parish Registers on microfiche in The Herbert Maxwell Wood Collection of Transcripts of Parish Registers of Newcastle and County Durham in Newcastle City Library.

Briggs   Katharine M. Briggs, *The Last of the Astrologers: Mr William Lilly's History of his Life and Times 1602-1681*, reprinted with notes and introduction (1974).

Broxap   Ernest Broxap, *The Great Civil War in Lancashire* 2nd ed. (Manchester, 1973).

Burnet   Gilbert Burnet, *The Memoires of the Lives and Actions of James and William Dukes of Hamilton and Castleherald* (1677).

CPCAM   *Calendar of the Proceedings of the Committee for Advance of Money, 1642-1660* ed. M.A.E. Green 3v. (1888).

CPCC   *Calendar of the Proceedings of the Committee for Compounding* ed. M.A.E. Green 5v. (1889-92).

CSPD   *Calendar of State Papers, Domestic* 1581-1590 – 1659-1660 46v. (1865-1886).

Camden   William Camden, *Britannia* (1607).

Capp   Bernard Capp, *Astrology and the Popular Press: English Almanacs 1500-1800* (1979).

Cary   Henry Cary, *Memorials of the Great Civil War of England from 1646-1652*, edited from original letters in the Bodleian Library 2v. (1842).

Clarendon   Calendar of the *Clarendon State Papers* preserved in the Bodleian Library 5v. (Oxford, 1872-1970).

Clarke MS   Sir William Clarke, *Manuscripts 1640-1664* (Microfilm).

Clarke Papers See Firth 1891-1901.

Clay   J.W. Clay ed., *Yorkshire Royalist Composition papers II.* (Yorkshire Record Series 18) (Leeds, 1895).

GEC 1900-06   G. E. C [okayne], *The complete Baronetage* 5v. (1900-06).

GEC 1910-59   G. E. C [okayne], *The complete Peerage* 13v. (1910-59).

Cosin   John Cosin, *The correspondence of John Cosin, D.D. Lord Bishop of Durham* v.2 (Surtees Society 55) (Durham, 1872).

Curwen   John F. Curwen, *The Castles and Fortified Towers of Cumberland, Westmorland, and Lancashire North-of-the-Sands* CWAAS Extra Series xiii (Kendal, 1913).

Dawson   William Harbutt Dawson, *Cromwell's Understudy: the life and times of General John Lambert* (1938).

Defoe   Daniel Defoe, *Memoirs of a Cavalier* (Oxford, 1972).

Dendy   F. W. Dendy, *Extracts from the Records of the Merchant Adventurers of Newcastle-upon-Tyne* 2v. (Surtees Society 93 & 101) (Durham, 1895-99).

DNB   *Dictionary of National Biography* 63v. (1895-1900).

Dixon   D. D. Dixon, *Upper Coquetdale, Northumberland: its history, traditions, folk-lore and scenery* (Newcastle-upon-Tyne, 1903).

Dodds   M. Hope, Dodds *Extracts from the Newcastle upon Tyne Council Minute Book 1639-1656* (Newcastle, 1920).

Drummond   Sir William Drummond, 'The Diary of Sir William Drummond of Hawthornden, 1657-1659' ed. H. W. Meikle *Miscellany of the Scottish History Society* 7 (Edinburgh, 1941) 3-52.

Dugdale   William Dugdale, *The Visitation of the County Palatine of*
Lancaster   *Lancaster*, ed. F.R. Raines (Chetham Society 88) (Manchester, 1873).

Dugdale   *Dugdale's Visitation of Yorkshire, with additions* ed. J.W. Clay
Yorkshire   v.2 (Exeter, 1907).

Dumble 1987   William Dumble 'The Durham Lilburnes and the English Revolution' in Marcombe, 227-252.

Ekwall   Eilert Ekwall *The Concise Oxford Dictionary of English Place-Names* 4th ed. (Oxford, 1960).

Edwards 1995   P.R. Edwards 'The Supply of Horses to the Parliamentarian and Royalist Armies in the English Civil War' *Historical Research* 68 (1995) 49-66.

Edwards 2000   Peter Edwards *Dealing in Death* (Stroud, 2000).

Fairfax-   J Fairfax-Blakeborough *Northern Turf History* v. I (1949).
Blakeborough

Farr   David Farr *John Lambert, Parliamentary Soldier and Cromwellian Major-General, 1619-1684* (Woodbridge, 2003).

Fawcett 1914   J.W. Fawcett *The Parish Registers of St Cuthbert's Church, Satley . . . 1560-1812* (Durham, 1914).

Fawcett 1921   J.W. Fawcett 'Notes on Northern events in 1648 and 1659-60' *PSAN*[3] ix, (1921) 46-8.

Firth CA   C.H. Firth *Cromwell's Army* 4th ed. (1962).

Firth RHCA   Sir Charles Firth *The Regimental History of Cromwell's Army* 2v. (Oxford, 1940).

Firth 1891-1901 C.H. Firth ed. *The Clarke Papers*, 4v. (Camden Society New Series 49, 54, 61, 62) (1891-1901).

Firth 1898   C.H. Firth 'The journal of Prince Rupert's marches, 5 Sept. 1642 to 4 July 1646' *English Historical Review* 13 (1898) 729-741.

Firth 1904   'Narratives illustrating the Duke of Hamilton's Expedition to England in 1648' ed. C.H. Firth *Miscellany of the Scottish History Society* 2 (Edinburgh, 1904) 289-311.

Firth and Rait   C.H. Firth and R.S. Rait eds *Acts and Ordinances of the Interregnum 1642-1660* 3v. (1911).

Foster   Joseph Foster ed. *Pedigrees recorded at the Visitation of the County Palatine of Durham* (1887).

Fraser   Antonia Fraser *Cromwell our Chief of Men* (1985)

FSPB   *Field Service Pocket Book* (1914).

Furgol   Edward M. Furgol *A Regimental History of the Covenanting Armies 1639-1651* (Edinburgh, 1990).

Gentles 1975   Ian Gentles 'The arrears of Pay of the Parliamentary Army at the End of the First Civil War' *Bulletin of the Institute of Historical Research* xlviii (1975) 52-63.

Gentles 1992   Ian Gentles *The New Model Army* (Oxford, 1992).

Gentles 2007   Ian Gentles *The English Revolution and the Wars in the Three Kingdoms 1638-1652* (Harlow, 2007).

Giggleswick   *The Giggleswick School Register 1499-1921* ed. H.B. Atkinson (Newcastle, 1922).

GRO   General Register Office, *Edinburgh Place names and population, Scotland: an alphabetical list of populated places derived from the Census of Scotland* (Edinburgh, 1967).

Grainger and   Francis Grainger and W.G. Collingwood *The Register and*
Collingwood   *Records of Holm Cultram* (CWAAS Record Series 7) (Kendal 1929).

Green   'The diary of John Green" ed. E.M. Symonds *English Historical Review* 63 (1928) 385-394, 598-604; 64 (1929) 106-117.

Groome   F.U. Groome ed. *Ordnance Gazetteer of Scotland* New ed. 7v. (Edinburgh, 1892).

Hay   'John Hay, earl of Tweeddale Autobiography, 1626-1670' ed. Maurice Lee Jnr. *Miscellany of the Scottish History Society* 12 (Edinburgh, 1994) 58-99.

Heath   James Heath *A Chronicle of the Late Intestine War in the Three Kingdoms of England, Scotland and Ireland* 2nd ed. (1676).

Hedley   W. Percy Hedley *Northumberland Families* 2v. (Newcastle, 1968-1970).

Heesom   Alan Heesom *Durham City and its MPs 1678-1992* (Durham, 1992).

Henry   Philip Henry *Diary January 1650-February 1684*, ed. M.H. Lee (1882).

Heywood   *Oliver Heywood's Life of John Angier of Denton … also Samuel Augier's Diary*…with introduction and notes by E. Axon (Chetham Society, New Series 97) (Manchester, 1937).

H of C   *Journal of the House of Commons* v.2-7 (1802).

H of L   *Journal of the House of Lords* v.6-10 (1802).

Hodgson   J.C. Hodgson's Ms Pedigrees . . . bequeathed to the Newcastle
Pedigrees   Public Library.

Hodgson 1806   *Original memoirs, written during the Great Civil War; being the Life of Sir Henry Slingsby and Memoirs of Capt. Hodgson etc* (Edinburgh, 1806).

Hodgson 1910   J.C. Hodgson ed. *Six North Country Diaries* v.1 (Surtees Society 118) (Durham, 1910).

Hollar   W. Hollar *The Bishop-ricke of Durram, and Cumberland, Westmoreland, Yorke-shire, Lancast-shire, and part of Lincon-shire: The second map of The kingdome of England & principality of Wales, exactly described whith euery sheere, & the small towns in euery one of them* … W. Hollar fecit. [1676?].

Holmes   Richard Holmes *Preston 1648* (Market Drayton, 1985).

Howell 1967   Roger Howell *Newcastle upon the Tyne and the Puritan Revolution* (Oxford, 1967).

Howell 1981   Roger Howell, Jr. 'The Army and the English Revolution: the case of Robert Lilburne' *AA*[5] ix (1981) 299-315.

Hudleston &   C. Roy Hudleston & R.S. Boumphrey *Cumberland Families*
Boumphrey   *and Heraldry* (CWAAS Extra Series 23) (Kendal, 1978).

Hughes   Edward Hughes *North Country Life in the Eighteenth Century: the North-East, 1700-1750* (1952).

Hunt   Tristam Hunt *The English Civil War at First Hand* (2003).

Hunter   Joseph Hunter *Familiae minorum gentium* ed. John W. Clay v.3 (Harleian Society 39) (1895).

Inglis   Harry R.G. Inglis *The 'Contour' Road Book of England (Northern Division)* (1911-12).

Jackson   W. Jackson 'The Curwens of Workington Hall and kindred families' *TCWAAS* 5 (1881) 181-232, 311-342.

James   Mervyn James *Family, Lineage, and Civil Society* (Oxford, 1974).

Ker   *Correspondence of Sir Robert Ker, First Earl of Ancram, and his son William, Third Earl of Lothian* ed. D. Laing. 2v. (Bannatyne Club) (Edinburgh, 1875).

King   D.W. King 'The higher command of the New Model Army' *Journal of the Society for Army Historical Research* 56 (1978).

Lamont   John Lamont *The Diary of Mr John Lamont of Newton, from the year 1649 to the year 1671* (Maitland Club) (Edinburgh, 1830).

Lancaster   M.E. Lancaster *The Tempests of Broughton* (Broughton, 1987).

Langdale   'An Impartiall Relation of the late Fight at Preston, being the Copy of a Letter written (as the tenor of it importeth) by Sir Marmaduke Langdale. Printed in the year 1648' in Ormerod, 267-270.

Lemmings   David Lemmings *Gentlemen and Barristers: the Inns of Court and the English Bar 1680-1730* (Oxford, 1990).

List of officers   *A List of Officers claiming the Sixty Thousand Pounds, &c Granted by His Sacred Majesty for the Relief of His Truly-Loyal and Indigent Party* (1663) (Wing L2402).

Macdonald Fraser George Macdonald Fraser *The Steel Bonnets* (1989).

Madge   Sidney J. Madge *The Domesday of Crown Lands* (1938).

Marcombe   David Marcombe ed. *The Last Principality* (Nottingham, 1987).

Matthews   *British Diaries: an annotated bibliography of British diaries written between 1442 and 1942,* compiled by William Matthews (1950).

Merrington   James P. Merrington & Mark P. Merrington *Brancepeth 900: the story of Brancepeth and its Rectors 1085-1985* (Brancepeth, 1985).

Military Engineering   *Military Engineering* v.5 (1935).

'Miscellaneous' 'Miscellaneous notes from various sources relating to Brancepeth' *PSAN*[3], ii (1907)170-181.

Musgrave   'Musgrave's relation' in Firth 1904, 302-311.

NCH   Northumberland County History Committee *A History of Northumberland* 15v. (1893-1940).

Newman   P.R. Newman *Royalist Officers in England and Wales 1642-1660* (1981).

Ogilby   John Ogilby *Britannia* (1675).

Oglander   Sir John Oglander *A royalists notebook* ed. Francis Bamford (1936).

Order Book   'Council of the Northern Parliamentary Army, 1647-8. A book containing a modern [before c.1900] transcript of part of the order book of the Council, found in some old buildings by Mr W[illia]m Murgatroyd (Councils of War at Ripon, Knaresbro', York, etc.)'. York Minster Library, Hailstone Collection BB53. (The work is usually referred to as the Order Book, although it is in fact a record of meetings of the Council of War of the Northern Army, chiefly concerned with courts martial.)

ODNB — *Oxford Dictionary of National Biography* 60v. (2004).

Ormerod — G. Ormerod ed. *Tracts relating to military proceedings in Lancashire during the great Civil War* (Chetham Society 2) (Manchester 1844), 267-270.

Oxberry — John Oxberry 'Diary of Major Sanderson, of Hedleyhope for 1648' *AA*³ xvi (1919) 103-116.

Parkinson — Elizabeth Parkinson, ed. *County Durham Hearth Tax Assessment* (British Record Society Index Library 119, Hearth Tax series IV) (2006).

Parkes — Joan Parkes *Travel in the Seventeenth Century* (Oxford, 1925).

Paul — Sir James Balfour Paul *The Scots Peerage* 9v. (Edinburgh, 1904-14).

Peacock — Edward Peacock, ed. *The Army Lists of the Roundheads and Cavaliers, containing the names of the Officers in the Royal and Parliamentary Armies of 1642* (1874).

Pease — Howard Pease *The Lord Wardens of the Marches of England and Scotland* (1913).

Pepys — *The Diary of Samuel Pepys*, ed. Robert Latham and William Matthews 11v. (1983).

Portland Papers — *The manuscripts of His Grace the Duke of Portland preserved at Welbeck Abbey* 10v (HMC) (1892-1931).

Raine — James Raine *The History and Antiquities of North Durham* (1852).

Reid — David S. Reid *The Durham Crown Lordships in the Sixteenth and Seventeenth centuries and the Aftermath* (Durham, 1990).

Roberts — Keith Roberts *Cromwell's War Machine: the New Model Army, 1645-1660* (Barnsley, 2005).

Rushworth — John Rushworth *Historical Collections* 4 parts in 7v. (1659-1701).

Sanderson 1648 — John Sanderson *A full, exact and particular relation of the chiefe passages of the Parliaments army*. Printed 1648. (Wing S578A).

Sanderson 1931 — John Sanderson *The Travels of John Sanderson in the Levant 1584-1602* ed. Sir William Foster (Haklyut Society 2nd Series 67) (1931).

Seton — Sir Bruce Gordon Seton *The House of Seton* 2v. (Edinburgh, 1939).

Sharp — Sharp ms, vol 12, Durham Cathedral Library.

Skirmish — *A skirmish in Northumberland*. Being a reprint of a very rare tract in quarto entitled "Packets of Letters . . . 1648" (Sunderland, 1842).

Smith — Tom Smith *A History of Longridge and District* (Preston, 1888).

Spence — Richard T. Spence *Skipton Castle in the Great Civil War 1642-1645* (Skipton, 1991).

Stocks   Helen Stocks ed. *Records of the Borough of Leicester 1603-88* (Cambridge, 1923).

Surtees   Conyers Surtees *The History of the Castle at Brancepeth, Co. Durham* (Mainsforth, 1920).

Surtees   Robert Surtees *The History and Antiquities of the County Palatine of Durham* 4v. (Durham, 1816-40).

Sweezy   Paul M. Sweezy *Monopoly and Competition in the English Coal Trade 1550-1850* (1996)

Taft   Barbara Taft 'Voting lists of the Council of Officers, December 1648' *Bulletin of the Institute of Historical Research* 52 (1979) 138-154.

TT   *Thomason Tracts*, British Library [Contemporary pamphlets and newspapers collected by George Thomason; the numbers are those assigned to the individual entries].

Thornton   Alice Thornton *The autobiography of Mrs Alice Thornton of East Newton, Co. York* ed. Charles Jackson (Surtees Society 62) (Durham, 1875).

Turner 1829   Sir James Turner *Memoirs of his own life and times 1632-1670* (Bannatyne Club) (Edinburgh, 1829).

Turner 1849   Edward Turner 'Extracts from the diary of Sir Richard Stapley, gent . . . from 1682 to 1724' *Sussex Archaeological Collections* ii (1849) 102-128.

Tylden   G. Tylden *Horses and Saddlery* (1965)

Upton   Anthony F. Upton *Sir Arthur Ingram, c.1565-1642: a study of the origins of an English landed family* (1961).

VCH Chester   Victoria County History of the County Palatine of Chester ed. B.E Harris (1979).

VCH Hampshire   *Victoria County History for Hampshire and the Isle of Wight* ed.William Page (1911).

VCH Lancaster   *Victoria County History of Lancaster* v.7 ed. William Farrer & J. Brownbill (1912).

VCH Leicester   *Victoria County History: A History of the County of Leicester* v.4 The City of Leicester ed. R.A. McKinley (1958).

VCH Yorks ER   *Victoria County History: A History of the County of York East Riding* v. 2 ed. K.J. Allinson (1974).

Venn   J.A. Venn *Alumni Cantabrigiensis* Part I (1927).

Watson   T. E. Watson *History and Pedigree of the Family of Lewen* (1919).

Wedgwood   C.V. Wedgwood *The King's War* (1974).

Welford 1895   Richard Welford *Men of Mark 'twixt Tyne and Tweed* 3v. (1895).

Welford 1905   Richard Welford *Records of the Committee for Compounding etc. with Delinquent Royalists in Durham and Northumberland during the Civil War etc. 1643-1660* (Surtees Society 111) (Durham, 1905).

Welford 1911   Richard Welford 'Newcastle householders in 1665: Assessment of Hearth or Chimney Tax' *AA*[3] vii (Newcastle 1911) 49-76.

Wing   Donald Wing *Short-title Catalogue of books printed in England, Scotland, Ireland, Wales, and British America 1641-1700* 2nd ed. (New York, 1972-1988).

Wood 1922	H.M. Wood ed. *Durham Protestations, or the Returns made to the House of Commons in 1641/2 for the Maintenance of the Protestant Religion for the County Palatine of Durham for the Borough of Berwick-upon-Tweed and the Parish of Morpeth* (Surtees Society 135) (Durham, 1922).
Wood 1929	Herbert Maxwell Wood, ed. *Wills and Inventories from the Registry at Durham* Part IV (Surtees Society 142) (Durham, 1929).
Woolrych 1961	Austin Woolrych *Battles of the English Civil War* (pb 1961).
Woolrych 1987	Austin Woolrych *Soldiers and Statesmen: the General Council of the Army and its debates 1647-1648* (Oxford, 1987).
Young	M.D. Young *The Parliament of Scotland* (Edinburgh, 1992).
Young and Holmes	Peter Young and Richard Holmes *The English Civil War* (Ware, 2000).

END NOTES

Chapter One Introduction

1 *PSAN*³ ix (1921), 8, 13-24; with Additions and Corrections, *ibid*. 44.
2 *ODNB*.
3 Atkyns and Gwyn, 108.
4 Firth, 1898.
5 Oxberry, 108.
6 Woolrych 1961, 160-1.
7 *TT* E436/24.
8 Birch, 15th, 25th June, 9th, 14th July 1648.
9 Rushworth IV, 1184, 1201, 10th July, 24th July; Portland Papers I, 488, 20th July.
10 Rushworth IV, 1218, 4th August.
11 H of C, v. 5, 5th August 1648; H of L, v. 10, 5th August 1648.
12 Oglander, 123.

Chapter Two The Sanderson family

1 James, 159-160.
2 Sweezy, 5-7.
3 *CSPD 1603-10*, 59, 66.
4 *CSPD 1595-1597*, 501.
5 Foster, 276-279.
6 Howell, 13 note 2.
7 Foster, 277.
8 Surtees II, 343.
9 Fawcett 1914, 188; *PSAN*³ ix (1921), 14.
10 BPR.
11 Sanderson 1931, 34-35.
12 Dendy II, 253.
13 *ibid*., 258.
14 Dendy I, 14.
15 Surtees II, 314.

16 Wood 1929, 132-3.
17 Sanderson 1931, xxx, 230.
18 Will of Barbara Sanderson, 25 March 1672, DULASC DPRI/1/1675/S2/1, not May as recorded by Surtees.
19 *CSPD 1619-23*, 154.
20 *ibid.*, 543.
21 'Miscellaneous' 175-9, which provides a review of references in *CSPD*.
22 Merrington, 15.
23 Wood, x-xi, 28, 39.
24 Giggleswick, 8.
25 Welford 1895, 635.
26 Heywood 157.
27 *DNB; ODNB.*
28 Firth & Rait I, 962,1079,1142.
29 Dendy II, 287; Jackson, pedigree facing 232.
30 Firth & Rait I, 707.
31 Cary I, 421.
32 Firth & Rait, 1430;1440.
33 Welford 1905, 252.
34 *ibid.*, 287.
35 Fawcett 1914, 189.
36 Parkinson, 28.
37 H of C, v. 7, 11th August 1659.
38 Welford 1911, 62; Heywood, 157.
39 Dendy II, 258, 273, 280; Dodds, *passim*; 129; Firth and Rait II, 672, 1330, 1376.
40 DULASC, DPRI/1/1650/S1/1, 3; National Archives, Kew, PROB 11/215.
41 DULASC, DPRI/1/1706/S2/f2.
42 Hughes, 77-82; Lemmings, 96.
43 Surtees II, 342; DULASC, DPRI/1/1669/S3/1.
44 Parkinson, 28.
45 *The Lord Generall Cromwell His march to Sterling . . .(TT* E613/16).
46 Abbott I, 262, letter to Sir William Springe and Mr Barrow, 28th September 1643.
47 Abbott I, 256, letter to Sir William Springe and Maurice Barrow 29th August 1643.
48 'List of the Army of Essex including officers 1642' (*TT* E64/4, 13).
49 H of C, v. 4, 27th August 1646. Reformadoes were officers whose regiments had been subsumed into another and were thus surplus to establishment and often served as rankers. Pepys uses the term of his brother-in-law Balty St. Michel when on board the *Swiftsure*, although he had never been a naval officer (Pepys I, 104, 6th April 1660). It seems that the term was used loosely for temporary as well as redundant officers.
50 H of C, v. 4, 2nd August 1645. Taunton was relieved in May 1645.
51 e.g. H of C, v. 1st July 1647.
52 *CPCC*, 147, gives this man as Colonel [Nich] Sanderson, but does not give a source for the Christian name. *CPCAM*, 705-8, has a Lt Nicholas Sanderson but the relationship to the colonel is not known.
53 Rushworth IV, 493-4, 25th May 1647.
54 *Victorious Nevves from the North . . . (TT* E463/14). In May a letter referred to

Major Sanderson and Major Cholmley with a party of Horse near Kendal
(Curwen, 473). This may also be Henry.

55 *Bloudy Newes from the North* . . . (*TT* E464/27).
56 *CSPD 1650*, 276, 510-511; *CPCC*, 815.
57 Hodgson 1806, 318-9.
58 Surtees II, 343.
59 *A Perfect Diurnall of some Passages* . . . *In Relation to the Armies* No. 59, 20th to
27th January 1651 (*TT* E781/35).
60 Stocks, 400.
61 Akerman *LFRO*, 44 (Letter no. 79, Cornet J. Baynes to Capt. A. Baynes,
Edenburgh, Janry 24th 1651[2]).
62 Grainger and Collingwood, 218. George Wilkinson is also named; he is
probably George Watkinson who was a captain in Lilburne's in the 1650s.
63 Akerman *LFRO*, 23 (Letter no. 40, Colonel Robert Lilburne to Capt. A.
Baynes, Swinton near Barwick, May 20 1651).
64 *ibid.*, 19-20 (Letter no. 33, Colonel Robert Lilburne to Capt. A. Baynes, Ap.
29th 1651).
65 H of C, v. 7, 13th June 1659. Baynes was a Captain in Lambert's Horse, and
acted as agent for some northern regiments.
66 BL Add. Mss, 21,419, f.331. This is the Captain Lister who served in
Lilburne's in 1649 (Firth *RCHA*, 264).
67 Madge, 223, note 2.
68 Order Book, f.33.

Chapter Three Background to the Diary

1 Clarendon II, 395, Document 2628, Jo. Wilcocks to Mr Edgeman, October
1647.
2 H of L, v. 7, 21st June 1645.
3 Considered in January and February (H of C and H of L *passim*), Ordinance
passed by the Commons 17th February, and Fairfax appointed 19th February
1645.
4 H of C, v. 4, 10th June 1645. The Lords agreed to a three month extension
of his command two days after Naseby, H of L, v. 7, 16th June 1645, with
subsequent three month extensions.
5 H of C, v. 5, 17th September 1648.
6 H of C, v. 5, 9th February 1648.
7 H of L, v. 10, 19th February 1648.
8 Gentles 1992, 47-8.
9 Firth *RHCA*, 267.
10 Rushworth IV, 1005, 21st February 1648.
11 *A Breviate of the New Allotment of Quarters in the Association* (*TT* E411/22).
12 Rushworth IV, 833, 1st October 1647.
13 Order Book, f.16.
14 *The Kingdoms Weekly Account* Numb. 4 From January 25. until February 2.
1647[8]. (*TT* E425/4).
15 *Ibid.*

16 Musgrave, 305, if he (a royalist) can be trusted to have exact figures for his opponent's strength.

17 Firth *RHCA*, 267.

18 Clarke MS 4/8 (Chequers MS 782) f.16. There were 43 non-commissioned officers to a regiment of horse, leaving in this case 567 troopers, or just under 95 per troop.

19 *ibid.*, ff.20 and 22.

20 Cary II, 116-7, Sir Thomas Fairfax to the Speaker, February 8 1648[9], quoting a letter from Lambert. Dawson, 64, quotes Lambert's letter under the impression that it refers to 1648, but a reference in it to the siege of Pontefract shows that it is 1649.

21 Birch, 16th June and 18th September 1648.

22 Monk *Observations* 61, quoted by Firth *CA*, 142.

23 Rushworth, 956-7, 5th January 1648, recording a Directive of the House of Commons. In December 1647 Parliament set a rate of 12d per day for troopers and non-commissioned officers (*TT* E421(9)). On 30th December the Northern Army set a rate of 1s 6d for the same ranks (*TT* E421/31).

24 *A Declaration of his Excellency Sir Thomas Fairfax, and his Council of War* Rushworth, 953-4, 3rd January 1648.

25 Order Book. The Order was signed by Thomas Margetts, Advocate, on 10th December 1647, confirmed by Lambert on 13th December, and included with the record of the Council of War for 28th January 1647[8].

26 See e.g. Roberts, chapter 3.

27 Gentles 1992, 43 implies that the cavalry of the New Model no longer carried carbines. H of C v. 4, 8th February 1645, has an order for "Two hundred Backs, Breasts, and Pots, and Four hundred pair of Pistols" for Sir Wm. Waller. This is cavalry equipment and makes no mention of carbines, although these were carried in Ireland.

28 The following history of Lilburne's regiment and its officers is based on Firth *RHCA*, 264-77, 432, 453-9, unless otherwise stated.

29 See Dumble, 235. Henry Lilburne changed sides on Wednesday 9th August (eight days before the battle of Preston) and held Tynemouth Castle for the king. It was recaptured by Hesilrige on Friday 11th during which action Lilburne was killed. A most untimely revolt, but it does not seem to have affected the standing of Robert Lilburne.

30 'List of the Army of Essex including officers 1642' (*TT* E64/4, 13).

31 Dumble gives an account of animosity between Hesilrige and the Lilburnes.

32 Howell 1981, 300.

33 Thomas Lilburne was cousin of John, Robert, and Henry (Dumble, 227).

34 There is some problem with the identity of Major Chomley, see Appendix 7a.

35 *Breviate of the New Allotment of Quarters in the Association* (*TT* October 1647, E411/22).

36 Diary, 29th September; Sanderson 1648.

37 Rushworth IV, 832-3, 1st October 1647.

38 *The Kingdoms Weekly Account* Numb. 9 March 1. till March 8 1647[8]. (*TT* E431/13).

39 *Perfect Occurrences of every daies Iournall* No 65 March 24-31 1647[8] (*TT* E522/10).

40 Order Book, 29th September, 20th September 1647, 12th December 1648 (mentioned twice on the latter date, once as Captain and once as Major).

41 *ibid*, 30th September 1647.

42 Firth *RHCA*, 264.

43 Clarke MS 4/8 (Chequers MS 782) f.11.

44 John Baynes to Adam Baynes, July 17 1649 (BL, Add Mss, 21,417, f.240).

45 Cary II, 342.

Chapter Four His early career

1 H of C, v. 3, 27th June 1643. He was commanding the troops stationed there, rather than being governor.

2 *Perfect Passages of each dayes Proceedings* Numb. 4 Novemb. 6. Novemb. 6. to Novemb. 13. 1644 (*TT* E17/1); *Mercurius Civicus* Numb. 77. 7. Novemb.to 14. Novemb. 1644 (*TT* E17/3). Sir Thomas Fairfax was besieging Helmsley.

3 H of C, v. 4, 27th August 1646.

4 Rushworth IV, 777, Monday August 16th 1647.

5 Order Book.

6 Rushworth IV, 832-3, 1st October 1647.

7 *Perfect Occurrences of every dayes Journall* Numb. 44 October 29. to Novemb. 5. 1647. (*TT* E520/2). Rushworth, 859, 1st November 1647 gives the place as Twisdale Castle, an obvious misreading of a manuscript report.

8 Rushworth IV, 870-1; *A Perfect Diurnall of some Passages in Parliament* Numb. 224 8. Till 15. of Novemb. 1647 (*TT* E520/5). The texts vary only slightly.

9 Rushworth IV, 832-3, 18th October 1647.

10 Rushworth IV, 847.

11 Order Book. Cholmley attended the Council on 30th September, but neither he, Sanderson, nor Capt. Lilburne were at any further meetings for the rest of 1647.

12 Liddesdale had been a notorious haunt of reivers in the previous century (see Macdonald Fraser, *passim*), and was clearly still troublesome.

13 A note in chapter 38 of Sir Walter Scott's *Guy Mannering* says "The roads in Liddesdale . . . could not be said to exist, and the district was only accessible through a succession of tremendous morasses." The description is of the 1790s.

14 The name could simply mean the area along Liddel Water, as in "Tyneside", but at Newcastleton they were already in Liddesdale. Newcastleton is now in Scotland, about three miles from the border.

15 *A Perfect Diurnall of some Passages in Parliament* Numb. 224 8. Till 15. of Novemb. 1647 (*TT* E520/5). Rushworth IV, 866, 8th November, has the same report.

16 *Perfect Occurrences of every dayes Journall* Numb. 55 Jan. 7 – 21 1647[8] (*TT* E520/27).

Chapter Five Capheaton to Appletreewick

1 *The Kingdoms Weekly Acccount* Numb. 4 January 25. until February 2. 1647 (*TT* E425/4).

2 Rushworth IV, 993, 9th February 1648. There are many other references to disbanding in both Rushworth and Thomason.
3 Rushworth IV, 981, 31st January 1648, reporting a letter of 29th January.
4 *TT* E424/11.
5 H of L, v. 10, 19th February 1648. A number of different pay scales and forage allowances for the army have been published (e.g Roberts 2005, 98-9) but this list is the closest in time to the Diary, and is used here throughout.
6 Pepys uses proffered in the same sense: "the secretary place which my Lord doth proffer me." (Pepys 1, 83, 8th March 1660.)
7 *A True Relation of Disbanding the Supernumerary Forces in the several counties of this Kingdom ... February 28. 1647* (*TT* E429/10)
8 Firth *RHCA* 271, 274-6. A Captain Levens is recorded in Lambert's regiment in Scotland in 1651 (Clarke MS, f.16, May 28 1651.
9 Rushworth IV, 982, 31st January, and 987, 7th February, respectively.
10 Rushworth IV, 1023, 11th March 1648.
11 *Clarke Papers*, v. II, 1, Thomas Margetts to William Clarke, York 8th April 1648.
12 Rushworth IV, 1054, April 10th.
13 Fairfax-Blakeborough, 169. Some commentators give Camden as describing racing at Gatherley, but he is in fact talking about the forest of Galtres, north of York.
14 Rushworth IV, 1031, 20th March, and 1040-41, 27th March, respectively.
15 Akerman 1856, 147.
16 Rushworth IV, 1099, 2nd May, and 1105, 8th May 1648.
17 Rushworth IV, 1105, 8th May. The point is relevant to Sanderson's activities in early June.
18 Cary I, 397.
19 *CSPD 1648-1649*, 136-137 (and see Appendix 3b).
20 Abbott I, 344-5, Cromwell to the Governor of the Garrison at Faringdon,. Later in the day he wrote a third letter, very civil in tone, about collection of the dead.
21 *CSPD 1648-1649*, pp 136-137.
22 Rushworth IV, 1113, May 15th 1648.
23 *The Moderate Intelligencer* Number 166 May 18 to May 25 1648 (*TT* E444/9).
24 *TT* E442/11, May 7 1648.
25 *The Moderate Intelligencer* Number No. 165 May 11 to May 18 1648 (*TT* E443/21).
26 Fawcett 1921, 47.
27 *Packets of Letters from Scotland, Berwick, Newcastle and York. ... Monday May 15 1648: the taking of Morpeth & Alnwick by the Cavaliers in the North* (*TT* E442/9).
28 *Perfect Occurrences of every dayes Journalll* March 24-31 1647[8] No. 65 (*TT* E522/10).
29 *The Moderate Intelligencer Numb. 168* June 1 to June 8 1648 (*TT* E446/28).
30 Hodgson 1910, 33.
31 *Perfect Occurrences of every dayes Journall* [No. illegible], *TT* E522/33.
32 *Packets of Letters from Scotland, Newcastle, York and Lancashire, number 11 May 29 1648.* (*TT* E445/5).

33 The times for sun and moon rise are taken from www.fourmilab.ch/cgi-bin/uncgi/Yoursky This gives uncorrected dates, and 10 days have to be added to allow for the correction of the calendar in September 1752 (see chapter 1 Calendar). Civil twilight is defined as ending at night and beginning in the morning "when the centre of the sun is geometrically 6 degrees below the horizon . . . Complete darkness, however, ends sometime prior to the beginning of morning civil twilight and begins sometime after the end of evening civil twilight." (US Naval Observatory, www.aa.usno.navy.mil/faq/docs/RST-defs.html). Both web sites were consulted in 2006.

34 See e.g. the letter from Cornet Pease to Captain Adam Baynes, Akerman *LFRO*, 78, Letter No. 143, 5th July 1654, and BL Add. Mss 21417, f.240, John Baynes to Adam Baynes, July 17 1649.

35 Drummond, 19.

36 *The Moderate Intelligencer No. 169,* June 8 to June 15 1648 (*TT* E447/24).

37 *Two Letters, one from Penrith another from Northumberland . .* 1648 (*TT* E450/12).

38 *Perfect Occurrences of every Dayes Journall in Parliament* Numb. 76. Fryday June 9 to 16 1648 (*TT* E522/40)

39 Portland Papers I, 508.

40 Information kindly provided by Dr. Robin Birley.

41 Mr Justin Blake of Haydon Bridge kindly supplied information on the South Tyne.

42 Rushworth IV, 1165, June 26th.

43 Letter from Sir Arthur Hesilrige, governor of Newcastle, in Bates 1891, 400-1. This is the full text of the letter précised in *Skirmish*.

44 Rushworth IV, 1165, Monday June 26th. Colonel Fenwick is George in other sources.

45 *Skirmish*, 1-7; *Packets of letters from Scotland, Lincoln, And Lancashire to Members of the House of Commons . . .brought by the Post on Thursday July 11 1648* (*TT* E452/17).

46 *A true and perfect Relation of A Great Victory obtained by Parliaments Forces in Northumberland…. In two Letters from Gentlemen of quality to their Friends in London.* (*TT* E451/22, and Bates 1891, 399). *The copy of a letter from one of our Commanders in the North July 2 1648* (*TT* E452/13) and a brief summary of a letter from "two Commanders of quality, from Newcastle and Hexam", (*TT* E451/18) add little.

47 Lilburne seems to have been with Lambert in the Stainmore-Carlisle area from early June (Rushworth IV, 1132/i.e 1140 [faulty pagination], 5th June 1648).

48 Portland Papers I, 474, Major-General Lambert, 4th July 1648.

49 *FSPB*, 37. Cavalry in half sections need a width of around 8' (*FSPB*, 111).

50 *ibid*.

51 Atkyns and Gwyn, 9, 10.

52 *FSPB*, 33.

53 Bates 1891, 402

54 *Military Engineering* 1935, 30.

55 Hodgson 1806, 109, also reports that it was "without the loss of one man of our party."

56 H of C, v. 5: 5th July 1648.

57 *The copy of a letter from one of our commanders in the North July 2 1648* (TT E452/13)
58 Bates 1895, 250.
59 Portland Papers I, 476-7, July 6th.
60 Hodgson 1806, 108.
61 Portland Papers I, 471, 474, Letters from Major-General Lambert 2nd and 4th July 1648. The quotation is from the letter of 4th.
62 Lambert's letter of 4th July (previous note) mentions the despatch of Colonel Harrison with his regiment and four troops of Cromwell's.
63 Rushworth IV, 1193 July 17th.
64 Young and Holmes, 280.
65 Portland Papers I, 474, Major-General Lambert to Sir William Lister, 4th July 1648.
66 *ibid.*, 488 Major-General Lambert to the Speaker, 20th July 1648; Rushworth 1200, Monday July 24th.
67 *ibid.*, 487.
68 *ibid.*, 505, 508.
69 *A True Relation of the fight between Maior Gen. Lambert, and the Scots Army near Appleby, July 24. 1648* (TT E454/14).
70 Hodgson 1806, 108.
71 Firth 1904, 305.
72 Gentles 1992, 49 and note 113; Gentles 2007, 107.
73 Abbott I, 631, August 14th 1648.
74 Lancaster, 66-7.
75 Sanderson 1648. This is now in the library of Worcester College, Oxford, Wing S578A, and reproduced in Appendix 4 by kind permission of the Provost and Fellows of Worcester College.
76 Abbott I, 634-8, Cromwell to the Speaker, Warrington 20th August 1648.
77 Holmes 1985, 32; Bull and Seed, 64.
78 *CPCC*, 808.
79 Dawson, 79.
80 During research for this book it became known that the first named writer is descended from the Salkelds. The precise relationship is unclear, but it may be that he has particular reason to be grateful for Major Sanderson's action.
81 Turner 1829, 64; Burnet, 360.
82 Heath, 178.
83 Turner 1829, 66. The altitude of the moon was 11.7° at 2130 hours, and 6° at 2330 (see note 33).
84 *ibid.*, 65.
85 Abbott I, 636, Cromwell to the Speaker, 20th August, referring to 18th.
86 *ibid.*, 640-2, Cromwell to the Committee at York, 23rd August; Cromwell to the Committee at Derby House, 23rd August.
87 Colonel Edward Rosseter to William Lenthall, 6th July 1648, Portland Papers I, 477; Firth *RHCA*, 166. For his wounds see H of C v. 5, 8th July 1648.
88 As a point of interest, Defoe, 232, 236, refers to Colonel Rossiter with the spelling Roseter, but the balance is still strongly in favour of Sanderson riding to Wroxeter.
89 Langdale, 269.

90 Abbott I, 637, Cromwell to the Speaker, 20th August 1648.
91 *ibid.*, 641, 646; Rushworth IV, 1249, September 2nd.
92 Oxberry, 108.
93 Rushworth IV, 1260, 1262, 1273, 12th, 14th, 25th September.
94 Lambert remained there until 27th (Abergavenny, 171). Cromwell made his own headquarters at Mordington on 20th September (Abbott I, 659).
95 Abbott I, 668, Cromwell to the Speaker, 9th October.
96 Taken at September 2007, (see www.army.mod.uk). For purchasing power see www. measuringworth.com, which does not calculate beyond 2006.
97 Rushworth IV, 1325, November 13th 1648.
98 *Packets of Letters from Scotland No 37, 25th November 1648 (TT E474/9).*
99 Rushworth IV, 1352, December 4th.
100 Abbott I, 683, Cromwell to the Committee at Derby House, 15th November 1648.
101 Rushworth IV, 1366, December 18th 1648. This will have been Adam Baynes who was in Lambert's.
102 E.g. Taft, 143.
103 Order Book, f.33.
104 BL Add. Mss 21,417, f.18. A letter from Margetts to Clarke, 13th December, also refers to Captain Baynes alone being sent with it (Dawson, 89).
105 Firth 1891-1901 II, 270-1; Taft, 148.
106 *Perfect Occurrences of every dayes Journall in Parliament* Fri. March 24-31 1647[8] [Numb. Illegible] (*TT* E522/10). Major Rokesby was killed at Dunbar in 1650.
107 Order Book, f.35.
108 Order book, f.32.
109 BL Add. Mss 21,417, f.22 (see Appendix 4).
110 BL Add. Mss 21,417, f.18, John Baynes to Adam Baynes 30th December 1648.
111 BL Add. Mss 21,417, f.231, John Baynes to Adam Baynes 14th July 1649.

Chapter Six His later career and his Will

1 BL Add. Mss 21,417, f.168, John Sanderson to A. Baynes
2 BL Add. Mss 21,417, f.199, W. Bradford to A. Baynes
3 BL Add. Mss 21,417, f.275, W. Bradford to A. Baynes
4 Firth *RHCA*, 264, quoting State Papers 28, Vol 138.
5 BL Add. Mss 21,418, f.177, Thos. Margetts to A. Baynes.
6 BL Add. Mss 21,418, f.252, Tho: Dickinson to A. Baynes, York, 5th January 1649[50],
7 BL Add. Mss 21,419, f.5, Lambert to A. Baynes, March 1650.
8 Surtees II, 14.
9 BL Add. Mss 21,419, f.16, Phillip Gouldsmith to A. Baynes, 2nd April 1650.
10 21st June 1650. 'Warrants of the Council of State for Payments of Money', *CSPD*: Interrregnum, 1650.
11 BL Add. Mss 21,419, f.224, G. Baynes to A. Baynes, 10th August 1650.
12 BL Add. Mss 21,419, f.227, G. Baynes to A. Baynes, 24th August 1650.
13 *Skirmish*, 11-15, and see Appendix 4.

14 DULASC, DPRI/1/1650/S1/1, 3.
15 National Archives, Kew, PROB 11/215.
16 Akerman *LFRO*, 14, Letter 22, 20th March 1650[1], refers to the governor as Major Sanderson.
17 Firth *RHCA*, 266.
18 Bates 1895, 250-252.
19 Fawcett 1921, 47.
20 www.northumberlandnationalpark.org.uk; Bull and Seed, 53, 93 and *passim*.
21 NCH XIV, 505.

Chapter Seven In conclusion

1 Oxberry, 109.
2 To judge by what was available to Pepys these could have been compasses, pantograph, protractor, slide rule, spy glass, night glasses etc (*Pepys* xi, Index).
3 'Advice', 357.

Appendix II The Diary volume and Almanacs

1 Briggs, 52, 63.
2 Heywood, 152.
3 Heywood, 157 where a footnote describes the probable reason as a visit to his 'academy contemporary', Peter's son Charles.
4 Turner 1849, 108
5 National Portrait Gallery, Archive Documents, Ms 18.

Appendix IIIa Sanderson's Accounts

1 Some names and words are in a simple code, using the previous letter in the alphabet.
2 He appears to have begun to write Russell in code, see three lines below.

Appendix IV Letters and Documents written by Sanderson

1 Words in italics were omitted from the version in *Skirmish*, or incorrectly transcribed, and have been added from the copy in DULASC. There are a number of other variations in spelling and punctuation but not of a material nature.

Appendix V Seventeenth century Roads and Maps

1 Parkes, 13; *Packets of Letters from Scotland No 37, 25th November 1648* (*TT* E474/9).

Appendix VI Horses

1 Tylden 1965, 5-6.
2 Edwards 1995; Edwards 2000.
3 Edwards 2000, 155-7.
4 Macdonald Fraser 1989, 85-6.
5 Pease 1913, 24-25 and note.
6 *A Perfect Diurnall of some Passages in Parliament* No 257 26 June- 3 July (*TT* E525/1).
7 Edwards 2000, 155.
8 *The Moderate Intelligencer* Numb. 155 2 March to March 9. 1648 (*TT* E431/18).
9 Rushworth IV, 1175, 4th July 1648.
10 *ibid.*, 1177, 5th July 1648.
11 *ibid.*, 1211. He gives the date as Monday 30th July, although 31st was Monday. If it did reach London on 30th, then it travelled at over 80 miles a day.

Appendix VIIa The Problem of Major Cholmley

1 Beaumont, 66 and note 122.
2 *CSPD 1656-1657*, 211.
3 National Archives, Kew, PROB 11/235.
4 Lambert to the Speaker, September 19th 1648 (Tanner mss., lvii, 297, quoted by Dawson 79-80).
5 Cromwell to the Speaker, 28th October 1648 (Abbott I, 672).

INDEX

Modern spelling is used for personal and place names. Officers are shown with the rank by which they were generally known at the time. The Transcript (Appendix 3) and Biographies (Appendix 7) are not indexed.